THE RISE
OF THE
WYRM
LORD

THE DOOR WITHIN TRILOGY CONTINUES . . .

BOOK

THE RISE
OF THE
WYRM
LORD

BY
WAYNE THOMAS BATSON

A Division of Thomas Nelson Publishers
Since 1798

www.thomasnelson.com

To the one true King,

you are my sword and my shield.

I enter the battle, and I am not afraid.

For I am not alone.

THE RISE OF THE WYRM LORD
Text copyright © 2006 Wayne Thomas Batson
Second in a series of three novels.
All rights reserved. No portion of this book may be reproduced in any form without the written permission
of the publisher, with the exception of brief excerpts in reviews.
Published in Nashville, Tennessee, by Tommy Nelson®, a Division of Thomas Nelson®, Inc. Visit us on the
Web at www.tommynelson.com.
Tommy Nelson® books may be purchased in bulk for educational, business, fund-raising, or sales promotional
use. For information, please email SpecialMarkets@ThomasNelson.com.

Library of Congress Cataloging-in-Publication Data

Batson, Wayne Thomas
      The rise of the wrym lord / by Wayne Thomas Batson
         p. cm.
Sequel to: The door within
Summary: Aidan's new friend Antoinette is called to the Realm, but when she arrives to rescue Robby through
his Glimpse-twin, the place is in turmoil and she must decide whether to stay loyal to the one true king or join
the evil side.
      ISBN-13: 978-1-4003-0737-1 (hardback)
      1. Space and time—Fiction. 2. Christian life—Fiction. 3. Fantasy.
   I. Title
      PZ7.B3238 Ri 2006
      [Fic] 22

                                                                                            2005030039

Printed in the United States of America
06 07 08 09 10 QW 9 8 7 6 5 4 3 2 1

CONTENTS

Principal Cast

AIDAN (AY-DEN) THOMAS
When Aidan's parents move the family to Colorado to take care
of his wheelchair-bound grandfather (Grampin), the teenager discovers
the Scrolls, which start him on an adventure of a lifetime.

ANTOINETTE (AN-TWA-NET) LYNN REED
Aidan's new friend at school, also a believer in King Eliam
and The Realm of Glimpses.

FAETHON (FAY-EH-THUN)
The last living son of Falon the Mortiwraith; guards King Eliam's treasuries.

FALON
The elder of all mortiwraiths, who are enormous,
venomous underground serpentine creatures.

FARIX (FAIR-IX)
Glimpse warrior, who does not wear armor.

KALIAM (KAL-EE-UM)
Glimpse warrior, former pathfinder,
now the fourth Sentinel of Alleble.

KING ELIAM (EE-LEE-UM)
The noble and wise monarch of Alleble, who invited Aidan to his kingdom.

LADY MEREWEN
Once a follower of Paragor, a capable silver-haired
swordmaiden in the service of Alleble.

LORD KEARN
One of Paragor's chief lieutenants, who leads the enemy through Yewland.

LORD RUCIFEL (ROO-SI-FELL)
Paragor's Lieutenant, who wields two swords.

MALLIK (MAL-ICK)
Glimpse warrior, who wields a massive war hammer.

MR. AND MRS. REED
Antoinette's father and mother.

MR. AND MRS. THOMAS
Aidan's father and mother.

NOCK
A highly skilled Glimpse archer and warrior from Yewland.
Twin of Bolt, who died in The Door Within #1.

PARAGAL (PAIR-A-GALL) / PARAGOR (PAIR-AH-GORE)
The first Sentinel of Alleble, who now rules over Paragory.

QUEEN ILLARIA (ILL-AIR-EE-AH)
Sovereign Queen of Yewland.

ROBBY PIERSON (PEER-SON)
Aidan's best friend in Maryland.

SIR AELIC
Aidan's Glimpse twin, prince of Mithegard. Grandfather was Captain
Valithor, a hero of Alleble. His father is King Ravelle, ruler of Mithegard.
His Glimpse twin in the Mirror Realm is Sir Aidan.

SIR OSWYN
Herb-meister, skilled with potions, cures, and salves.

SIR ROGAN
Tall blond warrior from Mithegard. He carries a broad-bladed battleaxe.

SIR TOBIAS (TOE-BYE-AHS)
Verbose pathfinder for the new Twelve Knights of Alleble's journey to Yewland.

SIR GABRIEL
Diplomatic envoy for the Twelve to Yewland. Very wise in the lore of Alleble.

TAL
Glimpse warrior, who likes to compete.

TRENNA SWIFTFOOT
Yewland Glimpse held in bondage by criminals in Baen-Edge.

Principal Settings

ACACIA (UH-KAY-SHUH)

Small kingdom to the south of Alleble. Once conquered by Paragory,
it was liberated and rebuilt by King Eliam.

ALLEBLE (AL-EH-BULL)

The first Kingdom of The Realm. After The Schism,
Alleble remained the center of The Realm.

BAEN-EDGE (BANE-EDJ)

Two cities divided by a river. It is a commerce center
and a trading partner for Paragory.

CLARION

Proud kingdom of artisans south of the Shattered Lands.

PARAGORY (PAIR-AH-GOR-EE)

A kingdom built by Paragor and his army.

MITHEGARD (MYTH-GUARD)

A kingdom in the northwestern part of The Realm.

SHATTERED LANDS

Desolate volcanic region; location of the Wyrm Lord's tomb.

THE BLACKWOOD

Forest of massive trees north of Yewland. Sinister things now dwell there.

THE REALM

The world of Glimpses, once united with our world,
was separated by The Schism.

YEWLAND

Forest city where Nock and Bolt were born.

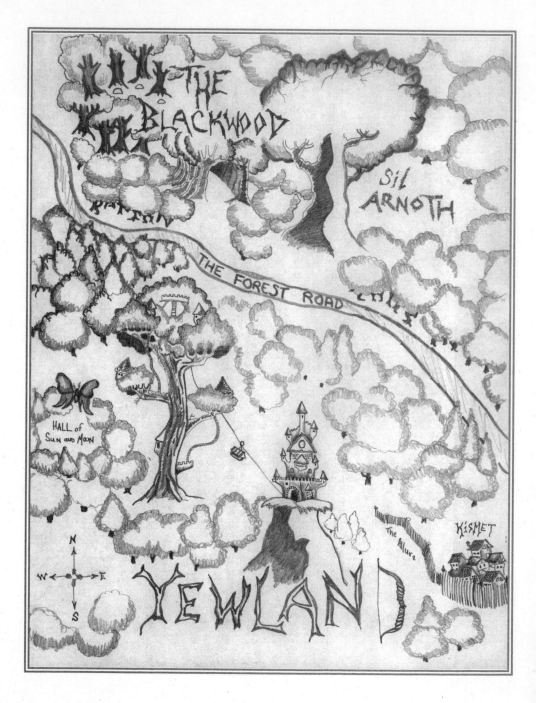

Adventures are
funny things.
Some streak down upon you
like a storm.
Others emerge only when many
years have passed
and something forgotten is
revealed.
They can be discovered upon a
dusty bookshelf or
even the yellowed pages of an
ancient map.
They promise great reward.
But no adventure is without risk.

THE SPECTRAL WINDOW

Thunder rolled, heavy and abrupt, shaking the windowpanes of Aidan's room. Aidan put down the scrolls he had been reading and got up to look out at the approaching storm. He could smell the rain in the air, but it hadn't actually started to fall. Aidan stood at the open window. A chill breeze swept in across his face and forearms. His skin tingled. The tiny hairs on his arms stood up.

The neighborhood lay in darkness. Few lights were on. *That's strange,* Aidan thought. *It's just nine o'clock.*

The whispering breeze swayed the pines in the front yard, but little else moved. The sky, thick with storm clouds, swelled and seemed to press down upon the shadowy houses.

Lightning flickered. In the brief blue flash, Aidan had seen eyes. He knew those eyes. Aidan blinked, and the eyes were gone. Thunder growled. The wind picked up. Aidan could not will himself to leave the window. *Something is wrong,* he thought.

Another flash bathed the neighborhood in intense blue light. For a moment a pale being appeared, just outside the window.

"Captain Valithor?" Aidan mouthed. Thunder cracked sharply and rolled away.

The next time the lightning came, the image of the Glimpse Captain appeared in more detail. He seemed to be standing by a smooth wall of stone. And, wait! There was another knight standing near . . . a very familiar knight.

Another bright flash, and the image grew wider still, a spectral window opening so that Aidan could see another time in another world. And this time, the vision did not fade. Aidan knew the scene. He had lived it—just weeks earlier in The Realm where the Glimpse twins of all humanity dwell.

Aidan had been dubbed a knight in the service of King Eliam, noble ruler of Alleble. The scene had taken place before dawn. Aidan had found the Captain alone, staring out over the seventh fountain in the courtyard before the castle. That fountain was dry and had ceased to flow since it had been used to fulfill Paragor's traitorous plan.

It was then that Captain Valithor had shown Aidan how Paragor's rebellion failed—how he and his horde of traitors had been cast out of the kingdom in disgrace.

Lightning split the sky. The neighborhood faded, and suddenly, Aidan was there in The Realm again.

"Captain, I've seen Paragor."

"What?" The Sentinel looked up, his eyes narrowed, posture tensed. "Where?"

"It was in a dream I had before I entered The Realm."
Tension melted from Captain Valithor. He sighed with

relief. "That is natural, Aidan. When you read the scrolls—it is bound to influence your dreams."

"But it was a dream I had before I found the scrolls."

Captain Valithor's eyes widened.

Aidan continued, "I had the same horrible dream over and over again. I was in the ruins of a kingdom. I was captured, and Paragor told me to deny my King. I refused, and . . . and he killed me."

Captain Valithor staggered backward and steadied himself on the wall of the fountain. "Aidan, I . . ."

"What is it?" Aidan was alarmed.

The Captain swallowed. Then he mastered himself. "Aidan, no matter what, tell no one else of this dream."

"But, why?"

"No one! Do you understand? I must seek the King's wisdom, for my own is found wanting in this. Remember, no one!"

Aidan's gut churned, and the hair stood up on the nape of his neck. "I won't tell anyone, Captain," he whispered. "I promise."

Thunder crashed. Aidan blinked until the disorientation passed. He was back in his room. The wind howled through the open window, and the rain began to fall in sheets. Aidan slammed the window shut and pulled the curtains. He looked at the scrolls on his bed and wondered: *Why did Captain Valithor become so disturbed when he heard about my dream? Why didn't he want me to tell anyone else about it?* Aidan went to his parents' bedroom. He knocked once.

"Come on in, Aidan," his mom said, and he entered. "All ready for your first day at your new school?" she asked, but then she stared at him. "Aidan, are you all right? You look pale."

"Yeah, I'm okay," he replied. "Where's Dad?"

"He's downstairs somewhere, I think," she said. She got out of bed and put her hand on his forehead.

"Mom, I'm fine."

She mussed the waves of his dark brown hair and smiled. "I can't believe you're getting so much older. Getting tall. You've lost those chubby cheeks you used to have. You look like your father when I met him—what with those bushy eyebrows and big ol' puppy-dog brown eyes."

"Oh, Mom," Aidan said, but he laughed and was pleased he was looking older. "So Dad's in the kitchen?"

"I'm not sure, honey. He went down about an hour ago. Haven't seen him since."

"Thanks," Aidan replied. Quickly Aidan went downstairs to look for his dad. Aidan spied him through the French doors of what was now the study. It had been Grampin's room. Aidan felt a tug at the pit of his stomach. Grampin had died the very day Aidan returned from The Realm, and Aidan still missed him terribly. Grampin had, after all, helped Aidan understand the message and answer the invitation in the mysterious scrolls Aidan had discovered in the basement.

Aidan's father sat on the floor with an old photo album in his lap and stared at it so intensely that he didn't even notice his son standing there. Aidan sighed. He'd talk to his dad later.

He went to the kitchen, poured himself a soda, and looked around as if to say, "Now what?" Thunder rolled softly in the distance. Aidan glanced at the clock. He didn't feel a bit sleepy. After this latest vision, he doubted very much that he could sleep anyway.

"I know!" Aidan stood up; he grabbed his drink and headed to the basement.

RED FOR THE EYES?

When he needed to think, Aidan often went to the basement to work on his latest art project. And after his last vision, he needed to think plenty. He looked up at the canvas. *I should have finished this days ago.* But he hadn't finished it.

Aidan frowned and then squeezed the tube of red acrylic paint until a small crimson pool formed in the bottom of his cup. *Too much red,* he thought. *Just a drop would have been enough for the eyes.*

He daubed his fine brush in the paint, lifted it slowly to the canvas, and stopped. *I don't want his eyes to be red. I want them to be blue!* Aidan put the paintbrush down and rubbed his temples. *How am I ever going to get Robby to understand, if I can't talk to him?*

Aidan shook his head and absently scanned the basement. *Funny,* he thought. *It all started down here with the scrolls.* He looked over toward the alcove beneath the stairs, now crammed full of cardboard boxes he and his dad had moved to make room for Aidan's art studio. Aidan shook his head and laughed quietly.

He glanced around the room at his finished paintings, all illuminated by the conical track lights he and his father had installed. The five paintings were a kind of visual history of Aidan's adventures—the Castle of Alleble, Grimwalk, Falon's Labyrinth, the Black Crescent, and the Glimpses of Paragor.

On the first canvas sprawled the Castle of Alleble and its vast courtyard, where Captain Valithor, the Sentinel and chief knight of Alleble, had trained an inexperienced and timid Aidan, turning him into a brave warrior and eventually a hero. "Stir your stumps, Aidan, thou lumpish tardy-gaited puttock!!" Aidan grinned, remembering the tongue-lashings the Captain used to give him. It had scared Aidan half to death at first, but it really did toughen him up. Aidan had much to thank his Captain for.

Valithor had sacrificed his own mighty life for Aidan. It was a sacrifice that still hit home in many ways, for Captain Valithor was the Glimpse of Aidan's grandfather. His death in The Realm had also meant Grampin's death on earth. Aidan often wished that he could have spoken to Grampin one last time before he died. There was still so much more Aidan yearned to know about The Realm—and about the visions. *Captain Valithor had seemed to know something . . . had Grampin known it too?*

The next painting was all stormy grays and wintry whites, depicting the cold and desolate Grimwalk. Paragor, the dark ruler of that inhospitable region, had conjured forth a devastating storm to waylay Aidan and his team of knights from Alleble. There, Aidan had saved the life of Gwenne, his closest Glimpse friend, and received a kiss on the cheek for his troubles. *Not a bad deal,* Aidan thought with a warm smile. He wondered what Gwenne had been doing in The Realm since he left. Probably out on an adventure—some mission for King Eliam, no doubt. He wondered if she thought of him as much as he thought of her. *If only I could . . .* but he shook the thought away. Aidan knew there was no going back . . . not until the end.

The next painting was of the subterranean maze known as Falon's Labyrinth. It was there that Aidan encountered a serpentine creature more fearsome than anything that lurked in his darkest nightmares. But in that fateful meeting, Aidan did not perish. Instead, he gained a powerful ally.

The last of Aidan's finished paintings was a panoramic view of the Black Crescent. It was there, under the inspiration of King Eliam, that Aidan had pulled off a victory so startling that it earned him the title Knight of the Dawn and saw his name added to a very select list of Alleble's heroes. Aidan ran his fingers across the long raised scar on his right forearm. The scar was a very real reminder of his adventures, but to Aidan's continuing frustration, his mother refused to believe that the sharp blade of a sword had caused that wound. Aidan wondered what it would take to convince her that King Eliam, The Scrolls of Alleble, The Realm, *and* her decision to believe were all very real. So real in fact that they were a matter of life and death.

And that brought Aidan back to the canvas in front of him. It was a scene from The Realm like the others, but not a place he had been personally. It had come from another one of his visions—the visions that came in dreams or when he traveled between earth and The Realm, like tonight with the lightning. Some of the visions had been foretelling, but not all had come true yet. There was one vision that Aidan desperately hoped would never come to pass. In this vision, there was a cavernous hall, lit from above by a flaming chandelier.

Beneath it, raising goblets as if in victory, were soldiers dressed in the dark armor of Paragory. Some of the Glimpse warriors had eyes that glinted green, the color of the undecided. Most of them had eyes that glinted red, a sign of service to Paragor. One of these red-eyed knights, Aidan recognized all too well. It was the Glimpse of Robby, his best friend from Maryland.

Aidan picked up the paintbrush, and instead of giving red eyes to the painted version of his friend, he dipped the brush into a clear cup of water and watched the color bleed away to nothing. *If there is a way to reach Robby,* he thought, *then King Eliam will show me.*

SLAM!! Aidan jumped, almost knocking over the stool and all his paints. Heavy footfalls bounded down the stairs, and there, looking breathless and feverishly excited, was Aidan's dad.

"Aidan!" he said. "I'm glad you're still awake. You've got to come see what I've found!"

"What?!"

"Well, I was boxing up some of Grampin's stuff in his old study, and I got this weird feeling I was being watched. When I looked up, one of the books on Grampin's bookshelves was sticking out."

Aidan smiled, but shrugged.

"Aidan, it was Grampin's diary. Inside, there's a note for you."

GRAMPIN'S DIARY

The first entry is dated March sixth 1940," Aidan's dad explained, holding the diary in both hands. "Can you believe Grampin wrote in this diary for more than sixty years?"

"It looks old," Aidan replied. Stains, cuts, scrapes, and smudges marred the dark brown leather cover. It had a tarnished coppery color at the binding. A ragged reddish tassel stuck out from the pages. "But how could he fit sixty years of writing into just one book? There can't be any more than three—four hundred pages in there."

"Well, from what I can tell, he didn't write every day. There are some places where he skipped whole years between entries. Maybe he just wrote about special occasions."

"So where's the note for me?" Aidan asked.

"It's at the end," his dad replied. "It's the last entry." As Aidan's father flipped through the yellowed pages, Aidan caught sight of innumerable passages written in Grampin's bold handwriting, as well as hand-drawn sketches and maps. Finally, Aidan's dad reached the last entry.

"I haven't read it yet," he said, closing the diary just enough to send Aidan's curiosity off the charts. "As soon as I saw the date of the entry and realized it was addressed to you, I came to find you. Do you want me to read it out—"

"Read it already, Dad!" Aidan interrupted.

"Okay, okay! Here goes!"

Dear Aidan,

I trust you'll find this when you get back from The Realm. I don't expect I'll be able to talk to you again, and that's a pity. This old heart of mine is about to quit, I think. Took every last bit of energy I had to send that bundle of scrolls into The Realm after you!

"Remember, Dad? I told you about that!"

"I still can't believe he got himself up and down the stairs," Aidan's father replied, shaking his head. "I guess I shouldn't be so shocked. Dad still had some strength in those arms of his."

"Keep reading, Dad!"

So I thought I'd best leave this old journal of mine to you, Aidan. It has been a long journey for me, and if my hunch is right, you're going to need a lot of what I discovered along the way. You might even be able to figure out some of the riddles I came across. At the very least, use the journal to convince your stubborn parents that The Realm is real. King Eliam has a heart for them. They just need to wake up and hear his call!

Aidan smirked. His father shrugged. "Okay, so I was stubborn!" he said. "But I came around."

"So what's keeping Mom?"

"I don't know, Aidan. She gives me an odd look every time I open up the scrolls to read. But you know how she is. She's a math teacher—everything has to be logical for her. If she can't see it, she won't believe it."

"But she's seen the scrolls, my scars . . ."

"She can invent explanations for those too easily. No, for her it's going to take something she can't rationalize away." They were quiet for some time, and then Aidan's dad continued reading from the journal.

The red tassel marks the first journal entry about my adventures in the Realm. I spent almost two years there, as Glimpses reckon time. I suppose you've already figured out that time works differently there. I guess I was gone about a month, our time, but anyway I learned a lot while I was there. I discovered that my Glimpse was named Valithor, and from what I learned, he was a formidable warrior. But then again, so was I. In my scrolls I read that Valithor eventually became Sentinel of the Realm! Imagine that! I wonder if you met him while you were there?

Anyhow, read this journal, Aidan. Start at the tassel. You'll find my adventures, sketches, and notes—even some maps I drew. There's a lot here that I figured out about the Realm, but much more I haven't figured out. So get all you can out of it. Study it. Read it to those hardheaded folks of yours. Maybe King Eliam will give you some wisdom beyond what I was able to learn. As I said before, I have a hunch you are going to need all the wisdom you can

get. You see, Aidan, I think there will come a time when you will
go back to The Realm.

"Go back?!" Aidan blurted out. "But Gwenne said—"
"Shhh!" Aidan's father said. "There's more."

But beware, Aidan. If I'm right and you do go the second time, it
won't be the same way you went before. And it may be that grave
challenges await you in The Realm if you return. Take heart, son,
and fear no darkness. You are never alone. My love to you and your
parents. This is not good-bye—only until later. The Sacred Realm
Beyond the Sun waits for me. And at last, I'll be able to get up
out of this old wheelchair once and for all.

Aidan sat back in a daze. "How am I going to go back to The
Realm?"

Aidan and his father sat in silence, each busy with his own thoughts.
They agreed to take turns reading Grampin's diary. Mr. Thomas would
read it first.

"How am I supposed to focus on anything with all this stuff
going on?"

"Stuff? You mean Grampin's diary?"

"Yeah, that. That and the visions," Aidan replied.

"You had another one?"

"Yes, but I don't know what it means."

Aidan told his father all about the flashback vision he'd had.

"I'll think about it, Aidan," Mr. Thomas said. "But it's late, and
you've got to get some sleep. School starts tomorrow."

When Aidan finally laid his head on his pillow, he still had no
answers—only questions.

THE BLUE-EYED MICROSCOPE

The rain the night before had left enough moisture to cause a swirling fog to form. The sun, a blotchy pale globe, rose and fought to burn through the drifting orange haze. Feeling like he too was in a fog, Aidan stood alone, waiting at the bus stop.

Things had seemed so clear when he left The Realm. He'd just come back, tell his parents and Robby about his amazing adventures serving King Eliam as a knight, and they'd all just believe. *Right. So far, Mom thinks I'm going through a "stage," and Robby seems to have dropped off the face of the earth! And the only reason Dad believes is because of Grampin.*

And then there was Gwenne. Aidan had thought he'd come up with a clever plan to see her again. "See you soon!" he had said just before kissing Gwenne on the cheek and leaving The Realm. He had figured that since every Glimpse had a human twin, he'd just find Gwenne's double, and everything would be happy ever after.

Good thinking. She could be anywhere in the whole world! And I might not even recognize her since time works differently between The Realm and earth. She could be three or thirty for all I know.

The visions he'd been having and Grampin's diary had muddled things further. And to top it all off, Aidan's mom—a high school math teacher—had called the math department chairman at Aidan's new school to get Aidan bumped up to honors math. *I barely scraped by with an A in general math, and she puts me in honors?* At last the bus turned onto Aidan's street. As it hissed to a stop, just inches from the curb, Aidan issued a silent plea to King Eliam for help.

Aidan boarded the bus. *Great! No open seats!* He'd just about given up hope of finding a seat when he reached the back of the bus and noticed that the second to the last seat on the left was occupied by only one person. It was a very tall male student wearing a black long-sleeved T-shirt and the baggiest jeans Aidan had ever seen. He had his knees and feet up on the dark green bench seat. The boy's hair was spiked and dark except for blue highlights on the pointy ends. He wore headphones and was completely oblivious to Aidan standing there.

Six other kids filled the seats near Mr. Bluehair. Black seemed to be their favorite color. Some wore leather jackets. Others wore trench coats. Most wore military boots. But it was all black. The most disturbing thing to Aidan, other than the group's black attire and various shocks of technicolored hair, was their makeup.

The boys all wore eyeliner, eye shadow—even lipstick. Black of course. There were two girls. The one with short, spiked, white-blond hair wore fierce blush and deep purple eye shadow. She had double eyeliner that streaked back from the corners of her eyes. *Cleopatra!* Aidan thought. *She looks like a punk version of Cleopatra.* The other girl, the one with very long, very red hair, didn't wear much makeup at all. Her wide eyes were startlingly blue.

The bus lurched. Aidan lurched. Finally, the girl with the long red hair glanced up sideways at Aidan. She brushed a wave of red hair over one ear that was pierced more than once, and she continued to stare. Aidan felt as if he was being sized up, analyzed, measured— like he was an insect under a blue-eyed microscope. Her stare felt oddly familiar, but uncomfortable at the same time.

At last, she reached over the seat and pushed Mr. Bluehair in the back of the head. He looked up and suddenly realized that Aidan was standing there. Without a word, he put his feet on the floor and scooted over so Aidan could sit down.

Although he felt very much alone in the back of the bus with the trench-coat clan, Aidan knew he was not alone. Recent events had taught him that much.

"Honors math. Great . . . just great!" Aidan grumbled as he left the main office. He looked down at his new schedule and wondered why his mom thought this was the best class for him. The bell rang. Now he was late for class! After bounding up a flight of stairs, he finally found the honors math classroom. Aidan eased open the door and tentatively walked in. The teacher had her back turned and was writing on the chalkboard.

"Uh, excuse me, Mrs. . . . , um—" Aidan looked down at the schedule. "Mrs. Van Der Ick?"

"That's VanDerEyck," said the teacher as she turned. "It's Dutch. Like *eye* with a 'k' at the end. VanDerEyck. And who are you?"

"I'm Aidan. Aidan Thomas."

"You aren't on my class list."

"I . . . I'm a new add."

"I see," said Mrs. VanDerEyck. She picked up a chart. "Thomas. That will put you in the seat behind Ms. Reed. We'll have to move Ms. Timmons, Mr. Young, and Ms. Zook."

She glanced up and three students immediately stood and moved to different desks.

The teacher nodded and then looked back at Aidan. "Order, Mr. Thomas. Get very used to order. It is the foundational principle that makes math worth our study. Keeping my seating chart in strict alphabetical order makes it possible for me to learn your names immediately. And in much the same way, I will teach you to recognize the order of all the operations of math, and you will learn deeply and at great speed. Now, Mr. Thomas, take your seat behind Ms. Reed."

Aidan looked nervously about, wishing he'd been watching the students who moved. There were two empty seats now, and he wasn't sure which student had left the seat he was now supposed to occupy.

Finally, the slightest of waves caught his attention. To Aidan's surprise, it was the red-haired girl from the bus. She waved again, more a ripple of fingers than a wave, but Aidan hurried over and took the seat behind her.

"Thanks!" he whispered to her.

"No problem," she whispered back. "You looked a little lost."

"She seems kind of strict," Aidan said.

"Confident, I think," she replied. "I like her."

And those were the last non-math-related words anyone said the rest of that class. Mrs. VanDerEyck became a hurricane of information, and it was all Aidan could do to hang on to a pencil.

In the hall after class, Aidan felt a tap on his shoulder. "Hey, it's Aidan, right?" It was the red-haired girl, Ms. Reed.

"Yeah, that's right, um—"

"Antoinette. I'm Antoinette Reed," she said. "You aren't from Red Rocks Middle—that's where I went last year. Are you from Breezewood?"

"No, I'm from Maryland. We just moved here in July."

"Oh, Maryland, huh? What's your next class?"

"Uh, art, I think."

"Art? With Mr. Kurtz?"

Aidan looked at his schedule. "Yeah, Mr. Kurtz, room 192."

"Me too," said Antoinette. "I'll walk with you."

Aidan wasn't quite sure what to say to that. The thought occurred to him that Mr. Bluehair and the rest of the trench-coat clan might not like it.

They easily found the class. Students filed in and checked the seating chart. Antoinette waltzed in and quickly found her seat. Aidan didn't have a seat on the chart and stood there like he'd just been hit by a bus. He had, in fact—a bus named Antoinette Reed.

Finally, Mr. Kurtz—a tall, slender man with a beak nose and big eyes—came over to Aidan.

"Your schedule, please," he said, drawing out each syllable ridiculously. "Yup, no doubt about it, you belong here."

He showed Aidan to a stool. In some ways, Aidan was relieved that it was on the other side of the room from Antoinette. In another way, he was a little disappointed.

Aidan glanced up at her. She immediately looked away. Had she been staring at him the whole time? *This is getting strange,* he thought.

LIVING ART

"Look at the book about master artists in front of you," Mr. Kurtz directed the class. "Each book is different. Your first assignment is to select one work of art and replicate it to the very best of your ability."

The textbook in front of Aidan was a collection of pencil and charcoal works by English artists.

"You may use pencil, pastille, pen and ink, or even watercolor paints, if you wish," the art teacher continued. "Do your very best work because I will be grouping you by your level of skill. When you finish, clothespin your work to the line above your head. You may begin now."

Aidan looked up. And sure enough there was some sort of clothesline-pulley contraption rigged all the way around the art room. Pictures could be hung from the clothesline and then rotated around the room by a master line near Mr. Kurtz's desk.

Cool! Aidan thought. *I wonder if Dad would let me put one in my r—*

"You ought to get started, Mr. Thomas."

Aidan turned three shades of red and hurriedly flipped open his book. The drawings were amazingly well done. But none of them really captured Aidan's creative eye. He was about to raise his hand when Mr. Kurtz broke the creative silence.

"A student has asked if something original could be drawn rather than imitating one of the masters. The answer to that question is yes. You may always be original, but be careful not to waste time thinking of what to draw or paint. You have only one hour remaining."

That was a relief to Aidan. Without any hesitation he grabbed a piece of sketch paper and launched into a rendering of the Seven Fountains of Alleble. Following the frenzied movements of Aidan's pencil, the fountains came to life. The perspective was from a castle balcony looking out over the dry seventh fountain. The other six fountains followed a gradual curl and nearly disappeared at the horizon. Aidan moistened the ends of his fingers several times and smeared the plumes of water spraying out from the center of each enormous fountain.

Tudor cottages, castle towers, and merchant shops sprang up on both sides of the fountains. Aidan even tried to draw in the cobblestones of Alleble's main thoroughfare.

It is looking very good, Aidan thought. So real, in fact, that for a few moments, it brought back the vision from the night before. There stood the tall Glimpse warrior Captain Valithor, leaning, staring into the dry fountain. Another vision of that fountain flooded into Aidan's mind, and there were Glimpse men, women, and children standing waist-deep in ugly black oil. A flaming torch arced into the night sky and plunged inevitably toward the fountain, toward the oil—

"All right, time's up," Mr. Kurtz announced. Aidan came racing out of the trance. "Please hang your works of art on the gallery line. And don't forget your autograph. An artist always signs his or her work!"

Aidan looked down at his work and signed his name at the bottom. He picked up the sketch and was about to clothespin it to the line, when he froze.

Beyond the last fountain in his drawing, beyond Alleble's outer walls, two dark jagged mountain peaks stabbed up through distant clouds. Aidan knew what they were. They were the mountains of Paragory, The Prince's Crown. Only, he did not remember drawing them into the scene.

"Mr. Thomas, please hang up your work," chided Mr. Kurtz.

Aidan did as he was told. Mr. Kurtz gave a yank on the master line, and the art show began. Swaying from the gallery, the artwork of thirty students cruised clockwise around the room. From time to time, Mr. Kurtz commented or criticized some of the works, but he kept the line moving.

"Hmmm, there's a fine piece of work," he said. "And that one is very nice. Oh, someone needs to work on color choice. There's a good still life. Oh, dear, now I wasn't aware that Van Gogh did stick figures, but I guess we all must begin somewhere."

But then, Mr. Kurtz actually did stop the rotating gallery. He let the master line fall from his hands, and he stood gazing at a picture. From Aidan's place in the room, all he could see was a lot of black and red ink.

"Now, this is interesting," Mr. Kurtz remarked. "The use of red draws the reader into the center. Brilliant, really. Now many of my students try to create something spooky or sinister, but they simply cannot pull it off. One child tried to draw a haunted castle, but it looked for all the world like Snow White and the seven dwarfs might come marching right along."

Laughter rippled through the art room. "But this," Mr. Kurtz continued. "This is positively chilling." The art teacher seemed to shudder involuntarily, and then he pulled on the main line to continue the art show.

The red-and-black work of art drew stares from the rest of the class as it sailed around the room. As it came closer to Aidan, he began to feel very cold. The scene showed dark, twisted leafless trees in the foreground and towering black mountains in the back. In the center of the image was a huge set of doors opening from the bony roots of the largest mountain. Red light spilled out from the doors, revealing a cavern within and bathing everything in bloody light. But what captivated the eye and strangled hope from the heart was the train of unfortunate souls being led into the red cavern. Silhouetted against the surge of red were hundreds of beings, obviously bound by chains at the neck, hands, and feet. They were being drawn relentlessly into the bowels of that horrid mountain by dark figures on horseback who had swords, spears, and whips. There seemed no escape for the prisoners. And though what was waiting for them in the blood-red blaze of the cavern could not be seen, it was clearly an end too horrible for words. "The Gates of Despair . . ." Aidan muffled a gasp as the scene passed.

The bell rang, and the class began to file out as the art teacher said, "Ms. Reed and Mr. Thomas, please stay after class. I wish to speak to you about your art."

"I'm glad you both chose to create something original," Mr. Kurtz said. "What do you call this piece?"

"I . . . I don't know," Antoinette Reed answered. "It came from a nightmare I've been having. I think I'll call it *Despair*."

Aidan's eyes narrowed. *Does she know? And if she does, which side is she on?*

"You have named it well, Ms. Reed," said Mr. Kurtz. "Something in my heart aches when I look at it. Very powerful work, yes. And what of yours, Mr. Thomas? Have you given it a name?"

"The Seven Fountains of Alleble," Aidan replied. He studied Antoinette.

"Your work, Mr. Thomas, is equally breathtaking. There is beauty and strength. There is also, I think . . . mystery. For instance, why is one fountain dry and empty?"

Aidan suddenly felt very awkward. Gwenne had told him once that he must go into his world and tell everyone he could about Alleble, but to tell a teacher he didn't even know? "Uh, it's a long story," Aidan muttered, and immediately he felt ashamed for not saying more.

"I enjoy long stories, Mr. Thomas. So another time, perhaps," said Mr. Kurtz. "In any case, I asked you to stay after because—well, quite frankly—your artistic skills are far superior to everyone else's in the class, and I fear what I have to teach will be a waste of your time."

Aidan thought, *Not another schedule change!* He looked at Antoinette; she looked back at him.

"Soooooo, I have decided to create a new section," explained Mr. Kurtz. "I'll call it advanced art. It will be four credits, not three, and will appear on your report card as an independent study class. I've never done this before, but math does it all the time, so I will too."

"Excuse me, Mr. Kurtz," Antoinette said, "but will we still come to your class at the same time?" Exactly what Aidan wanted to know.

"Yes, of course. But I will set up a little area at the back table where the two of you can work without being disturbed by my prattling. This is all up to you, though. Is this something you wish to do?"

They both nodded vigorously.

"Done then. We'll begin Thursday. Be thinking of a technique you would like to learn, and I will provide some resources for you. Now, let me write you each a pass so your next teacher doesn't throw you to the wolves for being late."

Mr. Kurtz closed the art room door. Aidan and Antoinette looked at each other.

"Do you believe?" they blurted out simultaneously.

"Yes!" Aidan answered.

"Me too," Antoinette said.

"But, what . . . what do you believe?" Aidan asked. He had to be sure.

"I believe in Alleble of The Realm," she began. "And King Eliam the King of all Kingdoms. He is everlasting, and seeks all who would follow the true King. I believe that one day I will go to be with King Eliam in the Sacred Realm Beyond the Sun. I believe everything in *The Book of Alleble*."

"*Book of Alleble?*"

"Yes," she replied, looking confused. "*The Book of Alleble*. You believe in it, don't you? Well, you must because of your drawing, *The Seven Fountains*. Those fountains are spoken of many times in the book. You must know."

"I believe everything you said, but I didn't learn it from a book. It came from The Scrolls of Alleble. But my dad told me there was a book. Bestseller, he said."

"That's right. You can find it in any bookstore. My parents gave me mine for my seventh birthday."

"This is incredible, Antoinette!" Aidan said. "Finally, someone else who believes. When I saw your picture I was afraid for a minute that you served the Prince."

"Aidan, what a horrible thing to say! I hope you weren't judging me. Just because my friends and I like to dress a little different doesn't mean that we are evil!"

Aidan wondered how she seemed to know what he was thinking. He smiled, remembering someone else who used to do that as well.

"No, Aidan, I would never serve the Prince. I only drew the picture because I keep having nightmares about it."

"It's a horrible place, Antoinette," Aidan said with a shudder. "You sound as if you've—"

"I've been there. I saw the Gates. I was nearly captured and taken inside."

A look of awe surged onto Antoinette's face. "We need to talk," she said.

"Maybe after school?"

"Okay," Antoinette said.

"I'll clear it with Mom," Aidan said.

"I'll call my mom on my cell phone to let her know where I am."

"Maybe you could help me with the math homework too. It's a little over my head," Aidan said.

"Sure. I better run. I've got honors English now. See ya later." And with that she left.

Aidan wondered if the bus ride home would be awkward. After all, Aidan didn't really fit in with the trench-coat clan. And he wondered what his parents would think of Antoinette. *Dad's bound to like her,* he thought as he wandered down the hall toward his next class. But he wasn't so sure about his mom.

Stories to Tell

The bus ride home wasn't at all awkward. Mr. Bluehair even saved a seat for Antoinette and Aidan. Apparently, being Antoinette's friend earned Aidan some points with the trench-coat clan.

The awkward part came when they reached his house. Aidan checked his pockets. He looked all through his backpack. "I can't believe it!" Aidan complained. He turned several shades of red.

"What?"

"I forgot my keys," he answered sheepishly. "But my mom should be home soon."

"S'okay," Antoinette replied with a shrug. "We can just spread the work out on your porch and knock out our math homework."

"Good idea," Aidan said.

Antoinette really is smart, Aidan had to admit, *and not just in the bookish kind of way.*

"Mom will probably faint from the shock of seeing me doing homework without having to be told to do it."

Three pages of trigonometry later, Aidan's mom arrived.

"Hello," she said, stepping onto the porch. "You must be Antoinette."

Antoinette stood and held out a gentle hand. "Pleased to meet you, Mrs. Thomas," she said.

"It's nice to meet you too. So, why are you two outside and not inside working on homework?" she asked.

"I forgot the key," Aidan said.

"Well, come on in," Mrs. Thomas said as she opened the door.

"Mom, Antoinette and I just finished our math assignment."

Aidan's mom looked at the completed assignments and stared blankly. "You even showed your work," she mumbled.

"Can Antoinette stay for dinner?" Aidan asked.

"We were just going to order pizza, but you're welcome to join us—if it's okay with your parents, of course."

"I'm sure they won't mind," Antoinette replied. "I'll call them to make sure, though."

"Mom, we're going to the basement," Aidan said as he led Antoinette into the house. "I want to show her my paintings of The Realm."

"All right. But Antoinette should call her parents before it gets too late."

"I'll call right now, Mrs. Thomas," she said and flipped open her cell phone. But Mrs. Reed didn't answer, so she left a message.

Aidan and Antoinette tromped down the stairs to Aidan's new art studio. "Did you see her?" Aidan asked. "She was still staring at my math papers. Probably checking my work."

"If she is, she'll be in for a treat. Every one of your answers is correct."

Aidan smiled as he clicked on the track lights that illuminated his artwork.

"Whoa!" Antoinette gasped, looking at the paintings. "These are incredible!"

Aidan blushed. "I'm just getting used to painting with acrylics, but I'm sure you could do just as good."

"No, I mean it, Aidan," she said, walking up to his picture of the Grimwalk. "I've read about these places . . . I've dreamed about them. They look just how I imagined they'd look. Have you actually been to all these places in The Realm?"

Aidan nodded.

"Okay, you have got to tell me everything!" Antoinette said, sitting on a stool. "Start with how you got into The Realm. I didn't think anyone went there until they died."

"King Eliam called me," Aidan said.

"How?"

"There were signs. Weird things happened to me."

"What kinds of weird things?"

"Well, as soon as we moved out here, I started having nightmares—horrible recurring dreams. Especially this one where Paragor himself kills me." Antoinette went very still and her eyes widened. But she said nothing.

"Then, one time when I was in my room, I felt like something was staring at me from outside the window . . . which didn't make any sense because my room's up on the second floor. When I looked, the pine tree shook violently as if something large had been perched in it and flown off. I ran outside and saw an enormous shadow."

"Wait," Antoinette said. "An enormous shadow?"

"Yes," Aidan replied. "It was huge—like something invisible was flying overhead."

Antoinette's brows furrowed and she rocked on the edge of the stool.

"I think King Eliam sent a dragon to watch over me," Aidan continued. "At the time, it really messed with my head. But the weirdest thing that happened was when I was down here in the basement. I was bored, and I came down to poke around. It was really dark—we didn't have the track lights up yet—and I started hearing strange scratching sounds. It came from right over there beneath the stairs."

Aidan pointed. Antoinette stared and held her breath. It was silent in the basement.

Suddenly, Antoinette's cell phone shrilled, and they both jumped.

Antoinette flipped open her phone. "Hi, Mom."

She smiled at first, but then her expression clouded. "What? Why? . . . I know, I know—it's important. Okay, I'll be ready. And, Mom, guess what? Aidan believes! I know. That is so cool, isn't it? *What?* Mom, that's a great idea. It'll almost make up for today. I'll ask him."

Antoinette lowered the phone. "I'm not going to be able to stay for dinner."

"Why not?" Aidan's shoulders sagged in disappointment.

"Our neighbor just had a baby, and we're going to go by the hospital tonight. But my mom said you could come to our house for dinner Friday . . . if you want."

"Uh, yeah," Aidan said. But he wondered what his parents would say.

Putting the phone back to her ear, Antoinette told her mom where Aidan lived and then closed the phone. "My mom said she'll be here in ten minutes. Quick, tell me! What happened after the scratching sounds?"

"Well, the sounds got louder, and blue sparks started swirling on the floor. Then, just like that, it all stopped, and there were three tall clay pots. In them, I found the scrolls—the scrolls that tell about Alleble and of Paragor's betrayal."

"That's what's in my book," Antoinette said quietly, half to herself.

"I needed my grandfather to help me understand the poem at the end of the story. That was how I went in. The poem was the invitation."

"Poem?" Antoinette echoed. "Aidan, I've been having dreams about The Realm too. And just the other day, I was out in my garden getting the last of the tomatoes, and I saw the same kind of shadow you described. Do you think King Eliam could be calling me to come to The Realm? But my book doesn't have a poem at the end—just blank pages. What could that mean?"

Aidan shook his head. "I don't know, but when I was in Alleble, I had a friend there who told me that King Eliam invites only a few from our world prior to death—and then only for special missions."

"What was your mission?"

"I was called to travel to a small kingdom called Mithegard. It was one of the isolated cities Paragor wanted to force into a dark alliance with his dark realm. I was part of a team of twelve sent to Mithegard to convince them to seek protection from Alleble."

"Did you succeed?" Antoinette asked.

Before Aidan could answer, the doorbell rang.

"Oh, that's probably my mom!" Antoinette said. Aidan started to head for the stairs, but Antoinette grabbed his arm. "Tell me one more thing before we go up. This painting you're working on now . . ." Antoinette pointed. "Why doesn't that knight have any eyes?"

Aidan looked at the painting of Robby's Glimpse and got goose bumps. If only there was some way he could reach Robby or his Glimpse. *Maybe . . .*, Aidan thought. But before he could answer her, his mother called downstairs.

"Aidan! Antoinette's mother is here. Come on up."

As Aidan and Antoinette came up the stairs, Mrs. Reed was saying, "Thank you so much for inviting Antoinette to stay for dinner. I'm terribly sorry that I have to take her away. But our neighbor had twins—"

"Twins?" Antoinette exclaimed. "How cool is that!"

"Very cool, indeed, Antoinette," Mrs. Reed said. Then, turning back to Aidan's mother, she asked, "Perhaps Aidan could have dinner with us Friday night?"

"Yes, that would work fine."

And it was settled that easily. Mrs. Reed would pick up Aidan and Antoinette on Friday after school. She would drive him home around nine. Aidan couldn't wait. There was so much left to tell about The Realm, about Alleble, about Glimpses. And there was the inkling of a plan Aidan was developing to follow up on. Aidan wondered if Antoinette would consider it. *Maybe*, he thought.

⌇

"Come on," Aidan said into the phone. "You gotta be home sooner or later." Since Antoinette left, he had dialed Robby's number every fifteen minutes, but no one ever answered. It didn't make sense. A month and a half earlier they were best friends. Then . . . nothing. It was like Robby had disappeared from the face of the planet. Aidan was just about to give up trying, when . . .

"Hello?" A voice with a pronounced Floridian drawl answered.

Aidan nearly jumped out of his chair. "Hello, Robby? It's me, Aidan!"

"Aidan, hey!" Robby answered. "I was fixin' to call you. But I've been kinda busy gettin' ready for school."

"Yeah, me too. My first day was today. How was soccer camp?"

"What?" Robby asked.

"Soccer camp at Camp Ramblesomething."

"Oh, that. It was fine. But that ended a few weeks ago."

Aidan frowned. He'd sent a dozen emails, called innumerable times—but no replies from Robby.

"Did you get any of my emails?" Aidan asked. He didn't know why, but he felt embarrassed for asking.

"Uh, yeah." Robby hesitated. "Sorry, but like I said, I've been real busy, so I haven't had a chance to reply. You know me, I'm not much for writin' anyway. And my sister Jill hogs the computer most nights."

It sounded like a lot of excuses to Aidan, but he knew an argument would not help him deliver the message he hoped to share. "Uh, okay. Robby, listen, I've been wanting to talk to you because something really cool has happened to me."

No reply.

"Remember in that email I sent you, the one where I told you about the strange thing in the tree outside the window of my new house?"

"Uh-huh."

"Well, okay, that was the first thing—well, that and the dreams. But anyway, I was looking through the basement and I found some ancient scrolls. They told me about this place called Alleble. It's a kingdom, and well, you can go there if you believe."

"Righ—ight," Robby replied. He always said the word that way, as if it had two syllables.

Something was not right, Aidan felt sure. It seemed like Robby wasn't hearing him, like he had his ear to the phone but was listening to someone else or watching television.

"Robby, did you read my email about the scrolls?"

"Uh, yeah, I think so. . . . What was it about again?"

Aidan expelled an angry sigh and launched into the account of all the adventures he'd had when he entered The Door Within—including Grampin's heart attack.

When he was finished, there was dead silence on the phone.

Finally, Robby spoke. "I'm real sorry about your granddaddy."

"Thanks," Aidan said, then swallowed hard. "Robby, did you hear what I said about my adventures?"

"Yeah, Aidan, but you kinda lose me when ya' go off on that imaginative stuff. So are you writin' a story or somethin'? Is that it?"

"No," Aidan barked. "I'm telling you, I went there. I became a knight! These people, er . . . Glimpses, I mean. They are twins of us. What they do affects us and what we do affects them."

Aidan thought for sure that would get a response, but then heard: "I know, Mama, I'm comin'. But it's Aidan on the phone. Aidan Thomas . . . the kid who lived around the block. Yeah, I know he told me not to. Okay, Mama, okay."

"Robby?"

"Uh, yeah, sorry. That was Mama. We're leavin' to do some shopping. I'll have to call you later."

"But, Robby—"

"Good hearin' from you, Aidan. Bye."

"Well, how'd it go?" Aidan's dad asked as he walked into the kitchen and saw Aidan hanging up.

"Awful, Dad. Robby was acting weird, almost like he didn't know me."

"Well, that's a shame, son."

"And when I tried to tell him about the scrolls and Alleble, he wouldn't listen. Thought I was writing a story."

Aidan's dad sat down at the kitchen table and gestured for Aidan to join him.

"Aidan, remember that the Scrolls, Alleble, Glimpses—it all sounds crazy to those who do not want to see. You cannot make him believe."

"I know, Dad, but he's my best friend. He ought to trust me."

"Just like I ought to have trusted you," Mr. Thomas said, and he glanced toward the study where Grampin had spent most of his time. "Just like I ought to have trusted my own father. He tried to convince me for twenty years, and I just didn't want to hear it. In one way, it sounds too good to be true. In another way, it's frightening."

"Frightening?"

"Well, yes. Most people believe only in the here and now—in what they can see in front of them. We get kind of comfortable living in the moment. Well, Alleble, Paragory, The Realm—it's a threat to that comfort. If it's true, then our whole idea of the way the world works and why we're here on this giant spinning mudball gets blown away."

Aidan grinned.

"What?"

"Grampin used to call the earth a mudball too."

"I catch myself talking like him all the time. I wish I had listened to him earlier. But I was hardheaded. Of course, your mother thinks I have truly lost my mind. She thinks it's my way of grieving for Grampin . . . but she'll come around. We'll gang up on her."

They shared a laugh, but later as Aidan lay on his bed, he felt anything but happy. Robby was in danger, and there seemed to be nothing he could do about it. When he had left Alleble, he had a plan—a plan to see Gwenne again, a plan to save Robby. Now, Aidan wasn't sure if any of it would work.

Aidan turned on his side and stared out the window over the whispering pine trees.

Neither Aidan nor Antoinette could anticipate what would happen later that night. For there was another plan at work in their lives.

A GHOST AND A MONSTER

Mr. Reed stopped by Antoinette's room to say good night. Sweat trickled down his face and his sleeveless sweatshirt was soaked.

"Been working out?" Antoinette asked.

"The heavy bag," he replied between deep breaths. "No matter how many times I hit the thing, it never falls down!"

Antoinette made a face. "Maybe you should try kicking it." And then she did a side kick within an inch of her father's chin. She let her foot hang there a few moments before slowly lowering it to the ground. She grinned.

"I think I've taught you too well," Mr. Reed said. "That was nice."

"So, what did you think of the twins?" he asked.

"Too cute, Dad," Antoinette replied. "But they are so tiny."

Antoinette's dad smiled. After a quiet moment, he said: "Mom tells me you made a new friend at school today."

"His name is Aidan. He and his family moved here from Maryland. And, Dad, he believes."

"So I hear. But don't sound so shocked. King Eliam is still very much at work in this world. I run into believers all the time."

"I know," Antoinette replied. "It's just that there aren't that many my age around here, I guess."

"Maybe you and Aidan can do something about that."

"Yeah, maybe we will." Antoinette grinned. "Dad, what do you think of this?" Antoinette held up a dark purple knitted poncho. "I was thinking of wearing this tomorrow."

"You mean you aren't wearing black?" Her dad feigned shock. "What will your trench-coated friends think?"

"Daaaad, please don't offend my friends like that," Antoinette said.

"No harm intended, sweetie," he said. "It's just, well . . . they look rough, and some of them smoke."

"I'm too smart to mess with cigarettes," she replied, hands on her hips. "And the clothes, it's a style. They may look a little different, but at least they'll listen when I talk about Alleble."

"I trust your judgment. I'm just protective of my little girl, that's all."

"I can take care of myself, Dad. You taught me. Now what about the poncho?"

"You're not wearing it to impress this Aidan fellow, are you?"

"Daaaad!"

"I know, I'm being overprotective again. I think the poncho looks great on you, but since I clearly have no concept of fashion whatsoever . . . you should ask Mom."

"Thanks, Dad. And anyway, I'll wear a black tee and black jeans underneath." They shared a laugh and said good night. Antoinette closed the bifold doors of her closet, turned out the light, and hopped into bed.

Ten minutes later, Antoinette was still awake. *A storm is coming*, she thought. Not long after, the curtains floated on a steady breeze. Soon, light flickered outside the window, followed by a long, low roll of thunder. *Still a ways off though,* she thought as she closed the window and got back under the covers.

Weather, especially severe weather, had always fascinated Antoinette, and as long as she could remember, she seemed to have the peculiar ability to sense when a storm was coming long before it arrived.

There had been a storm the night her birth parents lost their lives in a fire. A fire caused by lightning. *If only I had known about that storm.*

Antoinette shook her head. She had long ago accepted her parents' deaths, though in bad times she often needed to remind herself that King Eliam's plans always worked out for good. After all, it was her adoptive parents who first told her about Alleble.

Another flash of lightning. Thunder growled more conspicuously.

Antoinette closed her eyes, but they snapped right back open. *Who am I kidding?* she thought. *I don't even want to try to sleep.*

She was afraid that the nightmares would return. Lately, they were always there. She wished she could escape them. She wished she could enter The Realm as Aidan had. Maybe there, in the presence of King Eliam, the nightmares would go away. She nestled under her down comforter, a steady rain began, and she began to feel drowsy.

Antoinette awoke with a start. Had someone called her name?

Lightning lit up the room, but the thunder was distant. *The storm is leaving*, she thought. *How long was I asleep?*

Her heart hammered. She hadn't had a nightmare, but someone had called her.

"Dad?" she whispered urgently, sitting up. No answer.

Then she heard it.

"*Antoinette . . .*"

Her name faded in and out as if whispered by someone far away. She yanked the comforter up to her chin and scanned the shadows of her room.

The closet was open. *But I'm sure I closed it,* she thought. Even the hanging clothes within had parted to reveal the pale back wall of the closet. Antoinette thought of Aidan and the strange events that befell him just before he received the Scrolls. It was a sign, Aidan had said.

"*Antoinette . . .*"

The voice came from the closet.

"It's a sign. It's a sign. It's a sign!" Antoinette repeated to herself. She rocked back and forth on her bed and stared at the back of the closet. It was as if someone had been walled up behind the closet in a secret room. But Antoinette knew that could not be. There was nothing behind the closet. It was on an exterior wall.

"*Antoinette . . .*"

This time, a small flicker of blue appeared in the exact middle of the back wall of the closet. Then it was gone. The voice was less garbled, but still sounded far away.

"*Antoinette, hear me . . .*"

The flicker reappeared. At first just a twitching finger of blue electricity, it quickly formed into a quivering circle. The circle began to grow, and it rotated slowly. It reached three feet in diameter, stopped growing, and flickered white-hot. Within the circle, the closet wall went dark as if a tunnel had opened, a tunnel that went on and on, forever into darkness.

Entranced by the vision before her, Antoinette stared, but did not scream.

"Antoinette . . ."

In the center of the darkness within the electric circle, a shape appeared. It was an irregular shape. It seemed to be growing. As it moved closer, it became more recognizable. It was a person, but pale—very pale, possessing an eerie light of his own. And suddenly he was there, floating just outside the closet at the foot of Antoinette's bed.

Antoinette realized it was a young man. He was dressed in armor and had emblazoned upon his breastplate two mountains with a bright sun rising between them. An immense sword hung at his side. His skin, armor, and weapon were pale . . . ghostly. And he flickered as if he were struggling to stay visible, while an unseen force was drawing him away. But while his appearance was frightening, there was something about this being that was familiar and comforting.

"Antoinette . . . ," he spoke. He raised his spectral hand and pointed to her. His eyes bored into her. They were dark but flickered blue. And then, Antoinette knew him. It was Aidan! His hair was longer, and his face looked older, but Antoinette had no doubt it was Aidan.

She started to speak, but the ghostly Aidan spoke first.

"Antoinette, you have been called."

His image then began to fade and shrink. But all the while, his eyes beckoned, and he pointed to her.

The electric blue circle reversed course and shrank as well. Antoinette watched it disappear. *It's a sign,* she thought to herself. *But how could Aidan—*

She never finished the thought, for suddenly she felt a chill as if the temperature in her room had instantly dropped thirty degrees.

Wind gusted out of her closet. Lightning struck just outside her window. The thunder detonated like a cannon within a heartbeat. Antoinette screamed.

Aidan switched off his lamp. Thunder rumbled in the distance, and a steady rain began. *Another storm?* He stared out the window and wondered if he'd see Captain Valithor again.

Masses of gray clouds enveloped the mountains. The pines in the front yard whispered as the rain fell, and though Aidan was not sleepy, his eyelids drooped. Aidan felt suddenly disoriented and shook his head. He reached clumsily for his bundle of scrolls, but missed. He fell away from the window sill and dropped like a stone.

Aidan felt like he was falling forever. There was no sound, no wind in his hair, but he knew he was falling. He saw only darkness at first. Then, as he began to level out, he witnessed the most alien landscape he had ever seen.

An ocean of great jagged shards of broken rock stretched out before Aidan. Volcanoes rose up on both sides of a path. Some belched towering plumes of black smoke. Some vomited streams of molten rock. And still others stood quietly smoldering.

And upon the wretched path were torch-bearing soldiers in dark armor.

Aidan zoomed above the path through ash, smoke, and fire, slowing only when the path snaked around the greatest of all the volcanoes. Like an immense beast waiting to spring, the fiery giant seemed to stand guard at the top of the world.

The scene sent tremors through Aidan, and he knew that he should not be there. He struggled against his momentum but could not reverse course. He floated slowly but inevitably down into the charred chasm.

The great volcano sent a deluge of molten rock into the valley, but by machinations that Aidan did not at first understand, the flow of liquid fire diverted. Had the natural flow of magma not been interrupted, the empty, charred hollow would have been a lake of fire.

As Aidan descended lower he could see thousands upon thousands of knights standing in rigid lines. Weapons—swords, pikes, and bows—held vertically at each soldier's side. Their armor was black and polished. Their dark eyes glinted red. *This army must be from Paragory,* Aidan thought.

The pale knights in the dark armor did not notice Aidan. They were looking at a massive square excavation site. Layer upon layer of dark rock had been carved away. And by the guards' torchlights, Aidan saw a staircase leading into the pit.

At the top of the stairway stood Paragor. He wore the same black armor as the others, but a burgundy hooded cloak draped his shoulders—and upon his breastplate, gouged red into the dark iron like a black widow's hourglass, was the image of an inverted crown.

Once a powerful knight in service of Alleble, Paragor had betrayed his King. And as a consequence for his treachery, Paragor was cast out of Alleble and doomed to rule as a mere prince in a dark and hopeless land far away from the throne he desperately wanted.

Behind Paragor stood an attendant, nervously watching his master. Even from far away, Aidan could see the deep scars on the man's face and hands.

Paragor removed his helmet and handed it to the attendant, who ducked and scurried away.

Paragor's dark, dark eyes flashed red for an instant. He smiled at the approach of a second attendant who bore a case of black marble and offered it to his lord.

The Prince reached down, lifted the lid from the case, and removed a long, segmented piece of iron. He then held it aloft for all to see.

It was a key, and a loud murmur surged through the ranks of the soldiers. It seemed to Aidan that the key was something ancient, something powerful, and something dangerous in Paragor's hands.

His mission accomplished, the attendant bowed and turned to leave. Then he abruptly looked up. His cold eyes flashed red, and in that moment, Aidan knew him. It was Robby's Glimpse! And he was directly in the service of The Betrayer!

"Robby!" Aidan cried out. "Robby, no!" But with a flourish of his dark cape, Robby's Glimpse disappeared into the mass of enemy soldiers.

A blazing torch in one hand, the huge key in the other, Paragor descended the stairs into the pit. Unable to resist the strange gravity that compelled him, Aidan followed. They traveled through several layers of striated stone that reeked of centuries of burning.

Soon the smell of char was overpowered by a smell so foul and sharp that Aidan struggled for breath.

Paragor paused at the bottom of the stairs. Before him was an enormous steel door. Two men high and four wide. Its frame was secured to the stone wall by dozens of fist-sized rivets, and there was no handle or door ring. It seemed that whatever had been locked behind the door was meant to stay there.

Aidan watched as Paragor held his torch to the door. He uttered words in a strange language and moved the torch slowly over the surface of the door. Suddenly, licks of fire leaped from the torch to the door and burned away a hole for a key.

There came a thunderous booming from deep within the rock, and slowly the door began to open. A mist of darkness swirled out like tendrils of smoke from inside. But it was not smoke, rather a purposeful, groping darkness that reached and curled around Paragor's legs and spread up the stone walls like a black, creeping vine. Even Paragor stepped away from the door.

Then, unbearably slowly, Aidan began to rise out of the pit.

Suddenly, a hand emerged from the door and grasped the riveted doorframe. It was a huge hand, black and scaly, gnarled but sinewy and strong. There were long white talons protruding at the end of each finger, and they scraped along the metal as if trying to escape. The taloned hand and then a huge leathery wing emerged from the door, but that was all Aidan saw. He spiraled with greater speed upward into the night sky. Behind him he heard a hideous voice from the pit near the center of the emptied lake of fire.

The voice seemed ancient and harsh, as if it had not spoken for an eternity.

Aidan covered his ears with his hands. But it was in vain. The words pounded at his skull and roared into his mind: "They will all die."

THE WAY OF
THE SWORD

Events at school the next day seemed to conspire to steal away every chance Aidan and Antoinette had to talk. Mrs. VanDerEyck put them in separate groups to work on a series of math problems. The school counselor called Antoinette to the guidance office during lunch. And an assembly ate up the time they would have normally spent together in art. When Aidan and Antoinette finally climbed into the second seat of Mrs. Reed's truck, it all came out in a rush.

"I have something to tell you!" they said simultaneously.

"Last night I—" Again, speaking at the same time.

"You go first," Aidan said.

"Okay," Antoinette replied. She pushed aside her long red bangs, exhaled a deep breath, and said, "I saw you last night."

"What?" Aidan stole a glance at Mrs. Reed to see if she'd heard.

"Mom's cool, Aidan," Antoinette said. "She believes, remember?"

"I know. But, Antoinette, what do you mean, you saw me?"

"I had a vision," she replied. "But it wasn't actually you. I think it was your Glimpse."

"You know about Glimpses?" Aidan exclaimed.

"Of course, silly." Antoinette laughed. "I've believed in the story of Alleble since I was seven. My parents told me all about Glimpses a long time ago. Kind of cool, don't you think, to have a twin?"

Aidan was speechless.

"But, Aidan, none of us have ever been to The Realm," said Mrs. Reed from the front seat. "And none of us have ever seen a Glimpse . . . until now."

"He looked just like me?" Aidan asked.

"Well, not exactly. He looked older, his skin was superpale, his hair was longer, and he kind of floated there, flickering in the air. But other than that he looked just like you."

"All Glimpses have skin like that. It spooked me too," Aidan said.

"You look pretty cool in armor, you know."

Aidan blushed, and he was reminded of Gwenne, who also thought he looked handsome in armor.

"Aidan, why would I see a vision of your Glimpse?" Antoinette asked after telling him all about her vision.

"I think King Eliam wants to see you," Aidan replied.

"What?" Antoinette and her mom exclaimed at the same time.

"Didn't you say my Glimpse said you've been called?" Aidan asked.

"Yes."

"Do you have your copy of *The Story* with you?" he asked.

"It's at home, but—the poem!" Antoinette exclaimed. "You think the poem will be there."

Aidan, Antoinette, and her parents sat staring at the poem in the back of an old leather-bound copy of *The Story*.

There are passages and doors
And realms that lie unseen.
There are roads both wide and narrow
And no avenue between.
Doors remain closed for those
Who in sad vanity yet hide.
Yet when belief is chosen,
The key appears inside.
What is lived now will soon pass,
And what is not will come to be.
The Door Within must open,
For one to truly see.

"What's it mean?" Mr. Reed looked at Aidan for an answer.

"It's a riddle," Aidan explained. "I didn't get it at first either. Grampin, uh, my grandfather, had to explain it to me. It means—"

"When belief is chosen . . ." Antoinette interrupted, thinking out loud. "The key appears inside. I've got it! It means for people who choose to believe, they already have a key. The key is inside us. Of course, if it's The Door Within, then the key has to be within us too!"

Aidan couldn't believe it. He knew without Grampin's help he never would have figured out the poem. But Antoinette didn't need any help. She just charged ahead. *Was there no end to what this girl could do?*

"I guess this means you are going to Alleble!" Aidan said.

Antoinette turned to Aidan. Her glad blue eyes glimmered

through tears, and her smile held a thousand thank-yous. Then she turned to her father. "Well, Daddy, can I go?"

"Sweetheart, I don't think this is something you can rush into," he said, leaning back on the sofa and running fingers through his sandy brown hair.

"But, Dad—"

"No, Antoinette, he's right," Aidan interrupted. "Alleble is at war, and you may find yourself in the middle of it."

Antoinette looked indignantly at Aidan. "I can take care of myself."

"Your father and I need to talk, Antoinette," Mrs. Reed said sternly. "And before you go boasting again about what you can handle, I think you should listen to Aidan. He's been there, remember?"

Aidan saw the wounded look in Antoinette's eyes. He looked away quickly.

"Why don't you take Aidan downstairs and show him the gym," Mr. Reed suggested. Antoinette perked up at the idea.

"C'mon, Aidan!" And the next thing Aidan knew, they were headed down a steep flight of basement stairs.

"Wow!" Aidan said. "Your basement looks like a boxing ring."

The floor was a padded blue mat, and a battered red heavy-bag hung from the ceiling in the room's center. And around the perimeter of the room were racks of wooden staffs, crates of boxing gloves, and mannequin torsos dressed in what looked like a baseball umpire's mask and pads.

"What's all this?" Aidan asked.

"This is where we work out," Antoinette replied. "My whole family's into kendo."

"What's that?"

"It's Japanese. It means 'the way of the sword,'" Antoinette said, slowly drawing a long wooden blade from one of the racks. "We actually do spada-kendo, which is a European form. It combines medieval combat with Japanese fencing. It's sword fighting, basically."

Antoinette gracefully sliced the air a few times with the long wooden blade. "You said you were trained to be a knight in Alleble, right? Are you any good?"

Aidan grinned. "I'm okay," he said. "How about you?"

"I'm okay," she said, grinning back. "Grab a *shinai*."

"A what?"

"Shinai. It's a wooden sword for training."

"Oh." Aidan walked over to the rack and found a wooden blade that seemed about the right weight. It wasn't *Fury*, but it felt good to have any sword—even a wooden sword—in his hand again.

"My dad likes that kind," Antoinette said, grabbing some black pads. "Most of the time we spar down here, but let's go outside. There is more room to move around."

Antoinette unlocked a sliding glass door, and they walked up an areaway into Antoinette's backyard. It was flat and wide, like Antoinette said, with plenty of room to move around. Aidan wondered what to expect from his new red-headed friend.

The sun rained down through the trees, painting the unshaded patches of the backyard golden. Antoinette handed Aidan a harness of black pads. "You should put these on," she said as she put some on too. "Just in case I slip."

"That's not very comforting," Aidan replied. He quickly pulled the harness over his head. It fit like a life preserver.

"Remember, no shots at the head. Shinais may be wooden, but they can still do some serious damage."

"That's not very comforting either."

Antoinette laughed. "Ready then?"

Aidan shrugged. "I guess."

Antoinette held her wooden blade with both hands vertically out in front of her. Her back and neck were upright, perfectly straight, mirroring her sword. She flexed at the knees, one foot a pace in front of the other. She stood very, very still.

Aidan was about to speak, when Antoinette lunged forward with lightning quickness. Her wooden blade swept down with tremendous force. Aidan blocked it just in time. He sidestepped, but Antoinette pursued the attack. A combination high left chop followed by a low sweep at his right anklc. Aidan blocked and leaped, but the blows kept coming. Her sword moved with dizzying speed. Aidan didn't have time to think of a counter. All he could do was block.

She brought the blade down again and again. And all the time, she pressed forward. Aidan backed up a step.

Antoinette slashed left, right, and left again. Then she drove forward with two thrusts in succession. Aidan stumbled and found himself on his back with the tip of Antoinette's blade pressed into his chest pad.

"That is called *kakari-geiko*," Antoinette said, helping Aidan to his feet. "You charge forward with multiple strikes, never letting up, so that your opponent must abandon his own plan of attack."

"Well, it worked!" Aidan said, shaking his head. "And you said you were just *okay*."

"So . . . maybe I'm pretty good. Go again?"

Aidan nodded. He wasn't about to be taken off guard a second time.

They stood ready.

Once again, Antoinette launched forward, raining down blows. This time, Aidan was ready. He remembered that her slashing strikes came in threes with a slight pause between each series. He blocked and parried, playing defense and backing up—all the while counting her strikes. When she slashed the third time, Aidan snapped his wooden blade suddenly from outside in, driving her sword down almost to the turf. Maintaining control of her blade, Aidan let his elbow collapse in toward his side. Then he thrust forward before she could raise her sword to defend. The tip of his wooden sword stabbed into Antoinette's pads, and she jumped backward.

"Ouch!" she said. "That was amazing."

"It's called a *moulinet*," Aidan said, smiling. "A friend from Alleble taught me how."

"And you said you were just *okay*," Antoinette said, grinning.

"Maybe . . . I'm pretty good, then," Aidan replied with a wink.

"Well, we're even," Antoinette said. "Next strike wins?"

Aidan nodded, and once again they clashed. Wooden blades cracked against each other as Aidan and Antoinette ranged all over the backyard. Antoinette changed her strategy, and her attacks didn't seem to follow a pattern. She kept her slashes high, and Aidan couldn't find an opening for a moulinet.

For a moment, Antoinette pressed forward, driving Aidan back. But he countered with creative, sweeping combinations that forced Antoinette into awkward defensive backpedals. No one kept an advantage for very long.

Aidan pushed the attack. He figured Antoinette probably had not faced too many left-handers, so he went one-handed with his blade and came at her from left to right. It seemed to be working. He drove her into a sunny patch of the yard, and her guard seemed to be weakening. *A few more strikes*, he thought, *and then a moulinet!*

But as Aidan lunged forward, his foot turned on a tree root, and he stumbled. He went to one knee, and suddenly things went into slow motion.

He looked up at Antoinette, and with the sun directly behind her, her hair became brilliant gold. Details fell into place like puzzle pieces. The lavender poncho, the piercing blue eyes, the golden hair—

"Gwenne . . . ," Aidan said aloud. His sword fell. But it was so fast that Antoinette did not see. She was already swinging with all her might to block Aidan's next strike, which never came. Her wooden blade smacked Aidan across the nose, and he tumbled to the side with a yelp.

Antoinette dropped her shinai and knelt beside Aidan. "Oh, Aidan, I'm sorry! I'm so sorry! Oh, oh no, your nose is bleeding!"

Aidan sat up, clutched his nose, and tried to pinch shut the flow of blood. "Antoinette," he said nasally. "I can't believe I didn't see it before! I met your Glimpse in Alleble. Your Glimpse is Gwenne!"

And though his nose throbbed, and the blood flowed freely, Aidan smiled. For it was clear that King Eliam's plan was already in motion.

TRAVEL PLANS

I think the bleeding has stopped," Aidan said, tossing a red wad of paper towels into the trash. He joined Antoinette and her dad at the kitchen table.

"Y'know this isn't the first time Antoinette's done this," Mrs. Reed said, sitting down with a cup of coffee.

"Mom!" Antoinette exclaimed.

"She and her father were sparring in the basement," Mrs. Reed continued, ignoring Antoinette's pleas. "The Broncos scored a touchdown—"

"We had a TV down there at the time," explained Antoinette's dad. "I looked over for just a split second to watch the replay, and *WHAM,* Antoinette got me with a round kick."

"It was an accident!" Antoinette said.

"Boy, that was a gusher!" Mr. Reed said, absently pinching the bridge of his nose. "I probably should have seen a doctor. I bet it was broken."

"Dad, I feel bad enough already, okay?"

"I had it coming," Aidan said. "I shouldn't have dropped my guard, but when I saw you—that way—I just kind of lost it."

"So my Glimpse's name is Gwenne?"

"Yes, but she's a blond."

"Y'know, my hair is normally blond. I just like to dye it red." Antoinette tilted her head back and fluffed her hair like a model. "So tell me more about Gwenne."

"She is one of the twelve knights who went to Mithegard. We went through a lot together. She's . . . she's my friend."

Aidan hoped he wasn't blushing. From the moment he said good-bye to Gwenne, all he could think about was finding her human twin. Now that he had found her, he didn't know what to say. He certainly didn't want Antoinette to know how he felt about Gwenne.

"If Antoinette enters The Realm," Mr. Reed began, "what do you think her mission will be?"

"I don't know," Aidan replied. "It might be a mission like mine. I was told that there were many smaller kingdoms and cities still to be reached with the message of Alleble. But—" Aidan looked hopefully to Antoinette, "I was hoping that if you go, you might do something for me." Aidan held his breath.

"Just name it," Antoinette said.

Aidan felt a huge weight leave his shoulders. "I have this great friend, back in Maryland. His name is Robby Pierson. Well, when I left Alleble, I had a vision of him, and he was on Paragor's side."

Antoinette's parents stiffened. The room seemed to darken. Only Antoinette seemed unaffected by the mentioning of The Betrayer's name. "How do you know?" she asked.

"He was wearing the black and crimson armor of the enemy," Aidan explained sadly. "And his eyes . . . they flashed red."

"But it was a vision," Mrs. Reed asked. "Like a dream? Maybe you've just been so worried about him that it affected your dreams."

Aidan's stomach tightened uncomfortably. "Sometimes they are dreams," he said. "But other times they happen when I'm wide awake. They just come over me, and I see things. The events that I see . . . some of them have come true. I had another vision last night. I saw my friend Robby as an attendant to Paragor himself, and the two of them were setting something free from an underground cell. It was a monster. I'm afraid it will come true if someone doesn't reach Robby for the King."

"I don't like the sound of that, Aidan. Have you spoken to Robby since returning from The Realm?" Mr. Reed asked. "Have you told him about Alleble?"

"I've tried, Mr. Reed," Aidan said. "He just doesn't listen. He acts so strange on the phone—almost like he doesn't know me."

"That doesn't sound right," Mrs. Reed said.

"Okay, so you want me to find his Glimpse in The Realm, is that it?" Antoinette asked. Aidan continued to be amazed by her ability to quickly piece things together.

"Do you have a picture of Robby?" Mrs. Reed asked.

"No, but we can get one on the Net. His soccer team is ranked nationally. His picture's on their web site."

"I'll try, Aidan," Antoinette said. "It'll be like looking for a needle in a hay stack, but I'll try."

"Wait a minute," Mr. Reed objected. "You're assuming we're going to let you go to The Realm."

"But, Daddy, I've got to go," Antoinette pleaded. "I've been called. I can't just say no thanks, can I?"

Antoinette's father was quiet but struggling within. At last, he asked, "So, how does this work? How will Antoinette enter The Realm?"

Antoinette grinned. "Oh, thank you, Daddy! Thank you!"

"I didn't say yes, Antoinette. I just want more information."

Three sets of eyes turned to Aidan. He took a deep breath. "Like the poem says, Antoinette has to travel the narrow path," Aidan began. "It's what Glimpses call the path between worlds. My grandfather taught me to imagine a bridge over a deep chasm. Antoinette will need to picture this bridge in her mind and travel across it. Eventually, she will come to a door, The Door Within. When she passes through that door, she enters The Realm, and Gwenne, her Glimpse, will come here."

"She'll come here—like to our house?" Mrs. Reed asked.

"I'm not sure," Aidan replied. "But I don't think so. When I went to The Realm, Aelic, my Glimpse, didn't go to my house. All I know is that Gwenne told me a person and his or her Glimpse can never be in the same realm at the same time. And that's another thing . . . time works differently in The Realm."

"What do you mean?" Antoinette asked.

"Well, I was in The Realm for almost two weeks in Glimpse time, but when I returned, I discovered that I had only been missing for about five hours!"

"So Antoinette could be back by breakfast?" Mrs. Reed asked.

"Maybe," Aidan said. "I guess it depends on Antoinette's mission. But I don't think there's any way to compare the time exactly. My grandfather was in The Realm for a month our time. But in The Realm, he experienced two years of adventures!"

"Two years?" Mrs. Reed echoed. "Antoinette, a lot could happen in that time. And you don't even really know what you're getting into."

"You're right, Mom, I don't," Antoinette said. "But you know all I've ever wanted, since you first told me about King Eliam, was to do something for him . . . to serve him—if for no other reason than for the fact that he gave me hope that doesn't quit! Because of him, I will never be alone!"

Mr. Reed's shoulders sagged. He took his wife's hand. "A faithful servant of King Eliam would never ignore his call. It's just that—" His voice faltered. "The Realm is at war. What if something happened to you? What if you couldn't come back?"

Aidan stretched out on his bed and looked across the room to where he kept his scrolls. He thought about Antoinette. He wondered if she'd gone yet.

She probably left the moment I walked out the door, Aidan thought. *That's the way she is. Confident, brave, spirited. So much like Gwenne. Then again, Antoinette is not like Gwenne at all in some ways. She is too rash . . . too impatient.*

After dinner, Antoinette had pummeled Aidan with questions about entering The Door Within. He told her about the bridge, about being willing to take a risk and step out there, and most of all, about staying on the path no matter what the voices told her to do! *I hope she remembers,* Aidan thought with a laugh. *She wouldn't want her adventure to begin like mine did—by having to climb over the mountains of Paragory.*

Aidan scoured his mind, hoping he'd told her everything she'd need to know. He'd told her to try to find Kaliam when she got to Alleble. He'd told her she'd need to get fitted for armor. And he'd told her to expect to be trained—hard—for her mission. He hadn't told her about the chores she'd probably have to learn to do. No, that little tidbit, he'd left out. He wanted Antoinette to experience the joy of "refreshing the dragon pen" just as he had!

They'd printed a picture of Robby, and Antoinette taped it inside the cover of her copy of *The Story*. She promised to find him if she could. But Aidan knew it would really be a one in a million chance. If she did find Robby's Glimpse, Aidan hoped she would remember that anything that happens to a Glimpse would have an effect on his human twin. *That could be tricky*, Aidan thought. *Robby's Glimpse is an enemy knight. What will happen if there's a battle?*

Aidan sat up and looked out his window. *I wish Dad would come home soon*, he thought. *Ten o'clock. He's really late—and he's still got Grampin's diary!*

Aidan flopped back on the bed and exhaled. He wished he was the one going to Alleble. He wanted to clown around with Kaliam, Nock, and Mallik again. He wanted to watch the sun rise between the peaks of *Pennath Ador* and see its rays sparkle in the glorious fountains.

But more than anything else, he wanted to see Gwenne.

There was a soft knock at Aidan's bedroom door. His mom walked in carrying a cell phone. She did not look very happy.

"It's your father," she said abruptly. She handed the phone to Aidan and, without another word, shut the door behind her.

Aidan put the phone to his ear. "Dad?"

"Aidan, glad you're still up."

"You're at the office pretty late. Is that why Mom's mad?"

There was a brief pause. "Uh, no, that's only part of it. But listen, I wanted to talk to you. The reason I've been at the office is that there are some problems with an account I used to have at Riddick and Dunn's Baltimore office. We've been trying to hash it out over the phone, but it's just not working. They need me to fly in tomorrow morning. I'll probably need to be there a couple— maybe three days."

"So, anyway," Aidan's dad continued, "I was thinking that maybe you'd like to tag along. It'll give you and Robby a chance to talk about some things. What do you think?"

"Are you serious, Dad? I can go?"

"Well, you might have to miss a day of school, maybe two . . ."

No wonder Mom's mad, Aidan thought. *She never likes me to miss school.*

"Uh, I'll get over it!" Aidan said, laughing. "This is so cool! Thank you, Dad! Thank you!"

"You need to pack, and you should probably call Robby to see if it's okay for you to drop by while we're in town. But listen, don't stay up too late. Our flight leaves at seven A.M. from Colorado Springs Airport."

I won't be able to sleep! Aidan thought after he hung up the phone.

As he packed, Aidan thought it was rather funny that Robby was going to get the truth of Alleble from both sides—from Antoinette in The Realm, if she could find him, and from Aidan back in Maryland. And face-to-face, Robby would just have to listen, wouldn't he?

THE DOOR WITHIN

There it was, just as Aidan had described: a long, narrow bridge of planks and rope stretching across a vast chasm to a destination unseen.

Antoinette could still feel the bed beneath her, and she could still hear familiar house sounds. Aidan had told her that too. *Nothing to worry about. Don't open your eyes. The sounds of your room will go away as you travel across the bridge.*

She wondered if her parents would look in on her. Unable to have children, they had adopted three-year-old Antoinette and raised her as their own. Now, to allow their only child to enter a world at war was a huge risk for them, but in the end they trusted King Eliam enough to let their daughter go.

Back to the bridge, Antoinette told herself.

In her mind she walked to the edge of the cliff and looked down. It was a long way down—impossible to tell for sure how far to the ground because thick white mist swirled below.

Antoinette found a stone and hurled it out as far as she could. She watched it arc and fall. She saw it disappear into the cloud bank. And then she listened.

Nothing. *Okay, so it's a long, long way down.*

Antoinette shrugged. The height didn't worry her. She looked at the bridge. It looked sturdy. She looked at the sky. It was blue and cloudless, only the slightest breeze. She knew she'd make it across that bridge. In fact, she decided to run across.

Feeling invincible, Antoinette stepped out on the bridge. There, it was just as sturdy as it looked. So, off she went—a jog at first, confidence surging—then, a run. Then, an all-out sprint.

The planks went by in bunches. She started laughing as she reached the beginning of the upslope. Then she stopped running and stood very still.

She had heard something, and it was not a creak or a groan from the hallway or the rattle of the heat kicking on in her bedroom. It was not any house noise. It was a low roll of thunder, deep and menacing.

Antoinette slowly turned her head to the left. The sky, which had only a moment ago been peaceful and blue, had turned to a sickly yellow haze. And the horizon was black and spreading.

Lightning flickered. Thunder followed like the echo of a cannon. *Strange*, Antoinette thought. *Why didn't I sense the storm approaching?* And then Antoinette was afraid.

Lightning split the sky. Antoinette ducked as thunder crashed and echoed off the cliff walls. The wind picked up and swirled. The bridge began to sway.

If the storm caught her out in the open, suspended over the chasm. . . . Heavy raindrops began striking her. Antoinette held the *Book of Alleble* close to her body to keep it dry. Then she stumbled.

Shaking, Antoinette knelt there for a moment. She wanted the storm to go away. She wanted to make it go away.

Maybe I should just open my eyes. Then she realized her eyes were already open. She was no longer in her bedroom. It was no longer a vision.

When she looked up, it seemed that there were scowling faces in the clouds. Hideous, angry faces full of hate. Her skin prickled. The air grew chill.

Antoinette stood again, clutched the *Book of Alleble,* and sprinted, calling out to King Eliam as she ran. Her King would not let it end here, before her mission had really even begun.

The rain came harder now, obscuring her view of the way ahead. She slipped on the wet planks. One foot went over the edge for a moment.

Thunder crashed. It seemed to be laughing at her.

Antoinette pulled herself up and struggled forward. Then, through the sheets of rain, she saw it. *The door!* She pushed forward until, suddenly, she stood before it. The storm was gone as though it had never been. Antoinette exhaled, wiped back her sodden hair, and whispered, "Thank you."

The door was tall, hewn from gray stone and engraved intricately with castles, unicorns, warriors, and a long and winding road that led to two mountains. The sun rose between those peaks, and Antoinette's heart rejoiced.

Seeing the silver ring, she reached down and pulled. Light, fierce and startlingly pure, shone forth from behind the door. Antoinette shielded her eyes with one arm and walked through The Door Within.

PASSAGE

The light was warm, and all chill and dampness from the rain left. At last, the light dimmed and flew away to a pinpoint—one star among many in the darkness that seemed to stretch to forever all around her.

Antoinette now walked on a gray stone path. She felt light, almost as if she were floating. She began to hear voices, many voices, like echoes of all the conversations of history. But one voice rose above them all.

And though she did not recognize the language, she felt it was calling her. It was the voice of her King, and she knew it like a child knows the voice of her father. His voice drew her along, and she followed.

The darkness on both sides of the path began to flicker. Images arose—huge, vivid, moving images. Antoinette felt a tiny scratching in the back of her mind. Had Aidan said anything about this?

The first vision was of a deep forest where immense dark trees grew. In the center of the forest was a marvelous tree, older and taller than the rest. Its vast canopy suddenly withered and became smoke from the fiery cauldron of a volcano. Molten rock ran red down cliffs and into a cratered landscape spiked with jagged stone.

The vision changed again, and one dark crater became a tomb. Its door wrenched free and splintered. The vault was empty except for a rectangular altar of white marble in the exact center of the floor. The tomb vanished, but the white altar rested now on a wide balcony overlooking a sleeping city.

Suddenly, something blacker than night fell from the sky and shattered the white altar. It was a stone. In quick succession, another fell on the balcony. There was a marking in red on the stone. Soon stones like the first began to rain down from the sky, and the vision changed.

There were many visions, one after the other, accelerating so that Antoinette could not follow them all.

It is too much for you, an icy voice whispered. *You will fail.*

Aidan had told Antoinette of the voice that had warned him off of the path. She tried to ignore the voice, determined not to listen.

She looked at the path ahead. It was narrow.

Come, my darkness will save you, the voice called.

Antoinette did not veer right or left, but focused on maintaining her straight course. And there ahead was a window in the night.

You will not escape the storm again, the voice warned her.

With all her strength, Antoinette lunged for the window.

A Sort of
Homecoming

"M'lady? . . . M'lady, if you please," a voice persisted. "May I enter?"

Sleepy, Antoinette thought the voice sounded familiar. Perhaps a bit formal, but nice.

There was a knock on the door. And again the voice said, "M'lady? . . . M'lady, if you please. May I enter?"

Her eyes sprang open, and she sat bolt upright, looking around at unfamiliar surroundings. "Yes," she said.

A Glimpse knight opened the chamber door. He was backlit in gold from the hall's light.

"M'lord's Sentinel has summoned thee."

"Aidan?" Antoinette asked.

The Glimpse's eyes flickered blue, and he shifted uncomfortably. "Nay, m'lady. I am called Aelic. You speak of my twin in the Mirror Realm."

"I'm sorry," she said. "I just got confused because—"

"You have traveled the narrow path between our realms," Aelic said. "It is quite disorienting—I know. I made such a journey once upon a time."

"Am I . . . is this?" Antoinette looked hopefully around the chamber.

Aelic leaned a little farther into the chamber, but did not step in. "You are in King Eliam's castle in the city of Alleble. On behalf of my Lord, as well as the citizens of the Land of Seven Fountains, I bid thee welcome."

He bowed low with a flourish of his dark cape—all the while keeping the chamber door propped open with one foot.

"Thank you," Antoinette said. *Wow*, she thought, *Aidan really does look handsome in armor.*

"On the chest at the foot of your bed, you will find warm clothes and suitable armor," he said, gesturing and letting the door begin to close. "Elspeth will be along shortly to help you dress, and I suspect she will bring you a goodly assortment of victuals. I will return in due time to escort you to the Guard's Keep."

"Victuals?" Antoinette echoed.

"That is food, m'lady."

"Oh," Antoinette replied.

Aelic bowed again and turned to leave. "Wait!" Antoinette called, feeling a warm blush in her cheeks. "My name is Antoinette. Would you call me that instead of m'lady?"

Aelic smiled. "Yes, m'lady—um, Antoinette . . . as you wish." And with that, he was gone.

Antoinette chewed at her lower lip as she scanned the chamber. Large candles on tall silver stands lit the four corners of the room in soft blues and purples. Magnificent tapestries adorned the walls and gave the room a sense of history and grandeur.

I'm here! I'm really in Alleble! Antoinette thought. She threw off the covers, leaped out of bed, and ran to the chest to see the clothing and armor that had been laid out for her. A silver breastplate gleamed up at her, and she had to catch her breath. Engraved upon it were two mountains with the sun rising between them, the symbol, she knew, of King Eliam's great victory over Paragor's rebellion. She ran her fingers across it and smiled.

Next to the breastplate was a stack of plate armor and a light silver helmet. Aside from the helmet, Antoinette had no idea how to put the stuff on, but she could hardly wait to try! Then, she saw the clothing and laughed out loud for joy. She snatched up the dark breeches and the tunic and ran to the long mirror that stood in one of the corners next to a candlestand.

She held them up to herself and turned this way and that. She especially loved the black tunic she'd been given. It had intricate purple embroidery on the collar and sleeves and a braided black belt. *This is just my style. How did they know?* she wondered. She hurriedly slipped them on and modeled them in the mirror. *They're just the right size too!*

There came several rapid knocks at the door, and then a voice. "Hullo, dearie, Elspeth at your service! Are you decent?"

Antoinette ran and opened the chamber door. She found a round-faced Glimpse woman busily twirling a small white towel in one hand and balancing a tray on her rather large hip with the other hand. She smiled a broad cheeky smile and bustled into the chamber.

"Hullo, dearie!" she said again and placed the tray on a small table near the door. "Do have a seat, dearie, and have a bit to eat. There is good cheese there, some of my famous crusty bread, and a bit of beef. Fuel for the furnace, as I often says. Now, fill up when you can, for you never know when the next meal might come." She

cackled a laugh and patted her ample belly. "Now, sit here and eat."
Antoinette did as she was told.

"My name is Elspeth, but you can call me Mum. All me other
girls do. Now, what should I call you?"

"Antoinette."

"Antoinette. A beautiful name, that is."

Elspeth surveyed the room, then she busied herself gathering up
Antoinette's clothes.

"I see you found my Lady Gwenne's clothing that I put out for
you. It fits you well, it does. Makes sense, I suppose, seeing as how you
are her twin and all. But your red hair, that is different. Now, my Lady
Gwenne's hair is of golden blond like the King's wheat at the harvest."

"My real color is blond too," Antoinette said.

"I thought as much. Do not misunderstand me. Your hair is
long and lush—pretty enough in its own way," Elspeth said. Then
raising one eyebrow, she glanced at Antoinette and added, "Aelic
certainly thought so. But there I go again, flapping my lips like
dragon wings. You probably have so many questions."

Aelic thinks I'm pretty? Antoinette thought, and her mind
wandered.

"Antoinette, dear, are you there?"

Antoinette snapped out of her thoughts and nodded. "Uh, . . . well,
I guess my big question is, do you know what my mission will be?"

"Me? No," Elspeth replied. "I am sure I would not be able to
tell you anything of those matters. Some venture to put a crick in
the dark one's plans, like as not. War is coming, and maybe even
within our own borders this time—or so many claim. But swords,
shields, and battles are not where my wisdom falls. Mops, brooms,
cleaning, and cooking—now those I can tell a thing or two about.
Soon enough, you will be brought before Kaliam, our Sentinel. It is

from him you will learn all that you could want about missions and such. Was there anything else that you wanted to know?" Elspeth asked, as if she'd actually answered Antoinette's question.

Antoinette shook her head. Elspeth had carried on so long, Antoinette was afraid to ask her anything else. "No thank you," Antoinette said. "The food was very good."

"Did you like it, then?" Elspeth asked. "Just some old family recipes, really. But good enough for a fair number of knights, I can tell you. Take Sir Aelic, now. That one cannot seem to get enough of my stew. He is always pestering Lady Gwenne to get me to make that stew for him. Here now, enough about that. We must get you into your armor. It should fit just right, seeing as how it is also Lady Gwenne's. Her spare set, really. Kindle, our armory keeper, had it made up for her when she returned from Mithegard."

Elspeth was right. The armor fit almost perfectly. Antoinette looked at herself in the mirror and laughed. "I'm a knight!" she said.

"Well, a right, regular swordmaiden," Elspeth agreed.

"Swordmaiden?" Antoinette echoed, a broad grin forming. "I like the sound of that, but . . . uh, I don't have a sword."

"True enough, dearie. I expect you will need to see Kaliam about that."

Just then, there came a sharp rap at the door. Elspeth hurried to answer it.

"Sir Aelic has returned, m'lady," Elspeth said.

As Antoinette turned to greet him, Aelic stumbled backward, startled by the beautiful young woman before him.

"Even with your hair aflame and being younger, how much like Gwenne you look," he said. "It is strange to see a friend's likeness in one who is not Glimpse-kind. I imagine you must be thinking the same thing about me and my twin of your kind."

"Yes, it's kind of strange. I mean, I just saw Aidan earlier today." Antoinette laughed, remembering the duel she'd had with Aidan.

"Do you jest?"

"Jest? No, I'm sorry. I was just thinking of Aidan. We were sparring this afternoon, and I, uh, accidentally gave him a bloody nose."

Aelic smiled. "Then you are very much like Gwenne in more than appearance."

The two stood quietly staring at each other as if in a trance.

"Hullo, m'dears? Do you not have someplace to go?" Elspeth interrupted.

"Oh, yes. Kaliam awaits!" Aelic said.

Aelic led Antoinette through a half-dozen passages, and eventually past a pair of tall arched doors. "These are the doors to King Eliam's Throne Room," Aelic said.

"Will I . . . may I meet him?" Antoinette asked.

Aelic looked at her strangely. His eyes glinted bright blue, and he said, "You have already met him. You believed in the story of Alleble. You trusted him on the narrow path. You heard, and chose to follow his voice. You know him better than you think, and he knows you better than you know yourself."

"But I mean, may I see him?"

"King Eliam may reveal himself to you in time," Aelic replied. "But I am told that his countenance is painful to endure for those not of Glimpse-kind. Come, the Sentinel awaits upon the balcony."

At last they came to the end of a long hall. There was a stair there, and a door subtly set into the wall. Aelic opened the door. Sunlight blazed in.

"I shall take my leave of you for now, Antoinette," Aelic said. "But we shall meet again."

Antoinette stepped through the door out onto a vast balcony.

She was drawn to the parapet and beheld the Kingdom of Alleble. Towers, keeps, and cottages; courtyards, fields, and bustling markets—sprawled from left to right as far as her eyes could see. But in the center of it all were the fountains.

At last! she thought. And for a moment she was overwhelmed with emotion.

"The most wondrous city in all The Realm," a deep voice said behind her. She turned to see a tall, dark-haired knight. As he bowed low he said, "I am Kaliam, the fourth Sentinel of Alleble."

"I'm Antoinette," she managed to say. She felt slightly intimidated by this knight's size—he stood more than a foot taller than she. But at the same time, his smile and bearing radiated warmth, and Antoinette saw welcome in his eyes.

"Well-met," Kaliam said, and he laughed. "Though it seems strange to say we have just met. Gwenne's armor fits you well."

Antoinette blushed, surprising herself. He looked like a hero who had stepped out of a grand painting.

"You are a friend of Sir Aidan's?" he asked.

Antoinette nodded. "Yes, we met recently. And he helped me to understand that King Eliam was calling me here."

"Sir Aidan is a hero of this realm, a Knight of the Dawn. His Glimpse-kind, Sir Aelic, has carried Aidan's mantle well—just as, I am sure, you will carry Gwenne's."

"I'll do my best," Antoinette replied. It was quiet for a few moments, and then Antoinette said, "Aidan told me all about you and the others—Mallik, Nock, Tal, Farix. It's amazing to finally meet you. Will I meet the others?"

"In time," Kaliam answered.

"Oh, and Aidan told me to tell you not to say anything about the lantern spider incident. What's that all about?"

Kaliam's eyes flickered blue and he let out a howl of laughter. "M'lady," he said, clutching his sides, "with your pardon, I will, . . . honor Sir Aidan's request!"

Kaliam finally mastered his fit of laughter. "There are two reasons I required you to meet me here," he said. "But let us take one moment to admire the view. Aside from the Library Tower, this is the best view of the kingdom. I wanted you to see the kingdom—as it always should be—at peace. I fear Alleble will not remain at peace for much longer."

Antoinette knew why, and she looked to the west and stared.

"Yes, our enemy lies there," said Kaliam, and a shadow seemed to pass over his face. "Paragor has not been idle since Aidan left The Realm. Something has changed in his designs, and we do not yet know what it is. But it seems his influence in The Realm is waxing, for city after city has allied itself with Paragory. If our estimates be correct, Paragor now commands an immense army nearly equal to our forces here."

"What about Mithegard and the other allies?" Antoinette asked.

Kaliam looked at her gravely. "That is our greatest concern, Antoinette. Mithegard remains loyal, and with the help of Mallik's folk from the Blue Mountains, the Seven Towers are nearly rebuilt. But there have been troubling reports from many of Alleble's allies. Acacia, Clarion, and most recently Yewland have sent word that they may renounce our alliance."

"Why?" Antoinette asked.

"They claim that our new taxes are too severe," answered Kaliam. "They say that the Alleb Creed we impose is too strict. They threaten even to depose the governors we have sent." Kaliam gripped the balcony wall so tightly that his knuckles cracked. "But, Antoinette, we have sent no governors to our allies, we have levied no taxes, and there is no such thing as an Alleb Creed!"

"Is Paragor behind it?" Antoinette asked.

"He must be," said Kaliam. "We do not know how he could cause these things, but we intend to find out. We leave for Yewland in three days. I have determined to meet with one of these so-called governors!"

"You said *we*. Does that mean I'm coming on this mission?"

"Yes, Antoinette," Kaliam answered. He cocked an eyebrow and grinned. "You will become the Twelfth Knight on this journey—if you pass our tests."

"Tests?" Antoinette swallowed.

Kaliam nodded. "This mission is pressing, and there is no time to train you properly. Among reasons known only to him, King Eliam chose you because you already have some skills. You have held a sword before?"

"I can do more than hold it," Antoinette said bluntly. She grinned.

"And you can ride?"

"I ride horses very well," she said. "But Aidan told me you ride unicorns."

Kaliam laughed. "They are nearly the same, only unicorns are smarter and faster. I suppose then, you should pass your first two tests quite easily. But, ah, the third—well, now, that might be another matter. We shall see."

Antoinette waited for Kaliam to explain. But he did not. He turned and walked to the center of the balcony. There, something lay hidden under a beautiful silk tapestry.

"I told you there were two reasons I wanted you to meet me here. The first was to discuss the objective of your mission. The other is to show you . . . this!" With an effortless tug, he removed the tapestry, revealing a rectangular block of white marble. It was chest high, but its length and width were like that of a tomb.

Antoinette approached. She ran a hand along the length, and Kaliam watched her carefully. "I know this," she said. "It is the altar where Paragor killed the King."

"You have read the account of the Great Betrayal?" Kaliam asked.

"Yes."

"Is there anything more you recall when you look upon it?" Kaliam's eyes narrowed. He seemed hesitant, searching for but hoping not to find something to confirm what he suspected.

"Wait," Antoinette said slowly. "I remember something."

Kaliam closed his eyes and turned away. "What do you remember?"

"I saw this," she replied, gesturing to the altar, "in a vision when I walked between my world and The Realm. But at first it was somewhere else. It was in a cell or a crypt. I think it was underground."

"You saw visions between our worlds?" he asked, his deep voice reduced to a hoarse whisper.

"Yes," she replied. "Aidan told me I would. He saw visions too. Some of them came true when he was here."

"They are foretellings," Kaliam said. "Sights of what may come to pass. Captain Valithor was very aware of Aidan's visions. They troubled him greatly near the end, for not all who travel between realms see such visions. I too am troubled, but I will not speak now of what I fear. I must first visit the Library of Light. And then I will go to the King himself, for his wisdom has no end."

Antoinette swallowed. "Sir Kaliam, there's something else. In the vision, this altar faded from the tomb and reappeared on this balcony, I think. It was at night, so it was hard to tell. But suddenly, a dark stone that fell from the sky smashed the altar. Then many stones began to fall. I saw one of them close up, and there was something written on it, written in red."

Kaliam glanced to the west. "There is meaning in that also," he said, almost to himself. "Please, promise that you will not speak of these visions to anyone besides Aelic and me. There are many in Alleble who would make more of it than they ought."

Antoinette nodded. "I . . . I won't," she replied, suddenly feeling very nervous.

"Come, then, your first test awaits—that is, if you are ready."

"Lead on, Sir Kaliam. I am ready."

Kaliam's demeanor brightened, and he laughed. "Such like a younger Gwenne you are!"

OF SWORD
AND STEED

This is the Training Urchin," Kaliam said. He walked in a slow circle around the device in the center of the castle's southern courtyard. The urchin was a tall post with three segments that turned independently of the others. Wooden arms, each equipped with its own weapon or shield, protruded from the segments. Kaliam walked behind it and smiled.

"We use it to train knights in combat, or to test their skill," he explained with a wink. "I will control the limbs of the urchin. Your task is to attack—put a notch from your sword on each of the three segments without being thrown off balance, struck by one of its weapons, or knocked to the ground. You will have three strikes to succeed, and that is all. Do you have any questions?"

"Where is my sword?" she asked.

Kaliam gestured. Dozens of sword hilts jutted up from a barrel by the *palisade*. As she walked to the barrel to choose a weapon,

Antoinette noticed a small crowd had gathered. There were even a few curious eyes glimmering out from the cracks and knotholes of the fence. *Well, I'll give them a show*, she thought.

Antoinette sifted through the blades. Most of them were dull and notched from much use, but she found two swords that she liked. One was a two-fisted broadsword with a long, wide blade. The other was light with a narrow, tapered blade that looked much sharper than the others. She chose the sharp sword and turned back to the urchin.

"Ready?" Kaliam asked. He grasped the handles of the top and middle segments and stood, knees bent, feet at shoulder's width—combat stance.

Antoinette slashed the air in front of her. The sword felt good—not unlike her favorite shinai at home. "Ready."

Antoinette held her sword vertically out in front of her. Her back and neck were upright, perfectly straight, just as she had learned from years of spada-kendo training. She flexed at the knees, one foot a pace in front of the other. She stood very, very still.

Kaliam shifted in place behind the urchin. He turned the top segment so that its gray sword pointed at Antoinette. All the while, Antoinette remained motionless, watching intently. Finally, she thought she saw Kaliam's weight shift just slightly onto his back foot. It was the opening she had been waiting for.

Antoinette unleashed a kakari-geiko attack, rushing toward the urchin and raining down blows like a sudden storm. But Kaliam was not overwhelmed as she had hoped. With one hand, he maneuvered the top segment so that its sword parried away each of Antoinette's high attacks. With his other hand, he turned the middle segment so that its buckler shield swooshed toward Antoinette's midsection. She had to stay her attack for just a moment to bat away the shield.

And when she did so, Kaliam used his foot to jerk the bottom section of the urchin. It brought a mace with a long chain swinging so suddenly that Antoinette could not leap in time. The ball and chain wrapped around one of her boots, and Kaliam forced the segment back the other direction. Antoinette's leg was yanked out from under her, and she crashed to the ground flat on her back. Her sword flew out of her hands and clanged noisily across the cobblestone.

"Your speed is most impressive," Kaliam said.

"You're mocking me!" Antoinette said, leaping to her feet.

"I am most certainly not mocking you, Antoinette," Kaliam said sternly. "Your speed is absolutely impressive, as is your technique. But you made a grave mistake. You forgot your objective."

Antoinette winced as she bent over to pick up her sword. She thought she heard giggles from behind the fence. She went red with anger and turned back to Kaliam.

"What do you mean, I 'forgot my objective'?"

"You were simply caught up in the effectiveness of your own attack. Your slashes came at the blade and at the shield, but your goal is to put a notch in each segment of the urchin. You have only two strikes left. Make yourself ready."

Antoinette, sword out in front, approached the urchin. Her eyes darted from segment to segment. There was a sword and a blunt axe on the top segment, a sword and buckler on the middle, and only the mace on the bottom. Kaliam seemed able to move all three segments at once. Antoinette had to be wary.

Focus, she thought. *Remember the objective.*

She looked at the segments. One notch in each. Two strikes left. That meant she would need to get two notches in one turn. Antoinette moved side to side slowly, looking for an angle. She decided to attack the lowest segment first. Kaliam may swing the mace, but there was nothing there that could really block her attack.

Her mind made up, Antoinette lunged at the urchin. Her first swipe was a crushing high-to-low chop at the sword on the top segment. The urchin's wooden arm groaned as it absorbed Antoinette's fierce attack. Kaliam swiftly rotated the top segment. The blunt axe swung around. Antoinette ducked and raked her blade at the bottom segment, carving a notch into the base. But before she could swing again, Kaliam brought the middle section around hard. The buckler shield slammed into Antoinette's midsection and she sprawled backward, landing once again on her back.

"That was much better," Kaliam said.

Antoinette stood up, seething. "That's not fair!" she said. "No enemy can attack with three weapons at once."

Kaliam shook his head. "Do you think the knights of Paragory will fight fair? You are too used to rules of combat designed to keep opponents safe from serious injury. There are no such rules in war. Those rats from Paragor will hide daggers in their belts, throw sand in your eyes, or force you into a hidden fall—anything to gain the advantage. Anything to take your life. Now, you have one turn remaining, and two notches left. Be creative. It can be done."

Antoinette held her sword up and positioned herself just out of reach of the urchin's many arms. *I have only one sword*, she thought dejectedly. *How can I compete with so many weapons?*

Then she had an idea. She thought of a way to even the odds.

Antoinette stepped slowly to the left of the urchin. For this to work, she needed to swing hard from the outside.

Antoinette took her sword in both hands and battered the urchin's top sword hard to the right. Kaliam absorbed the blow and shifted to bring the buckler on the middle section through again. But Antoinette stayed far to the outside. And then she evened the odds.

Antoinette grabbed the buckler with her right hand and brought her sword down with a savage one-handed chop onto the wooden arm of the shield. The wood of that arm was old and battered, and it split in the center.

The urchin's buckler shield and half of its wooden arm clattered to the ground. But Antoinette was not finished. The mace came around hard, seeking her ankles, but she leaped and brought her sword down on the wooden arm that held the mace. It splintered, cracked, and fell away.

To Kaliam's astonishment, she did the same to the urchin's remaining two weapons. Then, she walked casually over and cut a notch into the top and middle sections. The crowd cheered. And Antoinette noticed that it was a much larger crowd than when she began the test. She stared, thinking for a moment that she saw Aelic, but she couldn't be sure.

"You, you have broken the urchin!" Kaliam bellowed. Antoinette's smile disappeared and she went red, wondering if she had gone a little too far. Then Kaliam laughed out loud and said, "Marvelous effort, Antoinette! Well done! Yes indeed, well done."

Antoinette grinned. "You said be creative."

Kaliam picked up one of the severed arms and said, "And it was creative! I am just glad that you were dueling a piece of wood and not me!"

Antoinette smiled and asked, "What's next?"

The crowd had grown yet again. They followed Kaliam and Antoinette to the fairgrounds behind the castle and filled the stands of the jousting arena. Antoinette sat atop a handsome white unicorn mare at one end of the arena. "She's beautiful," Antoinette said.

"Her name is Rael," Kaliam explained. "And she comes from a proud lineage. She is both surefooted and swift. Should you pass this test—and the test to come—Rael will bear you on our journey to Yewland."

Antoinette brushed Rael's silky white mane with her hand and leaned down to whisper in her ear. "You hear that? Help me win, and I'll take good care of you."

The unicorn bobbed its head and snorted.

"Look down the rail that runs the length of the arena," Kaliam said. "Do you see the three posts about midway?"

Antoinette nodded.

"They are spaced fifteen arms apart. Suspended from each one is a gold ring. You must ride your unicorn swiftly at the rings and steer her so that she spears all three rings with her horn."

"Sounds easy enough," Antoinette replied.

Kaliam grinned. "But you must do so before Sir Tal does."

Antoinette suddenly realized that at the far end of the arena was another mounted knight.

"Heralds, mark your place!" Kaliam yelled. Two Glimpses wearing dark blue tunics walked to the edge of the track in the center of the arena. Each of them had a green flag and a red one.

"Sir Tal has his own set of rings to spear on his side of the rail," Kaliam explained. "It would not do to have your unicorns knock heads at a full gallop."

Antoinette winced at that image.

"Your herald will raise a flag the moment you pass the three rings. A red flag if you miss a ring. A green flag if you get all three. The first herald to raise the green flag marks one of you the winner."

"I only get one try?" Antoinette protested.

"You told me you could ride," Kaliam replied.

"Yes, but I'm no seasoned unicorn rider. Sir Tal, he's probably done this before."

"Many times," Kaliam said with a laugh. "But Tal is much better with a blade or a bow than he is on a unicorn. I would say that you are well matched for this event. One try only."

Antoinette frowned.

"Riders, stand you ready!" Kaliam yelled. He strode quickly to a raised platform that stood behind the heralds. It was exactly in the middle so that both riders could see him.

Rael seemed to sense the competition, and she tensed like a compressed spring. Antoinette ran through everything she remembered from years of riding. Just subtle pressure from the legs or a slackening of the reins had definite meaning for a horse. Antoinette just hoped her commands had the same meaning for a unicorn.

"Riders, stand you ready?!" Kaliam bellowed from the dais.

Antoinette saw the other knight lift an arm in salute. She swallowed and did the same.

Kaliam held a large blue flag aloft.

"C'mon, Rael, we can do this," Antoinette said. She brushed the unicorn's mane once and grasped the reins. She looked at the golden rings and then back at Kaliam's blue flag.

The flag fell.

Antoinette kicked gently with her heels, and Rael responded by launching forward. The force of the movement overwhelmed Antoinette and she almost fell. But Rael adjusted her gait to allow her rider to regain her seat.

"Thanks!" Antoinette yelled. "Now go!" Rael surged forward even faster than before. It was more speed than Antoinette had ever experienced on a horse. The golden rings were just ahead. But Tal looked like he was going to reach his first.

"Stop staring at him," she told herself. "Focus on the objective! Focus on the objective!"

Rael raced forward. Antoinette pulled gently on the left rein, and the unicorn leaned to the left beside the rail. Antoinette leaned forward. Her armor bounced with the unicorn's thunderous gallop. The world was zooming by as they quickly closed in on the first ring.

Suddenly, Antoinette panicked. She didn't know how to ask the unicorn to lower its head so that it could spear the ring. She'd never had to command a horse to do such a thing. The ring was there, and there was no time to think. "Rael!" Antoinette yelled.

The second ring appeared a split second later. Then, the third. Rael suddenly slowed to a trot, and then came to a stop.

Antoinette brushed her wispy red hair out of her face and looked up. And swaying on Rael's white horn were three golden rings. "You did it, Rael!" Antoinette said, hugging the mare's velvety neck. "You got them!"

Antoinette pulled gently on the reins and wheeled Rael around. She rode toward the center of the arena and looked at the heralds. They both had their green flag raised high.

Antoinette looked at Kaliam. Tal came riding up as well.

"Congratulations are awarded to Tal!" Kaliam said. "For his flag rose first!"

Antoinette felt as if she had been kicked in the stomach. All her dreams of adventure in The Realm, her desire to serve Alleble as a knight, her errand for Aidan—it all swirled and vanished.

"Not so, m'lord!" came a deep, rhythmic voice Antoinette had not heard before. Antoinette looked up as Sir Tal approached. He had removed his helmet, and great locks of dark braided hair fell about his shoulders. His eyes were black and piercing beneath heavy bristling brows. He wore a thick mustache that tapered at the ends to a slight curl and a little inverted triangle of whiskers below his bottom lip. He reminded Antoinette of a good-natured pirate.

"I love to win more than any," he continued. "But I would rather be raked over hot coals than to be named the winner when victory was not earned."

Antoinette looked from Tal to Kaliam and back.

"My herald, it would seem," said Tal, "is in need of an eyeglass."

He gestured toward the ivory horn of his unicorn. Antoinette's heart leaped, for there were only two golden rings dangling from Tal's unicorn.

"I had a feeling I'd missed that first one." Tal laughed. "I looked up only for a moment to see where Antoinette was, but it seems that moment cost me the victory. Please tell me, m'lady, that this was not your first joust."

Antoinette hesitated. "Um . . . actually, it was."

"Not again!" Tal roared in mock anger. "First, Sir Aidan shows up and pulls off a moulinet in three days—a feat that took me three years to master! And now I am bested by Antoinette in the joust!"

"I've ridden horses for years, though," Antoinette said. "So I'm not a rookie."

"That is precious little consolation," Tal said, and he laughed. "But I say well-met to thee, m'lady. And should the King will it to be so, I will gladly ride by your side into battle!"

"Well, one thing is clear, Tal," Kaliam said with a wink, "your way with words is better than your riding ability. So therefore, Antoinette, I declare you the winner!"

The crowd roared its approval. Antoinette ruffled Rael's mane. "You hear that? We won!" She looked into the first row of the stands, and there was Aelic. He smiled and nodded his head just slightly. Antoinette smiled and nodded back, trying to will herself not to blush.

"Congratulations again, Antoinette," said Kaliam. "You have passed the first two tests. But one task still remains. It may prove to be the most difficult for you, for it is a very personal test. And from it you may learn more than you wished to know." Antoinette gave him a puzzled look.

Later, as Kaliam said good night to Antoinette, he tried to smile encouragingly, though, in truth, he was torn. The Library of Light had had very little mention about Antoinette's visions, but what little there was fed Kaliam's suspicions and left him with inescapable dread. For if Antoinette succeeded in the third test, she would journey to Yewland. *To what end?* Kaliam wondered. And if she failed, she would return to earth, and her life might be spared. *But at what cost to The Realm?*

Antoinette felt conflicted as she lay on the bed in her chamber and stared out the window at the quiet shadows of the slumbering kingdom. She had, after all, barely passed the first two tests. *What challenge would the final test bring?* It wasn't at all like trigonometry, where there were absolute rules—steadfast patterns she could count on to work the same way again and again. She could study for that sort of test. But there was no way to study this time. The third test could be anything!

Kaliam certainly hadn't given away much. He had told her that it would be a very personal test, and that the difficulty would be more than physical in nature. *Great.* But then she had a change of mind. *Maybe I can study for this test!*

Antoinette threw off the downy comforter, hopped out of bed, and grabbed a tall candle from the silver stand nearest her bed. She opened the chamber door and peeked both ways up the hall. No one in sight. She crept along the stone passage until she came to a torch, and held the candle's wick to the fire. Cupping the candle's small flame with her hand, Antoinette slowly made her way back to Gwenne's room.

Back in its holder, the candle cast flickering pale blue light upon the bed. Antoinette opened *The Story* and began to study. It was like visiting with a cherished old friend, and soon Antoinette was lost among the many adventures within the book's pages. Through every story, she found the steadfast presence of King Eliam's will. And there was great comfort in that. Whatever the third test would be, Antoinette knew she would not be alone.

＿✒

Hours later, a breath of wind blew out the candle near the bed. And for the first time in many days, Antoinette slept without the invasion of a nightmare. No, instead, she saw visions of rolling green hills blanketed with patches of white flowers, under a sky so blue that it must be from another time and another place.

A Walk and a Whoosel

"Now, that is the proper way to break the fast, eh, m'lady?" Elspeth asked, beaming with pride.

"Mmmm, yes," Antoinette mumbled, her mouth full of sweet, flaky goodness. Elspeth had prepared a plate full of triangular golden-brown biscuits called scones. Antoinette was already on her third.

"I added a touch of molasses, I did," Elspeth explained. "That is the secret, really. Like having the best of gingerbread and shortbread all in the same mouthful. Me mum always made them that way. She learned the art of scone-baking from a splendid old Glimpse from the Blue Mountain Provinces, and now she could ma—"

There was a firm knock on the door. Elspeth opened the door. It was Aelic.

"Good day, m'lady," he said, forgetting that Antoinette preferred to be called by her name. "Kaliam wishes me to inform you that your final test will be made ready late in the afternoon. I thought in the meantime you might like to see a little of this fair city."

"I would," she replied. "I would indeed."

_~~_

After a few passages and flights of stairs, Antoinette found herself walking the cobblestone streets of Alleble, Aelic by her side.

"Thanks!" she said.

Aelic's eyebrows rose in puzzlement. "Why do you thank me?"

Antoinette grinned. "You saved me!"

"Saved you? From what?"

"From Elspeth telling me the entire history of scone-making, that's what!"

"I thought I smelled scones!" Aelic laughed. "Yes, Elspeth does carry on a bit, but she means well. Though it may seem otherwise, she will listen more than she speaks if you have a need. And within that kindly mind of hers there is wisdom beyond that of pastry lore."

Antoinette smiled. "So where are we going?"

"To Kindle's place," Aelic replied. "To the Armory of Alleble. Then, if there's time, the market!"

_~~_

The Armory of Alleble was a place that instilled quiet. Visitors spoke in whispers out of respect, but Antoinette was speechless at the threshold of the great domed hall.

"But a small portion of the might of Alleble," Aelic said proudly.

Small portion? Antoinette wondered. To her it looked like enough armor and weaponry to equip an enormous army. Barrels full of spears, swords, and broad-bladed battleaxes, great casks filled with iron gauntlets, and row upon row of suits of gleaming armor that were mounted so they looked like scores of knights frozen in time. Antoinette wandered between them, here and there running a finger over the edge of a blade she fancied. "Will I get a sword soon?" she asked.

"Kaliam will provide you with a blade when you pass the third test," Aelic answered.

"Right," Antoinette replied. The test. She had put that out of her mind, enjoying the sights of Alleble—and the time with Aelic.

Aelic strode toward a high counter in the back of the armory. "M'lady, if you please," he said, motioning for Antoinette to join him.

"Would you please call me Antoinette?" she asked, feigning anger.

"I beg your forgiveness, Antoinette," he said. "But do come and look. Here you will see swords of special prominence."

Behind the counter, displayed in a case lined with lush red velvet, hung five spectacular blades. Antoinette gasped. Every one of the swords looked hard and strong, and each showed tremendous craftsmanship. Two were long-bladed broadswords of silver. Each had a dark wooden grip carved with intricate designs. The other three swords each had a single groove running from blade-tip to its massive winglike golden crossguard. Their grips were black and ribbed, a little longer than one hand, but shorter than the broadswords. The three blades were identical and matchless in splendor, though in some ways plainer than the others. Antoinette noticed that there was space in the display for more swords. "Where are the others?" she asked.

"They are with the knights who use them," Aelic said.

"And Kaliam owns one of them!" bellowed a stubbly-bearded Glimpse, and his voice echoed in the hall. He was clad in chain mail and possessed a stocky girth that gave him a squared appearance. He leaned on the other side of the counter as if he had been there all along. "The other belongs to Prince Aelic here!"

"Kindle!" Aelic objected.

"What?" complained the stout Glimpse, holding up his hands. "It is true."

Antoinette stared at Aelic. "You're a prince?"

"Not in Alleble," Aelic replied, glaring at Kindle. "My father is King of Mithegard. It is only there that I wear that title. And even there, I would rather not make much out of it."

"You're too humble," Antoinette said. And she laughed. "Prince Aelic. It has a good ring to it!" Aelic's cheeks reddened.

"Since the *prince* here has been rendered rather speechless," Kindle said, "I suppose I should introduce myself. I am Kindle, the keeper of this fine armory. And you must be Antoinette."

"How did you know?"

"Well, Sir Tal was here last night, shopping for a new lance. When I asked him why, he told me he was bested by a swordmaiden from the Mirror Realm . . . called Antoinette, with red hair."

"Oh," Antoinette replied. "These swords are amazing. Did you make them?"

"Me? Nay, m'lady. I make a fine buckler shield, and no one can surpass my skill with chain mail, but those blades are far beyond my reach. Those were forged and fashioned by Naysmithe, the second Sentinel of Alleble—now the chief metalworker to King Eliam."

"I really like them, especially those three," Antoinette said, pointing. "Do those belong to the Elder Guard?"

"Those three?" Kindle asked. "Those are Naysmithe's newest swords. But they do not belong to any of the Elder Guard. Naysmithe says they are to be wielded by the three heroes who are to come."

"Three heroes?"

"The Three Witnesses," Kindle explained. "There are some in Alleble who take to a legend about three mighty warriors who will save The Realm. I do not really hold to such tales, but Naysmithe does."

Kindle was quiet for a while, staring at the three identical swords. Finally, he said, "Did you notice, magnificent and strong as they are, the three swords have no engraving, no emblem, or mark? Naysmithe says the swords are not yet finished—that they will only be completed when the time comes for the Three Witnesses to appear." Kindle shook his head and laughed. "Naysmithe and his tales."

The market was already bustling with activity when Aelic and Antoinette arrived that afternoon. Shacks, carts, and stands filled the streets, and hundreds of Glimpses milled about or hurried by. Everywhere Antoinette looked there were gorgeous hand-woven tapestries, intricate beaded jewelry, and lovely crafts. Smoked meats hung above one stand. Wheels of cheese adorned another.

"This is marvelous!" Antoinette said.

Aelic nodded. "Artisans from all over The Realm bring their wares to trade and to sell, for Alleble is one of the few safe open markets left."

"Because of Paragor?"

"Yes, he is the root of most troubles in The Realm, and he has begun to move ranks of soldiers along some of the trade routes to the north and west. Still, here in Alleble merchants may find refuge, and just about anything can be found here in the marketplace—even some oddities."

"I love to shop," Antoinette said. "But I, uh, don't have any money."

Aelic frowned. "Did you think I brought you here to torture you with want? You have but to ask, and I will buy it for you."

"Aelic, I couldn't do tha—"

"Remember, I am a prince. I can afford it."

Just then, they heard a high-pitched squeal. Something orange and white darted out from under a table and scampered across their path. Whatever it was disappeared down an alley. Then, two sweating, rosy-cheeked Glimpse boys went running by, looking left and right, and hollering at each other. "You let him get away!"

"Did not. I told you not to scare it." And just like that, they too turned down the alley. Aelic looked at Antoinette. She shrugged and said, "Let's go."

At the end of the alley, they found the two boys with sticks poking at a small orange ball of fur. "Come on," one boy said.

"We just want to play a bit," said the other. Antoinette heard a tiny trilling whimper and caught a brief glimpse of two large brown eyes glimmering in the mass of fur.

"Stop that, boys!" Antoinette said in a tone harder than she intended. The two startled boys jumped and spun around.

"S-sorry, m'lady!" said one of the boys, staring wide-eyed at Aelic's and Antoinette's armor.

"You were hurting that—" She tried to get a better look, but the critter was balled up tight.

"Whoosel," Aelic answered for her. "I do not think any lads of Alleble should be about tormenting a defenseless animal."

"Begging your pardon, Sir Knight," said the other boy. "But we just bought this whoosel, and well, they are right cuddly most of the time, but this one nipped my finger, it did."

"And then it run off!" said the first boy.

"So you thought poking it with a stick would make it more friendly?" Antoinette asked. The two boys looked away and shifted back and forth on their feet.

"There you are!" came a booming voice from up the alley. A wide Glimpse wearing a soiled apron and what appeared to be a fur tunic came waddling up the alley. He had no beard but a very long mustache that bounced when he spoke. "I told you lads not to grab her by the tail! Whoosels do not take kindly to that."

He took no notice of Aelic and Antoinette. "Now, here is your shiny silver coin back," he said to the boys. "I will not be having anyone mistreating one of my whoosels."

He handed the first boy a large silver coin, and the two boys walked quickly out of the alley. Suddenly, Antoinette felt a strange scratching at her ankle. She looked down and saw the same pair of big brown eyes staring up at her. But the whoosel had uncoiled and now nuzzled back and forth between Antoinette's feet. It looked like a very long fox's tail with a small triangular face, large fuzzy ears, and a tiny pink nose. It squeaked and chattered, stopping now and then to look up at Antoinette.

"I think Brindle likes you," said the mustached Glimpse.

"Awww," Antoinette said. She reached down to pet it, but it sprang lightly onto the top of her hand, spiraled up her arm, and sat on her shoulder. "Aelic, look! How cute!"

"Yes, it looks quite at home in your fiery red hair," Aelic replied. "Perhaps it thinks you are its long-lost mother."

"Very funny, Aelic," Antoinette protested.

Aelic reached into a small brown leather pouch and handed the mustached Glimpse a gold coin. "I think we will take this whoosel, plus a little something for your trouble."

"Why, thank you, kind Sir Knight!" he replied, staring at the coin. "I may just close me shop early today! Very generous indeed!"

"Thank you, Aelic!" Antoinette looked at him with glad eyes. "Awww!"

"Take good care of Brindle now," said the mustached Glimpse, and he turned to walk away. It was then that Antoinette noticed the many pairs of bright eyes gleaming out from the Glimpse's fur garment. It was really no garment at all. The Glimpse was wearing a shirt of whoosels!

"I think we should be getting back to the castle," Aelic said. "Bring your furry new friend, and let us be on our way."

Antoinette patted Brindle on the head and followed Aelic back out of the alley. The lanky creature squeaked happily in Antoinette's ear, and she was grateful to have something to distract her. For the specter of the third test still loomed before her.

THE THIRD TEST

Too soon, it was time for Antoinette to meet Kaliam for the third test. Slowly, the Sentinel led the young swordmaiden down a steep flight of stairs in the Castle of Alleble. Brindle rode on her shoulder but stayed mostly hidden in her hair. Torches flickered ahead and behind, but aside from that and the steps, Antoinette saw nothing more. "Where are we going?" Antoinette asked.

"We are traveling a seldom-used stair to the old storehouse deep beneath the castle. In the storehouse there are many chambers. It is there you will face your final test."

"So what's the test?"

"The nature of the third test is not known to me," Kaliam replied. "But it is said that the challenge of the third test is not merely physical. All I know for certain is that within the first chamber below, you will be offered a choice of some kind. You must then pass into the second chamber. And there you will discover the consequences of your choice."

"Consequences?" Antoinette didn't much like the sound of that.

"Well," Kaliam said, "I do not know another way to put it. Something will happen to you in that second chamber. Depending upon your choice, it may not be pleasant."

They continued their descent in silence. At last they came to the final step, and before them, lit by torches on either side, loomed a massive wooden door. It was shrouded in cobwebs and looked as if it had not been opened in a century.

"I have to go in here?" she asked.

Kaliam nodded.

"Great," she replied, feeling uncertain. "Aidan didn't have to do this, did he?"

"No. As I said before, there is no time to train you as we did Aidan."

"Are you sure?" Antoinette asked, looking back at the door. "Because I think I'd rather do a week of training than go through that door. It gives me the creeps."

"The training Aidan endured was a greater trial for him than you know," Kaliam explained. "Aidan learned his knightcraft under the withering stare of Captain Valithor."

"Okay, fair enough," Antoinette replied. She knew about the demanding regimen of Captain Valithor's command from Aidan's stories. "But I still don't like this door."

"Nonetheless, you must pass through it," Kaliam said. "And now is the time."

"Right, yes . . . ," she said between taking deep breaths. "Give me just a moment."

Kaliam cocked an eyebrow and smiled.

Antoinette reached for the black iron knob and turned it. Brindle emitted a squeak that sounded strangely like "uh-oh!" The terrified whoosel leaped from Antoinette's shoulder and onto Kaliam's. It clambered atop his head and crouched warily. Its long orange-and-white tail whisked back and forth in front of Kaliam's nose.

"I see you have been to the market," Kaliam said.

"Aelic bought her for me," Antoinette said.

"It is better that she remain with me," he said, and he gestured toward the door as he gently removed Brindle from the top of his head.

Antoinette frowned and pushed hard on the door. The door protested a moment, came free, and groaned on its hinges as it swung into the room beyond. A smell like old books and mildew swirled out of the darkness.

"Uh, you aren't going anywhere, are you, Kaliam?" Antoinette asked. "I mean, in case I get into trouble. I can call you, right?"

Kaliam slowly shook his head. "I am not permitted to assist you in any way. The moment this door shuts behind you, I will ascend to the Guard's Keep. If you return, you will find me there."

"You mean *when* I return, right? Not *if*?"

Kaliam stared at her for a moment and then said, "I fully expect you to return, Antoinette. You have marvelous courage and tremendous skill, but the choice ahead of you may require more. Remember, you are never alone!"

Antoinette swallowed. She pushed the door open wider, slipped into the chamber, and slowly closed the door behind her. The moment the door was shut, she heard a ringing metallic click. The door had locked. There was no going back.

She found herself in near darkness. The vast chamber was lit in pale gray as if by moonlight, but Antoinette could not see the source of the illumination. In the center of the room were two white pedestals. There was something on each of them, but Antoinette could not tell what. Beyond the pedestals, on the other side of the chamber, loomed the dark outline of another door.

Antoinette approached the two pedestals. And, in the spectral light, the choice became clear. A sword lay upon one pedestal. A scroll lay on the other.

"Easy," Antoinette thought aloud. "There's probably a maze on the other side of that door, so I'll choose the scroll."

She took one step toward the scroll, but stopped short. She thought she should at least take a closer look at the sword. It seemed to be the only thing in the chamber not covered in a layer of dust or shrouded in cobwebs. It glimmered with pale light, and as Antoinette began to study it, her desire for the weapon grew.

The blade was about three feet long, both edges sharp and tapered to a subtly curved point. Near the base of the blade was an engraving of the sun, whose rays reached up the blade and curled decoratively into runelike letters of a language Antoinette did not understand.

The crossguard was like the outstretched wings of a great seabird perched above the grip. Upon its feathers were ornate designs: knights on horseback, shields, and more of the runelike writing. Crisscrossing banners spiraled down the grip to a large silver sunburst pommel.

Antoinette could imagine the weight of the sword in her hand. She knew somehow that it would feel just right, and she longed to pick up the weapon. But to pick it up would mean to choose. She began to reach for the sword.

Wait! Antoinette thought. Kaliam had said that the challenge was not merely physical. *And I've already been tested with the sword.*

She looked back to the scroll. King Eliam wrote The Scrolls of Alleble. His wisdom filled each page of parchment. *I could use some wisdom right about now.*

Antoinette froze.

A faint scratching sound came from the door on the other side of the chamber. It was like something was digging on the other side at the base of the door. Rapid—*scratch, scratch, scratch.*

Antoinette looked back to the sword. Then, there it was again. *Scratch, scratch, scratch.*

Something was there, behind that door. *Scratch, scratch, scratch.*

Antoinette approached as silently as she could, listening, straining to determine what would make such a sound. The scratches stopped as Antoinette drew near. Slowly, she leaned over and put her ear to the door.

WHAM!!

Something slammed into the other side of the door, sending Antoinette sprawling backward to the floor. A deep growl rolled out, until it seemed the whole chamber was filled with a menacing rumble.

Scratch, scratch, scratch. SCRATCH, SCRATCH, SCRATCH! Something tore into the bottom of the door.

It's trying to get in here! Antoinette's mind raced as a jagged chunk of wood was ripped free from the base of the door. A dark claw reached through, grasping, seeking. Then it withdrew. And just for the briefest moment, a yellow reptilian eye appeared.

Frantically, Antoinette slid backward. She screamed. A rivet from her armor pressed into her side. She rolled over on her stomach, the new wound burning.

The sword! I've got to get the sword!

She got to one knee. The scratching continued behind her. She heard another piece of the door being torn away. Another growl.

Antoinette struggled to her feet and ran awkwardly to the pedestal. Her hand was an inch from the sword.

No. The sword is not the answer, Antoinette suddenly realized. *I am not the answer. I need the King's word.*

The clawing continued. A larger chunk of the door broke off, and the taloned claw came through again.

Antoinette made the decision and grabbed the scroll. She unrolled it and read:

Fear is the enemy. And trust is your friend.
I will not leave you. Your life will not end.
The creature knows evil.
The creature knows good.
You must stand fast before him,
when he breaks down the wood.
The scent that you carry
is a song that you sing.
It carries the melody, your oath to the King.

Antoinette looked up from the scroll. A pair of three-toed claws reached through the gaping rent in the door. They clutched a ragged edge and began to pull with violent strength.

Stand fast? How can I just wait around for that thing? Antoinette looked to the other pedestal, but the sword was gone.

"Okay, I get it!" Antoinette yelled. Clutching the scroll, she edged closer to the door. Finally, just a few feet away, she stopped and closed her eyes. She could hear the relentless scrapes and scratches of the beast's sharp talons on the door. She could hear shards of wood cracking and being torn away. She could hear the anxious breaths of the creature on the other side. Antoinette knew, in moments, it would get in.

Through the terrifying ruckus, Antoinette repeated the words from the scroll, again and again in her mind. *I will not leave you. Your life will not end. I will not leave you. Your life will not end. I will not leave you . . .*

There was a tremendous, splintering crack, and then the sound of something heavy being thrown with great force into a corner of the chamber. Cold air washed over Antoinette. She stood very still. She felt something in the room with her.

There were footfalls, many footfalls. *There's more than one creature?!*

Antoinette struggled to keep her eyes shut. She struggled to keep still.

She felt an icy breath on her forearm. She heard it sniffing her. Then something wet touched her skin.

"Please don't kill me!" she whimpered.

"Kill you, hmmm? Is that what you thought I would do to you?" came a deep, rasping voice very near to Antoinette's face. "No, no, no, my dear. Faethon would rather be grilled in the open sunlight than to harm a servant of King Eliam. Besides, you are unarmed. It would be hardly sporting for me to attack a weaponless knight. Open your eyes, my dear. Open them and behold Faethon!"

Antoinette opened her eyes to a squint. A scaly creature was coiled in a wide circle around her. It was armored with dark scales on its long body. Some of the scales glimmered as if encrusted with jewels. The scales tapered off to gray leathery flesh on the creature's many limbs.

That's why I thought there was more than one! Antoinette thought.

"Impressive, hmmm?" The creature grinned. Its face was broad, its jaws long and filled with rows of fangs. Creased winglike ears swept back from its head. And large yellow reptilian eyes gleamed out from heavy lids. Antoinette was reminded of the dragons she had seen in Chinese New Year parades.

"I am Faethon, a mortiwraith," he said. "The last living son of Falon the Great! I serve King Eliam and guard his treasuries, among other things. And today, Antoinette, I became your challenge."

Antoinette sat down hard on the floor and winced in pain. The wound in her side stung.

"You are injured," Faethon said. "I smelled fresh blood. I am sorry. I suppose I got a little carried away when I ripped down the door."

"It's my armor," Antoinette said. "Something on the side here keeps poking me."

"Nothing Kindle in the armory cannot fix," Faethon replied. "Your wound shall be fixed as well. The leechcraft in this city is excellent. Perhaps Sir Oswyn is available . . . yessss, he is the best in The Realm. Ask Sir Aelic to take you to Oswyn's apothecary."

"You know Aelic?" Antoinette asked.

"Yes, though he has only been in Alleble for a short time," Faethon said. "Aelic comes down from the Guard's Keep to bring me meat. He keeps me company from time to time. I think he has become quite fond of you."

Antoinette blushed.

"Yessss, very fond of you indeed," Faethon said. His toothy grin widened. "He tried to make me promise not to harm you. I refused, of course."

"What if I had picked up that sword?" Antoinette asked.

"That is a good question," Faethon replied. "I most likely would have spared you anyway, as I sensed the purity of your heart from the moment you entered this chamber. But had you taken that blade and attacked me, hewed at one of my beautiful limbs through the door . . . then I do not know what I might have done. A mortiwraith provoked is a fearsome sight, indeed. But let us not think of such unpleasant things, hmmm? You have passed this test, Antoinette. It is time you enter the second chamber. Climb the spiral stair to the Guard's Keep. I believe Kaliam the Sentinel . . . and Sir Aelic are waiting."

"Congratulations, Antoinette. You survived your meeting with Faethon," Kaliam said when Antoinette entered the Guard's Keep. "Though not unscathed, I see."

"It's just a scratch," she said dismissively. "There's a rivet or something sticking out of this back thing—"

"The backplate," Aelic offered. Brindle sat on his shoulder, but scampered down when she saw Antoinette.

"Faethon said Kindle could fix the armor," Antoinette said. She winced as she stooped and Brindle returned to her new home in Antoinette's hair.

"Yes," Kaliam replied. "But your wound needs tending first. Aelic, escort Antoinette to Sir Oswyn's apothecary. Do you know it?"

Aelic nodded. "Who would not? Os plays his lute and sings to great crowds at dusk every evening! I know the way."

"Excellent," Kaliam said. "Make haste from there to Kindle's, and be sure that he will have Antoinette's backplate ready this evening for the gathering."

WOUNDS THAT
DO NOT HEAL

Aelic led Antoinette again through the market. Brindle bounded along behind them. Many of the shops were closing for the day, and there were fewer goods to see. But those Glimpse merchants selling food were very active and had lines waiting to be served. One Glimpse merchant stoked a mound of glowing embers till it cracked into a fire beneath dozens of hunks of meat turning on iron spits. Juices dripped from the roasts and fell with a hiss into the fire. The smell that wafted from that place was almost overwhelming, reminding Antoinette she had not eaten since the scones early in the morning.

"Do you think we could get a bite to eat?" Antoinette asked. "After we get my side taken care of. The final test took a lot out of me."

"Ah, you also have fallen prey to the scents of the marketplace, eh?" Aelic said, and he laughed. "There will be food in plenty at the gathering this evening. I think a morsel could be arranged prior to that. I know someone who makes a remarkably good stew—"

"Elspeth, right?"

"Oh, she told you about my insatiable appetite for her savory stew, did she?" Aelic grinned. "I am not surprised. Once Elspeth begins to talk, there is no telling when she will ever stop."

Antoinette laughed and then winced. "Owww," she said, clutching her side. "This stings! Stop making me laugh." She said nothing to Aelic, but blood was seeping through her tunic.

"We had better get to Oswyn's quick," Aelic replied. "For I do not know if I can restrain my jovial nature!"

"Ouch!" Antoinette said, coughing through a laugh. "Yeah, we better hurry."

They turned a corner and came at last to a little gray house with a thatched roof and an etched mortar-and-pestle sign hanging from its gables.

"Sir Oswyn!?" Aelic called, leaning inside the door. "Sir Oswyn, are you here?" There was no answer at first, so they walked in. There was no one in the shop, but there were candles burning.

"Wow!" Antoinette said, looking around. The square room they had entered was absolutely stuffed. Arched alcoves recessed into every wall were lined with shelves and stocked with ceramic or glass jars of every imaginable size and color. In the middle of the floor, turned this way and that, were several six-foot-high cabinets. And each of those had innumerable tiny drawers, each labeled in the same flowing script. *No doubt for herbs,* Antoinette thought. Brindle raced around the shop, stopping now and again to sniff at something.

Antoinette looked up. Larger ingredients webbed in fishing nets, strings of dried plants, and various vines hung even from the ceiling! At the back of the store was a wide counter made wholly of dark maple. Aelic approached and called out again. "Sir Oswyn!? Sir Oswyn, if you are here, I need you!"

"A moment!" a deep voice sang out from somewhere behind the counter. There was the sound of a door slamming, and a tall Glimpse appeared. He flung back the long, dark bangs of his thick mane, revealing bushy eyebrows and startlingly bright blue eyes. He saw Aelic and Antoinette and grinned broadly. Scores of wrinkles and dimples from a lifetime of smiling appeared, and his face took on the look of the happiest of souls. There was also, in the gleam of his eyes, a hint of mischief. He reminded Antoinette of a classical composer gone mad with laughter, and she wondered what sort of doctor he could be.

"Sir Aelic," he said, still grinning "what brings you to my humble apothecary? Oh-ho! Unless I have gone utterly mad, this must be Lady Gwenne's twin from the Mirror Realm! And her name is Antoinette."

"How did you know?" Aelic asked.

"Aelic, you should know by now that I never forget a name, and since her feats of yesterday in the arena, I daresay most of Alleble knows of Antoinette."

Antoinette smiled slightly and then winced. Oswyn immediately saw her wound. "A pox upon us, Sir Aelic," Oswyn said, and he ran around the counter to examine Antoinette. "For we have bandied words while a noble lady waits for treatment."

"Tell me, Antoinette," he said, looking up from the wound. "This knave here . . . he did not do this to you, did he? Practicing his beloved moulinet?"

"No," Antoinette said. She winced as Aelic held up the backplate.

"Ah, I see," said Oswyn. "Be at ease. It is not more than a scratch, though it bleeds more than it should. I have just the thing for that. I tended that very herb in my gardens this morning, as a matter of fact." Oswyn disappeared behind the counter. A door slammed, then slammed again, and Oswyn returned. He carried a long green plant with feathery leaves and tiny flowers of pale lilac blooming at its top.

"Yarrow," Oswyn explained as he laid it on the counter. "Most deem it a weed, and so it is—an aggressive one at that! Given the chance, its roots will spread beneath the surface until it takes over a garden! But yarrow has a virtue that few now remember: it stops a wound from bleeding and prevents infection! Staunchweed, some call it—an apt name. A little of this, and you will be as good as new."

Oswyn took out a ceramic mortar and began mashing the yarrow stalk. Every now and then, he poured a small amount of a milky liquid from a small dark bottle into the bowl. An acrid smell filled the air.

"This will sting a little," Oswyn said, daubing a clean cloth in the ointment. He pressed it into the wound and held it there for a few seconds. Antoinette grabbed Aelic's shoulder, and were it not for his armor, she would have made more wounds for Sir Oswyn to heal.

"You said it would sting a *little*!" Antoinette complained through gritted teeth. "I feel like my whole side is on fire!"

"It is doing its work, m'lady," Oswyn said, and he removed the cloth. "You see? There now, the wound is no longer bleeding. Allow me to put on a bandage, and you can be on your way."

———

"After all you have been through today, you must be anxious to find a place to recline," Aelic said as they left Oswyn's apothecary. "But I wonder if you might walk a little longer with me. There is something I would like you to see before I take leave to bear your back-plate to the armory."

"I'm intrigued," Antoinette replied. "But don't forget I'm hungry!"

"No, I will not forget. I will see to it that one of the guards at the gatehouse sends word to Elspeth to prepare copious amounts of her stew and bring it to the Guard's Keep."

"Aelic, I don't think I could eat that much stew," Antoinette said.

"Ah, but Antoinette, what you do not eat, I will."

Antoinette laughed and noticed that her side no longer hurt. "Wow, that stuff Sir Oswyn mixed up sure did the trick!"

"Sir Oswyn is as skilled a warrior as he is a healer," Aelic said.

They walked back through the streets of Alleble, Brindle bounding along behind them like a ball of yarn, keeping ever close to Antoinette. The streets were less crowded now, and all of the shops had closed at last. The sun had nearly set, and all but the rooftops were in shadow. Eventually they made their way to the main thoroughfare of the city.

"Now, Lady Antoinette, cover your eyes."

"Uh, okay," Antoinette replied, a little leery. Aelic led her a few more steps.

"Now, uncover your eyes!" he said dramatically. "And look upon the grandeur of Alleble!"

Antoinette lowered her hands and gasped. The sun was half hidden by the mountains on the distant horizon, but it spent its last rays dazzling the Fountains of Alleble. Great plumes of water and mist shot high into the air, and droplets of water sparkled like jewels thrown into the sky.

"It . . . it's breathtaking, Aelic," Antoinette said, and Aelic stood beside her.

"Yes," was all he said for many quiet moments. But then, his hand brushed against Antoinette's, and he stepped away abruptly. "I need to see to your armor," he said, dashing off through the thoroughfare. "And your meal!"

As Antoinette walked back to the castle, she looked at her hands and smiled. She was reminded of Faethon's words, "I believe Sir Aelic is quite fond of you." But she wondered. Was Aelic really fond of her? Or was it her resemblance to Gwenne? Another question spoke in a tiny, mostly ignored part of her mind: *And what about Aelic? Am I fond of him, or is it his resemblance to Aidan?* Antoinette shook her head. Having a twin in another world sure was getting weird! Antoinette laughed quietly to herself.

Just as she reached the castle's main gate, Antoinette thought she saw someone standing in the shadowy street behind her. She turned around to confront, but there was no one there—only the Seventh Fountain of Alleble stood behind her. Brindle raced down from her shoulder and disappeared into the gatehouse. But Antoinette was drawn to the presence of the fountain.

She found herself walking slowly up to the dry pool and peering into its gray emptiness. She put her hands on the cool stone rim, and suddenly, she began to see faces twisted in sadness and fear. And torches waiting to light the dark oil that filled the fountain.

"So, great King," said a voice that seemed to come from both above and behind. The thin, high-pitched, frenzied voice asked: "Will you lay aside your crown for your people?"

There was terror in the eyes of the Glimpses in the reflection.

"You do not command this!" another voice, weary, but still lordly and assured, declared. "I am allowing it. And nothing will ever rescue you from the doom you have chosen!"

There came a shriek and then the sound of a sword scraping across stone. The pool in front of Antoinette erupted in fire. Flames raced around the pool, and faces turned to terror and pain. Antoinette struggled to let go of the stone, but something held her to it. Helpless, she stared into the inferno.

Then she saw two people she seemed to recognize . . . a man and a woman. *They are not Glimpse-kind,* she thought. In vain the man embraced the woman, trying to shield her, but the flames engulfed them. Suddenly, to her own surprise, Antoinette screamed, "Mommy! Daddy! No, please, nooo!"

A hand grabbed Antoinette's shoulder, and as she fell backward, a single tear from her cheek fell into the dry fountain.

A Glimpse knight stood before her. He had long sandy brown hair drawn tightly back and a thin silver circlet above his restless blue eyes. "M'lady, are you all right?" he asked. Antoinette could not at first speak. She nodded weakly.

"You seemed in pain," he said. "I thought you ill . . . that you might fall."

"Fire," she said. "My birth parents . . ."

"Alas, m'lady. Now that the cruel shadows of night begin to fall, we are all haunted by the black deeds of our enemy. My brother Bolt fell to Paragor's dark army in the battle at Mithegard. But come; though some wounds do not heal, let us seek the light within the castle of our King. There we may find comfort and peace in times of trouble."

DREAMS AND DREAMERS

Antoinette, Aelic, and Nock sat at a long table in the Guard's Keep. In front of each was a giant bowl filled with stew. The moment one bowl was empty, Elspeth swooped down and refilled it from a great kettle of stew. She was kept busy enough, for Aelic and Nock put away enough stew to feed an army. At first, Antoinette thought that one bowl would have fed her whole family for a week, but she surprised herself by finishing it.

"Are you sure you don't want some more stew, dearie?" Elspeth asked.

"Maybe later, Elspeth. It is delicious," Antoinette said, feeling a bit chilled.

"Perhaps I've added too much garlic," Elspeth said.

Antoinette smiled at Elspeth. "The stew is perfect. I mean, look at Aelic." Caught slurping from his spoon, Aelic looked up. He slowly put the spoon down and then took a cloth and wiped his mouth.

"See what I mean?" Antoinette laughed. "Aelic can't get enough."

"Be glad that Mallik is not here," Nock chimed in, his intelligent eyes gleaming. "For we would not have enjoyed even a taste of Elspeth's fine stew if my hammer-wielding friend was here!"

"That rascal," Elspeth said playfully. "It would suit him to ignore the bowls altogether. Can you just see him sitting down with the whole kettle and a spoon?"

They all laughed at that. Elspeth beamed, obviously happy with the attention being paid to her cooking.

"What is going on here?" a voice bellowed from the doorway. "I tarry a few minutes and the stew is all gone?"

"I have put some to the side just for you, Sir Kaliam," Elspeth said. "You just sit down, and I will bring it right to you."

"Thank you, Elspeth," Kaliam said.

Kaliam turned to Antoinette and congratulated her once more. "You have passed the three tests—just as King Eliam said you would."

"King Eliam told you I'd pass the tests? He knew?"

"Of course he knew," Kaliam replied, looking at Antoinette strangely. "That is why he called you for this mission. He knew you would be ready."

"Then, what's the use of testing me? Why'd you make me go through all those . . . those stupid trials?"

Aelic glanced sideways at Nock. The jovial mood vanished like a candle being snuffed. Kaliam gripped the table and leaned over to look Antoinette in the eye. His forearms tensed. "Do not call anything stupid that has been arranged by the King," he said curtly. "And the tests were certainly not for our benefit. But sometimes a warrior must learn her own strengths—and weaknesses—before she can do any real good."

Antoinette looked away, feeling guilty.

"It may be that the lessons you learned from those tests will come back to you in some difficult place. They might even save your life."

Antoinette's shoulders sagged, and she shook her head. "I'm sorry, Sir Kaliam," she whispered. "I was wrong to say that. I know King Eliam knows what he's doing."

Kaliam straightened and nodded. "Antoinette, you have faced many challenges since arriving in The Realm. I cannot imagine what it has been like for you to leave the comforts of your home to face peril in another realm. But go now, and rest. For tonight is a very important night for you. Sir Aelic, escort Antoinette back to her chamber. Then see to it that she arrives in the Great Hall in two hours, not more."

"I am most happy to oblige, m'lord," Aelic said.

Outside her quarters, Antoinette asked Aelic to wait a moment while she went inside. When she returned she handed him the photograph of Robby from the soccer web site. "Have you seen him?"

Aelic stared at the image. "It is like a looking glass on parchment," he said, in awe of the photo. "And what unusual garments he wears. I have never seen a tunic that shade of green before. And his armor . . . it does not seem to protect much of his body."

"Those are his shin pads." Antoinette laughed. "And he's wearing a soccer uniform, not a tunic."

Aelic stared at her blankly.

"Soccer is a game we like to play in our world."

"Oh," Aelic replied.

"So have you ever seen a Glimpse that looks like him?"

"Alas, no, I am certain I have not," Aelic said. "I have only resided here in Alleble for a short time, but he is not here. Nor is he in Acacia where my mother resides, or Mithegard where my father rules. Why do you ask? Is this Robby in some sort of trouble?"

"I don't know. Robby is Aidan's best friend back in our world," said Antoinette, "and it's just that Aidan keeps having these dreams."

Aelic looked uncomfortable at the mention of Aidan's dreams.

"In the dream, Robby's Glimpse is a servant of Paragor, and he's involved in some kind of evil mission. Aidan asked me to find him and get him to follow King Eliam."

Aelic abruptly handed the photo back to Antoinette and stood up. "I am sorry, Antoinette, I have not seen him. I must go now, and you must rest."

"You've had dreams too, haven't you?" Antoinette asked.

"How . . . how did you know that?" Aelic asked.

"When I mentioned Aidan's dreams, you tensed up," she said. "And it made sense that if Aidan is having dreams, then you would too, right?"

"Yes, I have seen some haunting images," Aelic replied slowly, as if the very mention of them was too dreadful to think about. "Lady Gwenne confided in me that she too experiences similar dreams . . . strange, sometimes horrible—not easy for the mind to let go. And that must mean you also experience them."

"Yes," Antoinette replied quietly. "But Kaliam told me not to talk about them. It seems to mean something to him, something serious."

"I likewise have been so warned," Aelic replied. "Let us not speak of this again until we have Kaliam's counsel. Now, m'lady, do get some rest. I will bring your armor when I come for you later."

Aelic started to leave, but Antoinette motioned for him to wait.

"Sir Aelic, do you think I have a chance of finding Robby's Glimpse out of all the Glimpses in The Realm?"

"If that is what King Eliam called you here to do," Aelic replied, "then I am certain you will find him. But if he indeed serves The Betrayer, it will be no easy task to change his heart."

The Good Confession

Antoinette's repaired armor felt much more comfortable. And her side—it was as if the wound was never there. *Sir Oswyn knows his herbs!* she thought. She and Aelic had joined many other Glimpses in the Great Hall. There were knights in armor, ladies in long gowns, even a few children playing in the corner of the room.

"On your feet, you lot of lethargic widge-lumps!!" bellowed Kaliam as he stormed into the hall.

He startled Antoinette, Aelic, and most of the other Glimpses in the room. Antoinette and Aelic leaped up from their seats and stood very still.

Four other knights marched in with Kaliam and stood behind him at the head of the table. One of them was a stout Glimpse with dark eyes and a long coppery mustache and beard, who hefted an immense warhammer as he stepped forward.

"Very good, Sentinel!" he said. He smiled and elbowed Kaliam in the ribs. "You nearly sounded like the legendary Captain Valithor!"

"Mallik!" Kaliam exclaimed. "Do not ruin the moment!" But then he burst into laughter himself. Mallik grinned and stepped back in line as Kaliam turned and motioned for everyone to be seated.

"Citizens of Alleble!" he began. "Twelve knights will ride for Yewland at first light on the morrow. Joining me will be four members of the Elder Guard you see here: Sir Farix, Sir Tal, Sir Nock, and Sir Mallik, along with seven chosen from your ranks."

The Glimpses near Antoinette and Aelic murmured at this announcement. "The Sentinel *and* four Elder Guard?" one whispered.

"Something must have gone wrong in Yewland," said another.

Kaliam fired a harsh glare, silencing the gossip. Then he continued.

"The mighty and wise King of Alleble has chosen the twelve for this mission," he said, looking from knight to knight. "If I call your name, stand and join me at the head of the table. For those of you left behind, understand that the decision was made because of the skills needed for this mission. Do not despair. Your turn will come."

A wave of tension washed over the knights. Antoinette glanced at Aelic. His face was grim. His narrowed eyes glinted blue.

"Sir Aelic, as heir to Captain Valithor's mantle, you will journey to Yewland," Kaliam announced.

Aelic nodded and said, "My grandfather is a hero of Alleble, as is my twin in the Mirror Realm, Sir Aidan, Knight of the Dawn. Their mantles are beyond my grasp. I hope only to serve my King faithfully." Then he took a deep breath, stepped forward, and stood beside the Sentinel.

"Sir Tobias, come forward!" Kaliam said.

A tall, thin warrior rose to his feet. He had dark hair, immaculately cut to hang just above his shoulders, and smallish brown eyes that were close set, divided only by the narrow bridge of his sharp nose. He wore gleaming armor over a rich tunic of deep blue. He looked elegant and held his walking stick as if it were a royal scepter.

"You will serve as pathfinder on this journey," Kaliam continued. "But fear not. You will have a wealth of experience at your call. I am also a pathfinder—though, as Sentinel, I shall lead mostly in other ways. And no one in this room knows the southern routes and forest ways like Nock, for he was born in Yewland."

Sir Tobias stroked his neatly trimmed goatee thoughtfully and said, "Sentinel Kaliam, my Captain, it will be a significant honor to chart the prudent way to Yewland. It is my hope not to trouble you or our archer extraordinaire Nock with my own mundane pathfinding tasks."

Kaliam nodded. Sir Tobias went to the head of the table and stood proudly between Aelic and Kaliam.

"Sir Rogan," Kaliam said. "You have come to Alleble from the ruins of Mithegard. And like the city of Seven Towers, you are rebuilt, a new servant of King Eliam. Stand and join the twelve!"

A massive Glimpse warrior stood and without a word lumbered over to Kaliam. He bowed to his commander and took his place on Kaliam's left side. Sir Rogan was tall, and his aged leather armor could not contain his broad shoulders. He had long blond hair that fell like a cape behind his head. And his beard was just a thin goatee. Sir Rogan remained silent, but his intelligent green eyes scanned the hall restlessly. He seemed anxious as he fingered the edge of a great battleaxe at his side.

"Lady Merewen," said Kaliam as he looked to the back of the hall where stood a form all in gray, nearly blending into the shadows. "You will travel with us to Yewland, for we have need of brave hearts such as yours."

At first, the figure did not move. Then, slowly, Lady Merewen came forward and stood before Kaliam. Antoinette could not see her face for Lady Merewen's head was bowed and covered by a deep hood.

"M'lord," Lady Merewen said quietly, "you are gracious to speak to your servant with such kindness. My heart is filled with gratitude and yearns to serve the King if only in some small way. But among the Guard and the honored knights of this land? Surely there are many others more deserving and . . ." Her voice became only a whisper. "And more worthy."

Kaliam smiled kindly and gently pushed back her hood. Lady Merewen's hair was pure silver, but not the brittle gray of age, for it was like woven silk. And she wore it tied back in many intricate braids. A silver circlet with a single blue gem rested on her forehead above wet eyes. Antoinette marveled at her, for she was beautiful and queenly, but forlorn and sad like a queen in mourning.

"Lady Merewen," Kaliam said, and he lifted her chin until she looked at him. "Dwell not in dreary chambers of the past. For behold! You are not what you once were! You have crossed over from death into life. You have bravely forsaken The Betrayer and embraced the one true King of all The Realm. And it is he who now embraces you, Lady Merewen. Not one of us is worthy, and yet he calls us. King Eliam has called you, and so be glad. And let your sword join our number."

Lady Merewen smiled, and it seemed to Antoinette that it was a smile suddenly unburdened of a thousand cares. And if ever Antoinette had a doubt about the King she served, it was erased in that moment. Lady Merewen stood proudly among the others near the Sentinel's side.

"Sir Oswyn, come join us on our mission," Kaliam said. "And

bring with you your healing salves and knowledge of herbs, minerals, and curatives."

"Hail Kaliam!" Sir Oswyn's rich, musical voice sang out. He rose and flung back the dark bangs of his thick mane. "Hail, and well-met! Indeed I will bring all of my special mixtures—some for healing as you say, but others for inflicting! Ha-ha! I have some new flavors that I should like to test if a willing enemy should be so bold as to ask."

Sir Oswyn marched up to join the others, and Antoinette noticed a small lute bouncing on his back as he walked. *Does he sing as he rides into battle?* Antoinette wondered.

"Sir Gabriel," Kaliam continued, "thank you for agreeing to be Alleble's ambassador, for this journey may depend entirely upon shrewd negotiations. Yewland's ruler has made claims which need answering, and I can think of no one better to answer than you."

"Sentinel Kaliam," said a thin-caped Glimpse, "with such flattering words you could easily fill the negotiator's role. Queen Illaria is known to enjoy such quips that cater to her vanity. Nonetheless, I will not mince words with her. Something is amiss in Yewland, and her judgments of late have gone awry. The truth . . ." He patted scrolls that stuck out all along the seam of his waist belt. "The truth is what she needs. And in the King's name, I, Gabriel, will bring her the truth."

Sir Gabriel was noticeably older than the others. Lengthy waves of gray hair framed his long face. And unlike Sir Oswyn, whose wrinkles seemed to come from excessive humor, Sir Gabriel wore the care lines and heavy creases of much toil in thought. His beard dangled over his breastplate like the pendulum of a grandfather clock. But his age did not imply weakness. Hale and experienced, he seemed to Antoinette more like an old tree that had endured countless storms and stood defiantly on a hill waiting for more. And he wore, tucked into his belt among the parchments, two long fighting knives.

Sir Gabriel stood next to Sir Tobias, and they shared a quiet word. It seemed they'd had a friendship prior to being called as members of the twelve who would travel to Yewland.

"We stand now as eleven," Kaliam said to the crowded hall. "The Twelfth Knight is a place of honor on all such missions as this. And I must say that the first time King Eliam called one from the Mirror Realm and named him Twelfth Knight, I was doubtful that he would live up to that calling. Nay, he surpassed it even! For who shall forget Sir Aidan, Knight of the Dawn?!"

Some in the gathered crowd cheered and some raised their goblets in reverent silence.

"So today," Kaliam continued, "we name another Twelfth Knight from the Mirror Realm. She is Antoinette Lynn Reed. Antoinette, come forward and prepare your heart for the good confession."

What is this? Antoinette wondered. Aidan hadn't told her anything about a confession. She stood before Kaliam and looked questioningly into his eyes.

"Nock!" Kaliam gestured and the Glimpse archer came forward. His sandy brown hair was drawn back, and this time he wore a gold circlet above his arched brows and keen eyes. He handed a long bundle to Kaliam.

"Antoinette," Kaliam said as he unwrapped the bundle, "this sword is *Thil Galel*, the Daughter of Light, so named by your Glimpse twin, Lady Gwenne. It was by her own request that— should you become the Twelfth Knight—you use her sword on our mission."

He held the sword aloft. Torchlight gleamed off the keen double edge of the marvelous blade. Its winged silver crossguard curved slightly above the weapon's ivory grip. And as Kaliam slashed the blade down through the air, it made an odd half-musical metallic hum.

"This blade will be yours to wield, but tonight it will be symbolic of the step of faith you are about to take. Please kneel before me."

Antoinette knelt, and as she did so, it seemed the torchlight dimmed so that merely a small circle of light around Kaliam and herself remained.

"Antoinette, you have been called to be a valorous Knight for the Kingdom of Alleble. This is no small responsibility. And though by right of the passing of three tests, you have been found worthy, we require of you this confession. Do you, Antoinette, confess allegiance and absolute loyalty to the one true King, the provider of all that is just and good? Even were the hordes of darkness to assail you in hopeless demand of your life—even then do you swear devotion forever to the King?"

Kaliam lowered his voice so that only Antoinette could hear. "Think deeply on this, for nothing binds you to this choice. King Eliam will never force anyone to follow him. And even now, after all that you have been through, even now, you are free to choose. If you say nay, we will bear you no ill will and you will be returned swiftly to your realm. Another will be called, and you will carry on your life in much the same way as you ever did. Only reply aye if it is spoken with the deepest voice of your heart."

Even were the hordes of darkness to assail you . . .

Antoinette stared into the eyes of the other warriors called by the King. There was great courage in those eyes. And Antoinette knew she would need such courage. This was not a trivial decision.

When Antoinette looked at Lady Merewen, she saw courage, but also there glimmered a desperate cry of thankfulness. And glad tears streaked down her face. It seemed to Antoinette that Lady

Merewen was one who once had no hope but had been given hope anew, one who had nearly perished but had been rescued at the brink, one who had belonged to no one but had been adopted into the most loving of families. *That's like me,* Antoinette thought.

Antoinette looked into Kaliam's eyes and in a strangely confident voice answered, "Aye!"

"Then by the heartfelt confession of your lips," announced Kaliam as he gently tapped Antoinette's shoulders with the blade called Thil Galel, "I dub thee Lady Antoinette, Swordmaiden of Alleble and servant of King Eliam the Everlasting!"

After the deafening cheers died down, the celebration began. It carried on long after the twelve had left to prepare for their journey.

ON RAVEN'S WINGS

Antoinette lay on her bed in her chambers with Brindle curled up beside her. She stared out the window at the distant realm bathed in silver light from the waxing crescent moon. She held the photograph of Robby. "Where are you?" she whispered.

Her eyes drifted to the distant west and the jagged black peaks of The Prince's Crown. Antoinette shivered at the possibility that Robby was there.

Antoinette fell into a fitful sleep, not sure of what the morning would bring.

Antoinette could see a long pile of rocks heaped as a cairn. A raven stirred upon a sword hilt that had been driven into the frozen ground.

The black bird croaked harshly and then took to the air. Soaring into the cloud-smothered night sky, it floated above a wasteland of endless gray stone draped by miserable scabs of crusty snow.

The broken land rose into black ridges and severe mountains. Two peaks, taller and more jagged than the rest, pierced the lowest clouds like fangs. At the foot of these, as if thrust up through the world's stony armor, was a dark fortress.

Bastions, turrets, keeps, and strongholds—all irregular and rigid—fitted together diabolically like the gears of a torturing device.

Rising above all was a high tower, wreathed in sharp points of stone like a vine of thorns.

Into the topmost chamber of this tower, the raven flew. It landed on the sill of an open window. Inside was a tall warrior clad in black armor, except for a red inverted crown emblazoned upon his breastplate. The knight was ghostly pale and wore his long, dark hair swept back from his face and tied behind his head. His coal-black eyes flashed red for an instant as he stared down at an object in his hands.

Carefully, as if a father was laying his child to rest, the warrior placed the object into a sturdy chest of black marble. He looked up at the raven and smiled.

The raven jerked free of the window sill, into the night, and dove downward to an iron door ajar at the base of a keep.

It entered through a narrow opening and flew down a winding, torchlit passage. Finally, the raven emerged from the tunnel and perched on a wide chandelier in the midst of a vast chamber hall. Far below, teeming like a pit of black snakes, were ranks of soldiers. Rank upon rank of soldiers in dark armor. They filled the hall till it seemed there was nothing else. They were endless. Armed with spear, axe, blade, and bow, like a great thicket of brambles.

Arrows pierced the air, clanged off the chandelier. The raven flew again, swooshing back up the passage and through the narrow opening of the iron door. Between darkened dwellings, it careened through side streets and raced toward the enormous castle keep at the base of the tower of thorns. The black bird glided over a balcony high on its wall.

There was a feast within, a gathering, at a long, dark table with eleven chairs. The same warrior from the tower was at the head of the table. He raised a silver goblet. Ten other pale knights, grim and doughty, stood and raised their drinks. Their eyes flashed red as they all drank. But when they were finished drinking, their eyes flashed blue.

Antoinette gasped for breath, and started to fall . . .

Finding a Path
in the Dark

"Lady Antoinette!" called a voice. "Lady Antoinette!" There was a sharp knock on the chamber door. "It is Lady Merewen."

Antoinette struggled to wake up. She rubbed her eyes and slowly sat up in bed.

"Lady Antoinette," Lady Merewen called. "We leave within the hour! May I come in?"

"It was a dream," Antoinette said, relieved as she went to open the door.

"Lady Merewen, is it morning already?"

"No, the other knights have been restless and could not sleep. We are preparing to leave. I have been sent to help you with your armor, and Aelic is packing your steed. You must hurry."

"Okay, hold your horses," Antoinette said sleepily.

There was a silence, and then Lady Merewen explained, "We are not riding horses, Lady Antoinette. Our unicorns are more fleet-footed!"

Lady Merewen helped Antoinette quickly dress. They threw a few personal belongings into a satchel. Then, Antoinette patted the sleeping Brindle lightly on the head. "You'll be much safer here," she said.

In only moments, Lady Merewen was hurrying down the stairway to the main gatehouse. "Hurry, Lady Antoinette. Kaliam grows anxious about the situation in Yewland, and he is ready to leave."

"Has something changed?" Antoinette asked.

"Not long ago, a message arrived from Queen Illaria. It was ripe with veiled threats about dissolving our alliance. That would be a terrible loss to The Realm, to say nothing of the blow it would deal to Alleble's armies—Yewland's archers are unsurpassed."

"And this is all because someone pretending to be an ambassador from Alleble is ruining things over there?"

"An imposter, yes," Lady Merewen replied. "He has somehow convinced the Queen that Alleble requires tribute in gold—and Blackwood weaponry. The latter is more dear to them and most painfully would that be paid. It is Yewland's custom to gather timber only from limbs and trees that have fallen—and given the strength of those towering trees, that does not happen that often. Every bow, shaft, or staff made from the Blackwood is coveted throughout The Realm. Now it seems that the first messenger we sent to Yewland to warn them of the imposter has not returned, and Kaliam fears he is in the hands of our enemy. We must go now before the situation worsens beyond repair."

"How can Paragor get away with this?" Antoinette asked, following Lady Merewen. "Wouldn't the Queen be able to tell if this ambassador is really from Alleble? I mean, the eyes would give him away, right?"

"That has been so in the past," Lady Merewen replied. "But there was one other among the Prince's legions, whose eyes showed blue for a time though all the while his heart was red."

"Acsriot?"

"You know of his deeds then?" Lady Merewen asked.

Antoinette nodded solemnly. Aidan had told her a little about Acsriot's betrayal.

"To this day," Lady Merewen explained, "no one knows how he was able to mask his eyes. But one thing is certain . . . we cannot afford to be fooled again."

Antoinette wondered about the knights in her dream. Their eyes had changed color after they drank from the goblets. But remembering her promise to Kaliam, she did not speak of her dream.

"If he flees . . . ," Tobias said as he hunched over a map in the gatehouse. The other eleven knights gathered round. "If the imposter flees Yewland, he will no doubt take the main road out and head northwest, skirting the Endurel River. So I propose we take the trade route ourselves and then strike east just before Zin Lake."

"You seem so certain," said Kaliam.

"It is an elementary matter," Tobias replied. He straightened and gestured as if drawing a picture in the air. Antoinette thought he liked having an audience. "It is very possible that we will snare the imposter while he is still in Yewland. But if he is from Paragory as we suspect, then the western road will be his only escape."

"What of the Blackwood?" Mallik asked. "Could he not strike a straighter path by cutting across the Blackwood?"

No one answered. A cold wind whipped through the gate, and the torches flickered. The hair on Antoinette's arms stood up.

Finally, Nock spoke up. "If the imposter is foolish enough to venture into the Blackwood, then we will lose any opportunity to question him. He will not return."

"What do you mean?" Mallik laughed nervously. "It is merely a patch of woods."

"Nay, my hammer-wielding friend," said Nock, clapping Mallik on the shoulder. "That is no simple grove of trees. The Blackwood is the oldest forest in The Realm. It is said that before the first scroll of Alleble was written, King Eliam buried seven powerful ancient enemies there—the Seven Sleepers they were called. It is only the great dark roots of the blackwood trees that keep them from returning."

"Seven Sleepers?" Mallik scoffed. "You have been listening to too many harvest tales! Next you'll be spouting off about the Wyrm Lord!"

"Laugh if you wish, Mallik," Nock said. "But as for me, I would rather wrestle a dragon than go into the Blackwood—especially at night."

"Seven Sleepers or not," Kaliam said, "there are other foul things in the Blackwood, that is to be sure. Sir Tobias is right. If our imposter flees, he will strike the main road and run full into our snare. We will travel that way. Your steeds are saddled, ample provisions for the journey to Yewland are packed, and you have your weapons. Let us ride hard now. If we reach the ruins of Torin's Vale by daybreak, we will rest there for a short while. Then southwest following the road until it turns east before Zin Lake. May King Eliam's power fill us on this bold venture, for The Realm grows a more dangerous place with each passing day."

MIDNIGHT RIDE

The rush of the falling water filled the night with its steady hypnotic song. A light mist from six of the seven fountains fell upon the twelve as they rode past. Torchbearing guards saluted and raised the first and second gates. Led by Kaliam, the travelers passed beyond the safety of Alleble's grand walls and into the silent, waiting night.

Antoinette's thoughts lingered on the cold, dry stone of the seventh fountain. The vision she'd had there would not soon leave her thoughts. The fountain still seemed to call to her from the shadows.

"Will it always remain dry?" Antoinette asked Aelic, who rode beside her.

"Perhaps. Only King Eliam can say," Aelic replied. He glanced back at the barren fountain. "Our craftsmen have found no defect in its design which would hinder the flow of water from the springs below. But ever since the night of the Betrayal, the fountain has remained empty."

The unicorns seemed restless outside the walls of the city. Kaliam rode just ahead and turned. "Do you feel the tension in your steeds?" he called out. "They are spoiling to ride! I say let us give them their wish."

With a cheer of camaraderie Kaliam raised his broadsword high. The air filled with blades. Fury and the Daughter of Light were among them.

"To Yewland, we ride!" Kaliam roared. "For King and Kingdom!"

"Hurrah!!" his team responded.

Kaliam's unicorn needed no other prompt or spur. It bore Kaliam away as if by a sudden wind. The other knights thundered after him.

"Try to keep up," Aelic said to Antoinette. He winked and was gone.

"Oh, no, you don't!" Antoinette called after him. "Rael, go!" And the unicorn surged forward.

Aelic's steed was no slowcoach. Antoinette could see the beast's white flanks far ahead. But Rael would not be left behind. With Antoinette urging Rael on, she overtook Aelic and grinned as she passed. "It must be that I am lighter in the saddle!" she called out to him. Aelic pretended to glower for a moment, but then began to laugh.

The spirit of adventure swelling in each of them, the twelve raced on through the early morning darkness. Their steeds did not tire, and The Realm passed by in a shadowy blur. About an hour before sunup, they swooped into a misty valley littered with ruins. It was known as Torin's Vale.

The twelve slowed to a trot on the remnants of a cobblestone road, now overgrown with patches of tall grass. They passed under a pale stone arch, and before them lay the skeleton of a large ancient city. Wisps of gray mist enveloped the broken foundations of long-empty dwellings. Roofless cottages, empty manors, and fallen towers loomed in the shadows. Dark windows stared out at the riders as they passed.

Antoinette shuddered. "This place gives me the creeps," she whispered.

"It was once a great city," Nock said, "but it has long been abandoned. Nothing survives here now."

As she looked about Antoinette felt watched, as if something or someone was behind the darkened windows. She tried to shake off the feeling, but then she noticed Nock seemed exceptionally watchful and had his bow and arrow at the ready.

TORIN'S VALE

Moved by a chilling breeze, the mist reached for the ankles of their steeds, and all sounds were muted. Even the clip-clop of their unicorns sounded muffled and distant.

"I feel like I'm being watched," Antoinette whispered to Aelic.

"I feel it also. It is like the memories of the fallen watch us from the shadows."

"It must be the dark windows," she replied. "Or maybe it's those twisted clusters of trees—there must be a thousand places here where someone could hide!"

"That is precisely why our Sentinel led us here. Come morning, we will be forced to ride in the open, but we should remain hidden while we may."

"Still, this place gives me the creeps!" she said.

The twelve continued through the valley in silence until they came to a large stone wall. In the center was a huge arched gateway.

"This is Torin's Keep," Kaliam announced as he halted the team. "There were once magnificent tall doors of rich mahogany here—doors that opened to welcome the weary and bid them rest in the golden firelight of Torin's hospitality. These same doors closed to shut out the night, and no evil could pass them by force, or so the tales tell."

Antoinette imagined reclining in a great golden hall while dark stealthy creatures scratched at the powerful doors but could not get in.

"Nonetheless, even Torin's Gate could not stay the passing of time," Kaliam continued. "Still, we will rest here until the sun rises. We have made excellent time, my good knights, better even than I had hoped. Unburden your steeds, and let us kindle some small golden light to take the chill from the air. Torin's Keep will be glad once more."

The unicorns grazed in the tall grasses outside the keep. They seemed the least affected by the eerie surroundings of Torin's Vale. Farix volunteered for the first watch, and he patrolled the shadows around the perimeter of the camp. But inside Torin's Keep there was indeed cheery golden light rekindled. Eleven of the twelve knights gathered around a small but happy fire. They feasted on roasted beef and wedges from an aged wheel of cheese. Spirits were high, and they forgot for a time the dangerous nature of their mission.

"Do you remember that time, Kaliam," Mallik called across the fire, "when we camped near the Cold River? Sir Aidan woke us all with the fear that the enemy had found us!"

Kaliam smiled, and the firelight flickered in his dark eyes.

"Aye, no one could forget," said Nock, slapping Mallik on the back and sitting beside his burly friend. "Aidan saw the lantern spiders and took them for torches!"

"Lantern spiders?" Antoinette thought aloud, remembering the message Aidan had asked her to deliver to Kaliam.

"Yes, m'lady," Nock replied. "They spin great domes of—"

"Oh, do not tell that story again," pleaded Aelic. "You forget it was not me!"

Kaliam laughed. "It seems, Aelic, that you are always quick to point out Aidan's foibles were not you, but not so fast to deny his talents."

Aelic grinned. "Would it not be foolish of me to do otherwise?"

Everyone laughed in agreement.

"What of the lantern spiders?" Antoinette asked.

"I would not want Sir Aidan thinking ill of me. You will have to find that story out from him. It is you who told me he asked us not to tell of that event," Kaliam said. "You won't hear it from me."

"Yes, I can understand why a young knight would not want a lady to hear that story," Nock said.

"Nor an old knight for that matter," said Oswyn with a sly look toward Sir Gabriel. Sir Gabriel didn't even look up from the scrolls.

"I know!" Mallik announced. "What about the time when we surprised Sir Aidan as he refreshed the dragon pens?"

"Oh, no," Aelic muttered.

"Did Aidan request we not tell this story?" Kaliam asked Antoinette.

"Say yes!" Aelic whispered urgently to her.

Antoinette smiled gleefully at Aelic, then turned to Kaliam. "Oh, no. He only mentioned the lantern spiders."

Kaliam laughed. "Then I think we should."

"So there he was," Mallik began, "the Twelfth Knight-to-be, wearing a brand-new tunic and clean armor."

Nock laughed. "You can always tell a beginner in the pens! Ha!"

"Indeed," answered Mallik, and he turned to Antoinette. "For the dragon pens are fouled beyond words. Those who have had the misfortune of cleaning those pens know better than to wear anything clean!"

Beginning to imagine the events that followed, Antoinette put a hand to her lips.

"Oh, how Sir Aidan's armor gleamed, a crisp tunic, new breeches—"

"Oh, do go on," said Sir Tobias rather abruptly as he rubbed the tip of a long finger along the bridge of his nose. "You have already told us this part."

"Give him time. One must have patience for a story well told," Sir Oswyn said.

Antoinette felt uncomfortable, and for a moment she thought Sir Tobias would grow angry. But the aloof expression on his narrow face suddenly cracked into a grin and he laughed. "Well-met, herb-meister," he said. "Forgive my rudeness, Sir Mallik. It is just that I have not heard this tale, and I am dying to know what could be more embarrassing than mistaking lantern spiders for soldiers' torches."

Mallik smiled. "Aidan was supposed to be working. But Sir Aidan was anything but working. Daydreaming, I would say."

"Or knight-dreaming," said Tal, laughing at his own joke. "He was so lost in thought we could have marched right in front of him, and I doubt he would have noticed."

"It was Farix's idea to gather the rest of us, and hide behind the pen where Sir Aidan sat upon the fence wasting the night away."

"It is true," Nock said, smiling. "Farix had noticed that the king's largest dragon, Spryvern—"

"Not Spryvern the longtail! Why, he is the best-trained dragon in The Realm," Sir Oswyn said.

"Do not spoil the tale, now, Os," said Kaliam.

"So," Mallik continued, almost whispering, "Spryvern was sleeping in the pen next to the one Sir Aidan was supposed to be cleaning. And as it happens, Farix is good friends with Spryvern's trainer. So there sat Sir Aidan, lost in thought. Oblivious to us all. Sitting right above the pen he would soon wish he had cleaned!

"Now, Farix asked, 'Have you seen the dragon's new trick?' None of us had, of course. Quickly, Farix made three short whistles. That dragon jumped to its feet, made three loud screeches, and cracked its long tail like a whip!"

"Sir Aidan was so startled, he fell right off the fence!" Mallik bellowed. "He landed, ha! He landed face-first in the dragon pen! The poor fellow was so covered in dragon scat you could hardly tell who he was!"

Lady Merewen put a hand to her lips and laughed. Tobias rocked and nearly fell over. Kaliam tried to remain stoic, but he too broke down. Sensitive to Aelic beside her, Antoinette did everything she could to hold in the hysterical laughs that were bubbling up inside her, but it didn't work.

"You know," Aelic said finally, "it is kind of funny. Just remember—"

"I know," Antoinette interrupted. "It wasn't you!" And with that a new round of merriment began.

The laughter, like the fire, eventually died down. Everyone engaged in conversation, everyone except Sir Rogan and Sir Gabriel.

Sir Rogan, an empty dish and a wooden spoon in his hands, leaned forward, gazing into the fire. His long blond hair draped over his face, but his eyes gleamed.

"One piece of gold for your thoughts, Sir Rogan!" bellowed Mallik.

Sir Rogan straightened slightly, his eyes narrowed and focused for a moment on Mallik. "Hrmff," he grunted, and then he returned to staring at the fire.

Mallik smiled grimly. "Ah, I know what consumes your thoughts, axe-wielder. The burden of the fight to come mingles with the memory of battles past, does it not? We are brothers in that respect, for we all lost those dear to us in the fight at Mithegard."

Sir Rogan looked up once more from the fire. His eyes were glassy, but his jaw was set, and there seemed an air about him—a mixture of steely determination and barely restrained wrath.

"Let it not gnaw at your mind, my friend," said Mallik. "Vengeance, the thirst for blood, is the province of the enemy. But justice is of our King. We will seek peace, but be ever ready to deliver justice."

Sir Rogan nodded, and it seemed to the others that a bond had just been forged between axe and hammer.

"I don't think I'd want to be a Paragor Knight caught between those two," Antoinette whispered to Aelic.

"Nor I," Aelic replied. "Sir Mallik is unassailable when he swings that hammer of his, just as Sir Rogan with his broad-bladed axe. No, indeed, I would not like to face either upon the field of battle. Nor Sir Gabriel and his long knives—what say you to that, Sir Gabriel?"

Sir Gabriel did not answer. He sat on a wide log across the fire from Aelic and scrutinized the scroll he had spread on his lap. There were several scrolls lying unbound at his side.

Aelic looked at Antoinette and shrugged.

But Sir Gabriel's inattention did not bypass Sir Oswyn, who had been inconspicuously watching Sir Gabriel for some time.

"Gabriel," he called out. But when Sir Gabriel did not respond, Sir Oswyn prodded him softly with a stick. "Gabriel!"

"What is it?"

"You have done nothing but devour those scrolls since we arrived in Torin's Vale, when you ought to be devouring meat, bread, and cheese to keep your strength up!" Sir Oswyn said.

"He is right, Sir Gabriel," Nock said, offering a huge crust of bread. "We will not likely have another occasion to stop and eat before Yewland."

Sir Gabriel looked up disdainfully. "No, thank you, Master Bowman. I have fed from the wisdom of King Eliam, and that is enough."

"Surely it is not the plan of King Eliam that you feed only your mind with his word, while starving the body, Sir Gabriel," Sir Oswyn said.

Sir Gabriel frowned and returned to the scrolls before him, but before he could begin reading, Sir Oswyn once again poked him with a stick.

"Stop that!" Sir Gabriel said, becoming annoyed.

"Sir Gabriel," Sir Oswyn said, "you have great wisdom in lore and diplomacy, but you will eat before we break camp even if I have to feed you myself."

Sir Gabriel raised one eyebrow, took some food from Nock, and reluctantly began eating while continuing to read the scrolls.

Nock then turned his attention to Antoinette. "Would you like something more to eat?"

"No, thank you," Antoinette said. She was quiet a moment, but then turned to the archer. "Sir Nock, I guess being from Yewland, you've always been pretty good with a bow?"

"Yes," Nock answered. "My brother Bolt and I were always

practicing to see who could shoot the fastest, or the farthest, or the smoothest. I do not recall a time when I did not have a bow nearby. Even as children we carved our bows were carved from blackwood."

"Blackwood is the best wood?"

"Yes. In fact, my bow was carved from the root of a fallen blackwood. The wood is supple, resilient, and stronger than that of any other bough in The Realm," he said while handing her his bow. "A Blackwood bow can launch an arrow a great distance and with immense force. Blackwood Arrows fly straighter, penetrate deeper, and do not break."

Antoinette held the dark bow reverently. "I wish I knew how to shoot," she said.

"I could show you," said Aelic.

"Yes, you could, Sir Aelic," replied Nock with a sly grin. "But then I would have to help Lady Antoinette unlearn all the poor habits you would teach her."

Insulted, Aelic stood.

"I beg your pardon, Sir Aelic," said Nock, motioning for Aelic to sit. "Forgive my choice of words. But if mastering a bow is what Lady Antoinette wishes, then she should be tutored by a master of the bow. I would not dare to presume such a stance, if she required a lesson on the sword."

Aelic nodded. "I'm not that bad," he grumbled. Nock slapped him on the back, and they laughed.

"Come, Lady Antoinette," Nock said. "Allow me to reveal to you the art of bow and shaft!"

As they were leaving the camp, a sad melody reached their ears. Antoinette stopped to listen. The singer's voice was rich and clear, and he strummed his lute as he sang. *Sir Oswyn*, Antoinette thought. It was in a language Antoinette did not understand, but there was emotion within the melody. Antoinette felt it wash over her and stood transfixed.

> *Sil Minabryn son'ealyth. Sil pennathar son'bru.*
> *Sil gurethyn mare annocet, m'reavow alas rue.*
> *Nadar gurethyn nal fleurithyn*
> *Sil ridinel sil pereniel, sil guld pur gorithyn.*
> *A, Torin, kae trennethet sila waye?*
> *Sil brun Wyrm 'ycorason son'grae.*
> *A, Torin son ill Minabryn m'reave' thei',*
> *Endurie minabrie bru aelythei.*

"It is part of the lay of Torin," Nock said softly. "The melody is haunting, and to hear Os sing it in the old language . . . nearly breaks my heart."

Antoinette found herself staring at the opening where Torin's gate once stood. A cold tear rolled down her cheek. "What is a lay? Do you know what it means?" she asked. "Can you understand the old language? I . . . I'd really like to know what it means."

"I do not speak the old language," Nock said. "But a lay is a poem or a song. I can retell the lay, for I too was compelled to discover its meaning. It is a story about these ruins around us. Some call it a legend, for no one really knows who dwelt here or why they dwell here no longer. It tells of Torin, one of King Eliam's oldest and most trusted servants, and of how he died at the hands of the Wyrm Lord."

As Nock spoke the words of the lay, Antoinette found that she could no longer see the ruins. In its place stood a white castle manor surrounded by flowering trees and a myriad of living creatures. But the flittering birds and gathering squirrels hastened away suddenly, for something was coming.

The Realm was young and the mountains were new.
The sea birds cried, mourning as they flew.
Even birds on the wing could not escape,
The choice of the firstborn, and the cost of innocent blood.
Oh, Torin, why did you open that door?
The Old Wyrm's heart was black.
Oh, Torin, the poisoned world weeps
For you and waits for all things to be made new.

When Nock finished, Antoinette looked away. Her wet face glistened, and she hastily wiped her tears. "Was Torin very dear to King Eliam?" she asked.

"Yes," Nock replied sadly. "But no scroll in Alleble records his tale."

"The Wyrm Lord killed Torin?" Antoinette asked. "Is that the legend that Sir Gabriel spoke about?"

"Sir Gabriel dismisses Torin's story as a myth because none of his scrolls contain it. He is one of the wisest in The Realm, but I say he has erred in this judgment. The story goes that when King Eliam went away on a journey, he told Torin not to open the door to anyone until he returned. But the Wyrm Lord in his guile was very persuasive. Torin opened the door, and the Wyrm Lord slew him. How else could *The Schism* occur? It was innocent blood, I say. When the Wyrm Lord spilled the noble blood of King Eliam's servant, that is when The Realm divided, or so I believe. There, now, I have spoken too much of your time away. Enough! I promised you a lesson with the bow!"

The Eye of
the Archer

"Is this right?" Antoinette asked. She had an arrow fitted to the string of Nock's Blackwood bow.

"Almost," Nock replied. He moved closer to Antoinette and made a few adjustments to her form. "You must keep your release hand, your right hand, flat and close to your cheek. Otherwise you will hook the bowstring and have a sluggish release. Also, raise your elbow so that it is level with the arrow's shaft. Yes, that's better! Think of your right arm and the arrow as one long shaft and line it up with the target. . . . Um, we need a target, don't we?"

Nock went about twenty feet away from where Antoinette was standing, looked around, then lifted an old tree stump and positioned it against a tree so that the tree's rings would face them.

"That should work as a target," he said as he walked back to her. "When you feel the shot is lined up, use the muscles in your back to draw your arm a little farther back. The string should feel like it slips from your grasp rather than like you let it go. Try."

Antoinette looked down her arm and down the length of the arrow at the center ring on the target beyond. The bowstring was already taut and the bow felt ready to spring. She eased back her arm and released the string. The arrow left the bow so fast it seemed it was never there in the first place.

"Owww!" Antoinette exclaimed, and she shook her left arm. "I felt the bowstring through the armor!"

"A *vambrace* will keep your forearm from being cut," Nock said. "But the bowstring on a Blackwood bow impacts with such force that the, uh . . . inexperienced will still feel its bite."

"But where did the arrow go?" Antoinette asked.

"Ah, well . . . nowhere near the target, I am afraid," Nock replied. "But try it again. This time, remember, your task is to aim and pull. The string decides when to release."

Nock gave Antoinette another shaft. She fitted it to the string as before. And this time, she focused on lining up the shot without a single thought about releasing the arrow. Suddenly, she heard a sharp *twang* and a shaft was stuck deep in the target. The Blackwood bow felt warm in her hands.

"Well done, Lady Antoinette!" Nock clapped. "Well done, indeed!"

"But I didn't hit the bull's-eye!" she said.

"Did you expect to?" Nock's arched brows arched even more and he grinned. "That is good! Archers must always expect to hit the target. Always. But one flaw hindered your success. You were thinking too much about protecting your arm from the burn of the string. I saw the bend in your elbow. You must have proper form. And you must focus on the target!"

Focus on the objective—that's what Kaliam says too, Antoinette thought.

"Here, now, try it again. Allow the string to slip from your fingers in its own good time. And this time . . . use this arrow." Nock handed Antoinette a black-shafted arrow with white fletchings, the exact opposite of the first shaft she had fired.

"Why this one?" she asked.

"That is an arrow made from blackwood," said Nock, grinning. "I think you will enjoy the result!"

Antoinette held the shaft gently as if handling something volatile that might explode. Then she lifted it to the string and began to take aim.

"I hope we are not intruding!" came a voice from behind. Antoinette spun around. It was Tal, followed by Mallik, Kaliam, Lady Merewen, Aelic, and several others. Tal had a bow in his hand.

"Forgive me for interrupting your lesson, m'lady!" Tal bowed. "I overheard Nock's offer to train you, and knowing his impressive skill, I presume you have become a fair shot already."

Tal glanced around Antoinette at the target. "Yes, I see you already possess some luck."

"Skill, not luck, I would say," Lady Merewen said, and she grinned slyly at Antoinette.

"Yes, hmmm," Tal replied, scratching at his beard. "Skill."

"Tal, what do you want?" Nock asked, frowning on his way to retrieve the arrows. "As if I did not know."

"I just wished a little sport before we must return to the business of Yewland," he replied. "To be honest, my pride still smarts from losing to Lady Antoinette in the jousting arena. I thought she might be up for another challenge."

"Tal, why do you not challenge me?" asked Nock, returning with the arrows. "She has fired but two shafts thus far."

"Nay, Master Archer, I am no match for thee," Tal said. And he bowed again. "I simply thought tha—"

"I accept the challenge!" Antoinette said, surprising them both. "What's the contest?"

"Excellent, m'lady," Tal said. "A simple contest of accuracy I think will be best. Given your, uh, lack of experience, it would not be fair to add speed to the equation. We shall each fire one arrow. The shaft closest to the center of the bull's-eye shall be declared the winner. And, uh, to keep the competition fair, we will both use my bow."

Tal snatched the Blackwood bow—but not the arrow—from Antoinette and handed it to Nock. Then he took his firing position, drew back his bowstring, and was still for a moment. The bow sang, the arrow whistled to the target, and stuck directly in the center of the bull's-eye.

"Ha-ha!" Tal bellowed. His thick dark locks bounced. He reminded Antoinette of the guys in the reggae band that had come to her school the previous year. "Let us see if Master Nock's tutelage has served you well!"

Tal strutted over to Antoinette and handed her his bow. Antoinette looked at the target, which suddenly looked very far away. She frowned at Nock.

Strangely, Nock winked and nodded. *What?* Antoinette wondered. *Why are*—and then she looked down at the Blackwood Arrow in her hand. She smiled.

Antoinette fit the Blackwood Arrow to the bowstring, with three fingers stretched the string back to her cheek, and took aim. The arrow was sleek, from its narrow razor point to its close-cropped fletchings. It looked like it was built for speed. She flexed the muscles in her upper back, slowly drawing her right elbow back. *Any moment now*, she thought as she stared at the bull's-eye. *Any moment n—*"

ZING! The arrow was gone. It struck the target about an inch below the bull's-eye, but it struck with such force that the stump split. Tal's arrow wobbled and then fell out of the target.

"Lady Antoinette wins!" Nock announced joyously.

Tal stood for a moment, eyes bulging and mouth hanging slack. Then he cried out, "She most certainly does not win! My arrow was in the bull's-eye! It was by far the closest to center!"

"*Was* is the operative word, my competitive friend," said Nock. "It would seem that your aim was not true, for the target spat out your arrow!"

"My arrow is the closest to center now!" Antoinette said sternly, all the while trying to hold back laughter. Aelic clapped.

"Those confounded Blackwood Arrows!" Tal ranted. "She had an unfair advantage—Nock, you have cheated me."

"Advantage?" Lady Merewen objected. "You have been shooting your bow for most of your life, but Lady Antoinette had only fired three arrows! She won fair and square."

Tal scowled. "Let us fire again," he said. "But this ti—"

"Uh, pardon me!" Mallik interrupted. He stood next to the target. "I can see this competition has reached its due end. Allow me to settle this squabble!"

And then, Mallik hoisted his immense hammer high in the air and brought it crashing down on the target and the arrows. With a variety of sharp cracks, Mallik's weapon crushed the stump to splinters.

"I daresay that settles all disputes," Kaliam said, putting a hand on Antoinette's shoulder. "I do not suppose we will be able to find either arrow. Pieces, perhaps, but nothing more."

"Mallik, your hammer strike is fierce indeed," Nock said. "I did not know that anything could shatter a Blackwood shaft! You realize, of course, you owe me a replacement—and they do not come cheaply."

"My dear Nock," said Mallik, "when we get to Yewland, I will buy you a whole quiver if you de—"

"Silence!" Kaliam suddenly hissed. "Be still! I heard something. Nock!"

"I heard it too," he whispered. "It was dragon wings or I am a turnip."

"A spy?" Kaliam mouthed.

Nock nodded. Then they all heard it. A faint swoosh to the west. Nock leaped up into the lowest bough of a great tree. In a moment he clambered up to the top limb and unleashed a shot. Something screeched and crashed in the distance.

"Good shot, Nock!" Mallik blurted. "Come, let us see what game you have bagged!"

"Yes, we will go and see," said Kaliam. "But be cautious. There may be other spies in the area. And they certainly know we are here now. Tobias, Tal, return to the camp. See if you can find Farix, for we cannot leave our steeds or supplies unguarded."

So nine of the knights of Alleble sped off to the west. Sir Rogan bounded ahead of them, his great axe at the ready. They came to a clearing near a broad tree. Sprawled awkwardly on the weedy cobblestone was a gray dragon. A dark arrow pierced its lower jaw and protruded from the top of its skull.

"That shot was one in a million!" Mallik bellowed. Sir Rogan looked at Nock and smiled grimly.

"Yes," agreed Kaliam. "But where is its rider?"

"There," Antoinette said, pointing. "Up in the tree."

Strewn and twisted in the highest boughs was a dark figure. "Oswyn, if you please," said Kaliam.

"I will not climb up a tree with an enemy perhaps still alive," Os said. "Not unless I have to. On the other hand, if you want me to blow the tree up . . ."

"No, Os, that is quite all right," Kaliam said.

"I will get it done," Sir Rogan growled. He lifted his axe and strode to the base of the tree.

"No, Sir Rogan!" Kaliam cried. "Not with the axe."

But Sir Rogan did not use the axe. He placed the axe carefully on the cobblestone and then turned toward the tree. He wrapped his enormous arms around the trunk and began to shake. The tree swayed slowly at first but gained momentum. The topmost boughs began to quiver violently, and suddenly, the dark figure shifted, cartwheeled through the branches, and fell with a dull thud to the ground.

"Well, he is most certainly dead now!" Mallik blurted out.

"That was some display of strength, Sir Rogan," said Sir Gabriel. "But now he will not give us the answers to our questions."

"Do not be so sure of that," said Farix, appearing from the shadows.

"Master Farix," Lady Merewen said, "you, uh, do have a way of showing up rather suddenly." A corner of Farix's mouth turned just slightly in a smile.

Gabriel argued, "You cannot possibly mean that he is alive."

"Alive? Nay, ambassador. He was dead even before Sir Rogan shook him from the tree. But he may yet answer some of our questions." Farix rolled up his sleeves and walked over to the body. "He is clearly in the service of Paragory. But he is not a spy. You see the pair of dragon wings etched into his breastplate?"

"Let me look," Lady Merewen said, stepping forward. "Those markings show that this rider is a scout of the enemy."

"Spy, scout—what is the difference?" Mallik asked.

"There is a telling difference, Sir Mallik," Lady Merewen explained. "A spy is sent into a known situation to gather information. A scout, on the other hand, ventures into unknown places to locate potential dangers or to seek a better way."

"That is strange," said Nock. "The scout would have no business this far southeast. He should have been making his way up the main road."

"Yes," agreed Kaliam. "But now I see that I was careless to suggest that glad fire in Torin's Keep. The dragons of the enemy have a keen sense of smell. It is my judgment that this rider was one of several, scattered forward in many directions. This one dragon picked up our scent and veered this way."

Kaliam turned and stared off into the distance. The snowcapped peaks of faraway Pennath Ador were pink with the dawn sun. "This troubles me," Kaliam said. "If my theory is true, and there were several scouts, then what size force would there be? Lady Merewen?"

"A legion," she replied quietly. "Maybe more."

Antoinette looked at Aelic. "A legion? What does that mean?"

"It means a large force of enemy soldiers . . . very large," Aelic said.

"We leave at once," Kaliam ordered.

RIDDLE AT THE
FOREST ROAD

The twelve rode in haste from Torin's Vale, and now lay hidden on a ridge overlooking the main forest road. The unicorns grazed in a thicket out of sight.

"It is worse than I feared," Kaliam whispered.

"How many?" asked Nock.

"See for yourself, but stay low. They will not see you from the ground at this distance, but if the sun be allowed to glint off of exposed armor, they may."

Nock, Aelic, Mallik, and Antoinette crawled up the ridge and peered over the edge.

A seemingly endless river of dark soldiers flowed into the forest.

"Three legions there at least!" Mallik quietly exclaimed.

"At least," Kaliam agreed. "And more on the road ahead concealed by the woods."

Nock slid down next to Kaliam. "Kaliam, Paragor is set to invade my homeland! My people!"

"It seems so," Kaliam said. "Though I did not see their war engines or their catapults. There may be some hope in that. Tobias, Gabriel?"

Gabriel the wise and Tobias the pathfinder looked over the ridge.

"I would say four legions," Tobias said. "For if you look closely, you can see that the heralds are just entering the tree line. Given the timing of the scout we encountered at Torin's Vale, I cannot believe that more than a rank has passed under the cover of the trees before now."

"I agree," said Sir Gabriel. "And take hope, Master Archer, I do not believe they will invade Yewland."

"How can you tell?" Nock asked, eager to believe.

Sir Gabriel stroked his long beard. "As Kaliam pointed out, they have no war machines. And if you look closely, there are very few mounted soldiers. Even their pace is telling. They are moving slowly, deliberately. There would be no element of surprise at that rate. Your kinsmen would know they were coming long before they attacked."

"Why, then, would such a force be traveling to Yewland?" Kaliam asked.

"It looks like a military escort to me," Tobias said.

Mallik looked from face to face, confused. "But who would demand an escort of such size and grandeur?" He blinked a few times, turning his head back and forth. Then he became very still.

Antoinette suddenly felt very afraid.

"But why would *he* go to Yewland?" Sir Oswyn asked.

Sir Gabriel drew a scroll from his belt and wrung it slowly in his hands. "*He* was invited."

"Invited?" Nock scowled. "My kin would never invite The Betrayer to cross Yewland's borders."

"I agree," said Kaliam. "Many long years has Yewland been allied with the Kingdom of Alleble. Many who dwell in Yewland have eyes that glint blue and matching purity in their hearts. I do not believe Queen Illaria would welcome Paragor."

"She might welcome his gold," said Tobias.

Nock bit his tongue.

"No," Kaliam argued. "In spite of her love of things that glitter, Queen Illaria is too shrewd and far too proud to allow Yewland to fall under the harsh yoke of The Betrayer. She would return Yewland to an independent province as it was before."

"But she might allow him passage," Sir Gabriel said.

Nock looked away, exhaled a breath of complaint, and then clambered back up the ridge to look again upon the advancing army. Kaliam stood in silence.

"Why do you debate?" Mallik asked, turning his smoldering eyes to his troubled commander. "Given the new developments, there can be only one course of action. Attack! Attack immediately, I say."

Antoinette and the others could not believe their ears.

"If The Betrayer is there among his festering troops, let him meet the business end of my hammer, and we can be done with this war once and for all."

Tobias snorted out a laugh. "Right, Sir Mallik. Twelve knights against four legions—those are rather steep odds, would you not say?"

"That cannot be more than a thousand soldiers for each of us," Mallik replied. "I have seen worse!"

"And to think I was to be the jester on this journey!" Sir Oswyn said. He smacked Mallik on the shoulder. "You make me smile, my hammer-wielding friend, in the face of a very grim discovery."

"Mallik is correct in one respect," Sir Gabriel said. "There really is only one course of action. We must return to Alleble. Return in haste to seek the King's will. Perhaps our enemy, in leaving his dark strongholds, has put his neck out too far. This may be the occasion for King Eliam to send forth the full might of his armies, led, I am certain, by Mallik's hammer and Sir Rogan's sharp axe."

Mallik grinned. "What say you to that, Kaliam?"

Kaliam took a deep breath as if preparing to plunge into cold water. "I say there is wisdom in what we have heard. Wise guesses to be sure, but guesses nonetheless. We do not know for certain if Paragor leads this force in person. We do not know the intent of this huge army. Certainly there are enough soldiers to invade, but the manner of their approach does indeed suggest otherwise. If not to conquer . . . what then? Could it be an escort? If it is, then what is their destination? Would Paragor need a force this big for a diplomatic mission to Yewland? Nay, my heart implores me that there is something far more wicked afoot. To return to Alleble, albeit swiftly, may mean that we never discover the answer to this dark riddle."

"I am with you," Farix agreed. He sat cross-legged with his hands hidden in the wide sleeves of his surcoat. "In my mind it is like the calm before a dreadful storm. We must find out where that army is going and what purpose it hides."

Antoinette flinched. A sudden image of the open tomb flashed in her mind.

"Are you all right?" Aelic asked. She shook her head dismissively.

"Therein lies my struggle," Kaliam said. "How might we discover the enemy's plans? The main road is closed to us now—save perhaps if we delay until the enemy's untold thousands pass under the boughs, and then follow in what stealth we can manage. If we wait on the other side of Forest Road, things may go ill for Yewland. If only we had dragon steeds, we could fly to Yewland."

They all became silent. An answer was there, looming in the midst of them, but no one wished to make it known. Finally, Antoinette spoke up. "Couldn't we cut through the Blackwood?"

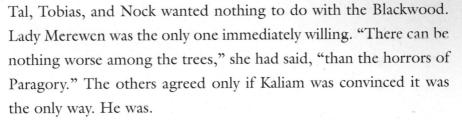

Tal, Tobias, and Nock wanted nothing to do with the Blackwood. Lady Merewen was the only one immediately willing. "There can be nothing worse among the trees," she had said, "than the horrors of Paragory." The others agreed only if Kaliam was convinced it was the only way. He was.

And so the twelve rode their unicorns at top speed to the northern fringe of the forest where Nock thought he remembered the location of an ancient path. He searched in vain at the edge of the forest, but the groundcover was thick and widespread.

"Ha, here it is at last!" he announced. "Come, it was well hidden, but now that I have found it, I will not lose it again!"

The twelve left the sunshine and slowly disappeared under the forest's massive boughs. Tree limbs, lush with foliage, flexed as the knights passed, and sprang back behind them as if a living door had closed. The Knights of Alleble were immediately surrounded by the glad green tones of living things: shrubs, ferns, sprawling canopy trees, and climbing vines.

Small golden insects teemed in the air and took no notice of the travelers. The air smelled of lilac and honeysuckle. There was also the music of the forest: the rustle of leaves in the wind, the happy chirruping of birds, and an odd, warbling trill sound that reminded Antoinette of the spring peeper frogs back home.

"This doesn't seem so bad," Antoinette said. The unicorns too seemed quite comfortable. They bobbed their heads and were allowed to occasionally munch leaves from protruding branches.

"Verily," replied Sir Oswyn, "nothing stirs my soul like a pleasant walk in the woods. Why, I feel almost merry!" And, in a flash, he fished out his lute and began a happy little melody.

Of all the forest creatures that dwell under forest eaves,
Perched upon the branches or feasting on its leaves,
There lives a mighty mite more mighty than them all.
It does not claw or scratch and stands only one inch tall.

It will not strangle like a serpent or stalk you like a cat.
It does not beat you like a bugbear or bite you like a bat.
It cannot crush its prey or maim it or drop it down a hole.
It has no deadly poison but is as deadly as a troll.

So what is this fell and mighty beast? And what terror does it hold
That rules the sprawling forest and makes faint hearts of the bold?
Why, it is the purple spotted meep frog, a truly perilous pest.
And lest you laugh, I promise it is more fearsome than the rest.

For doughty knight may face a panther or the fiery dragon slay,
But if he sees the purple meep, he'll clutch his ears and run away.
For one little meeper is bad enough, its meeping song annoys.
But when there are ten thousand, they will drive you mad with noise!

And so Oswyn's song went on, lifting the spirits of the team. But Nock was pensive. "I thought this was to be a beastly place," said Mallik, and he spurred his unicorn to trot next to Nock's.

"Full of nasty creatures and pitfalls—was not that what you said, Nock my friend?"

"The reason you still feel glad," said Nock, "is that we are not yet in the Blackwood."

"What?" said several of the knights in unison. Sir Oswyn's song ended abruptly.

"There is an apron of undefiled forest several leagues deep around the Blackwood," Nock explained. "That is where we are now. Alas that the Blackwood was once teeming like this and pure."

"Well, how will we know, then?" Aelic asked. "How will we know when we enter the Blackwood?"

"You will know, Sir Aelic, because the unicorns we ride will halt and refuse to go another step. You will know when the sounds of living things go dreadfully quiet. And you will know when the only trees you see are massive, dark, and brooding. Then you will know that we draw near to the real Blackwood."

Mallik's mustache twitched, and he let his unicorn drop back a few paces.

"Come, Knights of Alleble," said Kaliam. "It is nearly midday. We must quicken our pace. I for one do not wish to walk through the Blackwood at night."

They rode for hours as quickly as their surefooted steeds could bear them on the ancient path, broken and strewn with root and vine. Though the forest was still alive with green leaves and golden light, the twelve spoke very little, for each was busy with his own thoughts. And Sir Oswyn's lute stayed securely on his back.

Antoinette was nibbling at a crust of bread when they came to a strange sight. The bread dropped from her hands. Row upon row of tall trees stood before them, but they were without bark and bone white. And the groundcover died off as if fire had swept through a wide swatch of the forest.

"Beneath the ground," Nock said in a quiet voice, "the roots of the Blackwood stretch out to protect their realm. They will suffer no other living plant to pollute their soil."

The unicorns ground their teeth. Some of them reared. The twelve tried in vain to calm them, to urge them forward. "They will not pass this skeleton hedge of dead trees," Nock said. "To force them into the black forest beyond would drive them mad."

"We must dismount!" Kaliam commanded. "Our steeds have borne us well, but Nock is right. They will not enter the Blackwood. Take whatever food provisions you can carry and the waterskins. Leave spare garments and other comforts behind. We can purchase such necessities in Yewland."

"What will happen to the unicorns?" Antoinette asked. She stroked Rael's neck affectionately.

"They are clever beasts," answered Kaliam. "They will find their way back to Alleble. They will be far safer on their journey, I fear, than we will be on ours."

THE BLACKWOOD

Continuing their journey on foot, the twelve wove their way through the dead barrier of pale trees until at last the blackwood loomed before them. Immense black trees, they were, with great limbs and crowns of broad crimson leaves. The bark of the blackwood trees was smooth and featureless except that it was as black as a pool of cave water.

"Keep your weapon at the ready," Kaliam said, reaching over and adjusting the angle of Antoinette's sword. "By my reckoning, we have about four hours before the sun begins to set. Even if we are not delayed, that will be a challenge."

They stepped into the realm of the black trees and walked as briskly as they could, constantly ducking low-hanging boughs or stepping over the massive roots. Antoinette noticed that the warble of birds and the meeping of the frogs had ceased. In fact, no sound of any living thing could be heard. A cold breeze whispered between the dark trunks and swirled through the broad crimson leaves here and there as if quiet secrets were being shared from tree to tree. That was the only sound, and it was not comforting.

Aelic noticed Antoinette draw her cloak tight around her neck.

"There is a chill that seeps up through one's boots," Aelic said. "And through the cloak—right to one's bones. No garment seems to hinder it. It is not natural."

"It is a summons that you feel," said Nock. "A call to all evil in The Realm. The call of the Seven Sleepers."

"Do not fill their minds with such nonsense," said Sir Gabriel sharply.

"It is not nonsense," argued Nock. "Say that you cannot feel it. They are here, somewhere in the Blackwood, waiting."

"Rubbish, Master Archer," said Sir Gabriel with a dismissive wave. "In all your years in Yewland, did you ever find their final resting place, the Sepulcher, I believe it is called? Did any Yewland Brave in the history of your homeland ever find it?"

Nock frowned. "No," he said reluctantly. "My brother Bolt and I rarely ventured deep into the Blackwood, nor did most of my kinsmen, for it is vast and treacherous. We did not wish to find the Sepulcher of the Seven Sleepers. But you do not need to see evil to know that it is there."

"And yet, what one fears in the dark may not be there at all," replied Sir Gabriel.

Nock grumbled.

"Nock, can you tell me more about the Seven Sleepers?" Antoinette asked. "They don't sound pleasant, but I'd like to know what we may be up against."

"I do not wish to speak of them now," Nock replied, and he threw up his hood and hurried to catch up to Mallik.

"I would like to know also," said Tal, turning to Antoinette. "My friend Matthias, a worthy knight who fell in Mithegard, spoke of them to me once, but that was long ago."

"Yes," agreed Lady Merewen. "I am intrigued. Is there any among us besides our disgruntled archer who knows more of this?"

"I will tell you the tale," said Sir Oswyn.

"Kaliam, will you not stop this nonsense?" complained Sir Gabriel.

"No, I think we should all listen," said Kaliam firmly. "It will at the very least help pass the time. And it may be wise to hear of the dangers if they should turn out to be more than legend."

Sir Gabriel snorted and covered his head with his hood.

Oswyn began the story: "The Realm was new and no scrolls had yet been written. It is in the unwritten history of the Wyrm Lord where we find the lore of the Seven Sleepers."

As he spoke, it seemed to Antoinette that it became darker in the woods. *Is it getting late?* she wondered.

"King Eliam discovered a magnificent dragon in the wild—the region we now call the Shattered Lands, some say. And behold, this wyrm was exceptionally intelligent and endowed with extraordinary powers—not only a breather of fire, but it could change form such that it looked like one of us. It could even speak. It was, in fact, the firstborn dragon in all The Realm, the lord of all wyrms. King Eliam grew fond of it, and the wyrm grew very fond of King Eliam.

"But when King Eliam took on a servant by the name of Torin, the friendship between the King and the Wyrm Lord became strained. The dragon grew jealous. While the King was hunting in the forest, the dragon assailed Torin's Keep. Some say the Wyrm Lord broke down the gate. Others contend that he subtly tricked Torin into opening it of his own free will. But in any case, King

Eliam returned and found Torin and his family slain. The King sought the Wyrm Lord everywhere, but the creature escaped for a time to the mountains. There a pack of seven wolvins agreed to hide him in exchange for the power to shape-shift. And—"

"But what of The Schism?" Nock interrupted. "When the Wyrm Lord killed Torin, that is when The Schism occurred. Right, Sir Oswyn?"

"That is a matter for scholars like Sir Gabriel to debate," said Sir Oswyn. He turned to their ambassador, who lowered his hood and nodded respectfully at the compliment.

Antoinette thought something had moved high in the branches, and she looked into the treetops. But it was too dark to see anything distinctly. *Why is it getting dark so quickly?* she wondered. She started to ask, but Sir Oswyn continued his tale.

"The wolvins attempted to deceive King Eliam when he sought the Wyrm Lord in the mountains. By being able to change form at will, the villains escaped justice for a time. But the Master of the Realm, King Eliam the Everlasting, was not fooled. He eventually found the wyrm and his seven conspirators. He delayed judgment of the villains, but rather imprisoned them each according to his due. The wolvins he doomed to the long sleep, held beneath the earth by the roots of The Realm's strongest trees, the blackwood. He locked the Wyrm Lord in a cell of stone beneath a lake of fire. It is said by many that one day, both the Wyrm Lord and the Seven Sleepers will be set free from their containment, but on what that may mean, there is much disagreement. Some contend that the villains will face final judgment at that time, while others believe that they will roam The Realm once more to wreak havoc upon the innocent. That is all I know of the Seven Sleepers."

Sir Gabriel clapped in an exaggerated fashion. "Splendid, Sir

Oswyn," he said. "I do not believe a word of it, but it was a tale well-told. See Aelic and Lady Antoinette—they look stricken. You have them believing that at any moment we could trod upon the ancient burial sight of a sleeping horror."

"I'm not afraid!" Antoinette blurted out. But in truth, she felt very uneasy. "Anyway, if the Seven Sleepers appear, Mallik will hit them so hard with his hammer that they'll go deeper underground than they were before!"

The knights laughed quietly—all except for Aelic. "Are you okay?" Antoinette asked him.

Aelic shook his head. He was not okay. "It is not the Seven Sleepers, but rather a dream I had—" But remembering his promise to Kaliam not to speak of it, he would say no more.

They walked on for some time, and with each step, the tension grew. They were mostly bunched together, but Tobias and Gabriel walked a little apart and spoke in whispers. Tal had strategically placed himself between Mallik and Sir Rogan. Nock suddenly strode forward to catch up to Kaliam. Antoinette was convinced that Kaliam had goofed on his estimate of the time.

Maybe that's why Nock went up to talk to him. He's afraid we're going to be stuck in the Blackwood after dark.

The sun was clearly on its way down. There didn't seem to be any other explanation for the quickening darkness. Antoinette watched Nock whisper something to Kaliam. The Sentinel looked up and nodded. Slowly Kaliam turned and went from knight to knight, whispering something in each one's ear. Each time he did so, the recipient of the message hastily put on a helmet and looked warily upward. *What?* Antoinette wanted to know. *What's up there? I can't see anything. It's too dark!*

Finally, he came to Antoinette. "There are illgrets in the trees," he said. "Do not move suddenly, but put on your helmet and ready your weapon."

And just like that, he was gone to Oswyn and Farix behind her. *Illgrets?!*

"Aelic!" she whispered, urgently strapping on her helmet. "What are illgrets?"

"They are flying predators," he said. He turned and drew near to Antoinette. "They gather in the trees above us."

Antoinette strained to see into the dark of the treetops. "I don't see anything," she said.

"Illgrets are as black as night, and there are many. Did you notice that it seems near dusk even though there are yet several hours until sundown? That is because there is such a great number of them waiting above us that light is shut out. They do not need the light themselves, for they have dull eyes and see little but movement. They are drawn very accurately to our body heat. They wait until they have sufficient numbers to overwhelm their prey."

"Can't we run?" Antoinette asked.

"It is too late."

Antoinette looked up. If possible, it seemed darker still. And the shadows seemed to be undulating. Antoinette tensed, clutched the hilt of her sword. Then came a shrill cry from above, and Kaliam shouted, "Now, warriors, draw your weapons! Stand back to back, and fight them off!"

Aelic drew Fury and backed up to Antoinette. And she drew the Daughter of Light. The darkness above swirled down on top of them. Then there was chaos.

Shrill cries exploded from every direction. A myriad of dark shapes swooped down on her. She swung her blade, felt a half-dozen strikes, and heard desperate screeches. She swung again, but illgrets were everywhere in greater and greater numbers. She felt like she was in a storm of claws, teeth, and dark wings. The only thing that kept her sane was the constant pressure of Aelic's back behind her.

"Away from me, cursed fowl!" Mallik roared. Antoinette heard and felt his great hammer smashing clouds of the creatures to the ground. She heard a bowstring singing from somewhere up high, and she wondered where Nock was. But she could not linger on any thought for very long, for the illgrets came at her in fresh waves.

"Aelic!" she cried out. "There are too many!"

"Guard any exposed flesh!" he yelled. "Illgrets are drawn to your heat! And whatever you do, do not let one perch on you long enough to bite! There is sleeping poison in their saliva!"

"I won't!" Antoinette screamed. She slashed her blade as if it were a machete through tall grass. Dozens of winged black shapes fell with each slash, but still more came. She heard Aelic grunting and heard wet snaps as Fury swept through a cloud of winged enemies.

Suddenly, one ducked under Antoinette's sword and dove for her face. She screamed and dodged, but something sharp opened a gash on her cheekbone. She felt the thing on her shoulder, and tried to bat it away, but her armor made it nearly impossible.

Then Farix was there, and barehanded he grabbed the illgret from her shoulder. Antoinette heard a series of cracks and snaps and watched Farix throw what was left of the creature into the forest.

"It cut me!" Antoinette yelled furiously. She swung wildly, carving illgrets out of the air with every stroke.

"It was a talon strike!" Farix said. "Or you would be on the ground, dreaming dark dreams!" And then Farix disappeared into a swirling mass of black.

Another illgret swooped toward her face, tangled for a moment in her hair. Antoinette ducked frantically away and yelled, "Get away from me!" She went one-handed with her sword and whipped it low to high and at the same time backfisted an illgret with her left hand. They were everywhere.

"Antoinette!" Aelic cried out. She felt his body slide to the ground behind her. She slapped away several dark shapes, then turned to Aelic's prone form. Fury was no longer in Aelic's hand, and he lay very still. In an instant several dark shapes landed on Aelic and began to peck at him. Antoinette let out a rage-filled shriek, grabbed Fury with her left hand, and cut the heads off the scavengers. She stood over Aelic and began to swing both swords rhythmically in an undulating figure eight pattern. Illgrets fell in severed piles all around her, as if they had flown into a buzz saw.

But that didn't stop them. They came at Antoinette from every direction. And now that Aelic was not at her back, she felt them pelting her from behind. The armor kept them at bay, but then one landed on her collar and went for her neck. But Antoinette whipped her head back, and the creature fell away. *This isn't working! Focus on the objective,* Antoinette told herself. She kept both blades churning, but at the same time scanned the area. Through the cloud of black wings, she saw a broad tree just a few yards away. *That's it!*

She suddenly sheathed her sword, grabbed at Aelic's armor, and pulled with all her might. He was heavy, and the illgrets began to land on them both immediately. Still she managed to drag him a few feet. Then Sir Rogan appeared. He hoisted Aelic over his shoulder, and they ran to the tree. He eased Aelic down to the ground so that he lay against the tree as if napping. He turned to Antoinette.

"Does he live?!" he barked.

Antoinette knelt at Aelic's side and felt for a pulse on his neck. She did not feel anything. "Come on!" she yelled, placing her fingers in different places. Finally, she found it, a beat, faint but steady. "Yes!" she almost choked. "Yes, he's alive!"

Sir Rogan smiled. His eyes flashed blue and narrowed in such a way that even Antoinette was afraid. "Stay low," he said, and then he unleashed his axe. Antoinette watched with dark fascination as Sir Rogan swept his broadaxe back and forth so quickly it seemed he had two axes—no, three! Swarms of illgrets exploded in midair as the axe carved a wet swatch through the oncoming clouds. Pieces of the dark creatures were scattered everywhere.

Thok! Antoinette heard a loud impact and ducked reflexively, thinking that Sir Rogan had embedded his axe in the tree behind her. But when she looked up, she saw a Blackwood Arrow stuck in the tree. And impaled on its shaft were seven dead illgrets!

Thank you, Nock! she thought. Then she saw the illgrets up close for the first time. They were large and birdlike with scaly bodies and clawed limbs. But their eyes were what caused Antoinette to step back and shudder. Their eyes were milky white and slanted as if bent on malice.

"To me!! Warriors of Alleble!" a voice sang out. Antoinette thought it was Sir Oswyn's. "Rally to me all who can! Hurry! Follow my voice!"

"Come!" Sir Rogan said. He again slung Aelic over his shoulder, and they ran through the clawing, scratching clouds to follow Sir Oswyn's call. They found him and the others in a clearing of sorts, a place where the large trees around them were distant, but their long limbs still formed a kind of wooded roof.

"At last!" Sir Oswyn yelled. "Kaliam! That is everyone! Now?"

"Yes, now!" Kaliam answered. "The illgrets are regrouping!"

Sir Oswyn sheathed his sword and removed one of the long leather tubes that hung at his side. He popped the cap off the tube, grabbed the bottom of it, and slung it up with a snapping motion. A fine white powder shot out of the open end and fell slowly in a mist. Sir Oswyn ran around the outside perimeter of where the knights were huddled, waving the tube up and down until a ghostly cloud surrounded the entire team, including Sir Oswyn.

Then he took two stones out of a pouch. "You might want to close your eyes!" he said with a mischievous wink. Antoinette covered her eyes with her arms, but she did not close them. She watched Sir Oswyn strike the stones together several times. Finally, there was a spark, and . . .

WHOOOOSH!!!

Bright yellow fire leaped into the air, igniting the white powder and wreathing the twelve in a protective wall of flame. The illgrets who had been unlucky enough to be in close range burst into crackling fireballs. And sensing the heat and mistaking it for prey, the illgrets began to dive toward the flames. Wave after wave of illgrets ignited as the fire spread from wingtip to wingtip.

Flaming illgrets fell from the sky and landed in smoldering heaps, and the air filled with a horrible greasy smell. And suddenly, the unnatural darkness was lifted.

"What do you think of that?!" Sir Oswyn stood tall and grinned.

"Great, clever knight!" barked Mallik as he wiped blood off his gouged forearm. "But you could have done that sooner!"

"And harm the trees?" Sir Oswyn objected. "Do you not know that the Blackwood is the firstborn forest of the entire Realm?"

"Incredible stuff, that powder!" Sir Gabriel said. "I have never seen a nonliquid substance burn like that."

"I made it by grinding up the stalks of a most extraordinary plant that I found growing on the shores of the Mirror Lakes."

"What in The Realm made you think of burning it?" asked Tobias.

Oswyn winked. "I burn everything."

"What about reviving our two victims?" Kaliam asked. "Tal and Aelic were bitten. Do you have something to wake them?"

"Of course," Sir Oswyn replied, beginning to look through the many pockets on his jerkin. "Just a whiff of the milikynne pod ought to—"

From somewhere in the distant woods came a mournful howl. A few seconds later there was another, then another, until a chorus filled the woods.

"Wolvins," Kaliam whispered. "Nock, how close?"

Nock's eyes narrowed. "Not far enough. A quarter league or less."

"Have they scented us?"

"There is your answer," Nock said. He pointed to the tree line just beyond a pile of burning illgrets. A pair of keen yellow eyes stared out of the shadows.

"Take your best shot, archer," said Sir Gabriel.

Nock drew back his bowstring, released, and his black shaft streaked into the woods. There was a strangled cry, and the shadow dropped to the ground. Suddenly, a ruckus of growls and barks broke out in the woods.

"The pack draws near!" Nock cried.

"Mallik, take Tal," Kaliam commanded. "Rogan, take Aelic. Run south, follow the path as best you can! The rest follow, and I will guard the rear!"

"I will take the rearguard with you," Lady Merewen said. "I know something of these beasts, for they are the pets of the enemy!"

"Good," Kaliam replied. "Now, knights, fly! It is too late to avoid the Blackwood at night, but we must hope in our King's provision that we make it through to see the dawn! Fly! The hounds of Paragory are upon us!"

THE SEPULCHER OF THE SEVEN SLEEPERS

The Alleb Knights hurdled massive bulging roots and fallen branches, but they could not escape the pursuing wolvins. The creatures' mournful cries haunted every step of the fleeing knights. And worse yet, they had lost the path.

Sir Rogan, with Aelic slung on his back like a sack of grain, thundered through the darkening woods but had no idea which direction he was headed. "Just as likely to come out where we came in as we might to Yewland," he mumbled to himself. "If we come out at all."

Still, Sir Rogan plunged deeper into the woods. Mallik, with Tal on his broad shoulders, raced after him. Antoinette and the others followed with Kaliam and Lady Merewen guarding the rear.

"Fly!" Kaliam yelled, his voice strained and urgent. "They are at our heels! Fly or find a place we can defend!!"

Antoinette's heart hammered. She could run well on a track, but the weight of her armor and the perilous terrain robbed her of any such speed. "C'mon, legs!" she urged herself. "Go!"

Suddenly, a huge dark blur crashed out of the trees on the left and slammed into Mallik. Tal flew off Mallik's shoulders and landed with a flop at the base of a tree. Antoinette saw that Mallik lay still on the ground, but something huge was there beside him.

The thing was wolflike in shape, covered in dark fur, but much larger. And its upper body was massive. Its barrel chest heaved as it slowly rose up on all fours. It shook its head as if disoriented and then growled at the downed knight. Mallik rolled onto his back and frantically shoved himself backward. He reached for his hammer, but it had landed beyond his grasp. The beast stepped toward Mallik.

"Don't you touch him!" Antoinette found herself yelling.

The wolvin sniffed the air and then turned its head toward Antoinette. Huge black ears lowered and pressed back into its thick collar of dark fur. Its pale yellow eyes stared at her coldly, pupils small and absent of mercy. The wolvin's muzzle quivered. It bared its large white teeth and snarled with such slow, deep ferocity that Antoinette felt it.

The blood drained from Antoinette's face. Her hands went cold. She took a careful step backward, holding her sword out in front. The beast pawed toward her and then rose up on its hind legs like a bear and howled. But the howl was cut short.

"Time for you to join your friends!" Mallik bellowed. And he swept such a two-fisted hammer stroke into the body of the wolvin that it flew over Antoinette's head and up into the treetops. At that moment the rest of the team came stumbling to a stop behind them.

"Why do you halt?" Sir Oswyn asked breathlessly. "They are right behind us!"

"Where is Sir Rogan?" asked Tobias. "And what happened to Tal?"

Mallik growled and ran over to the sleeping warrior. "Tal is none the worse for wear, Master Pathfinder. He fares much better than the wolvin that delayed us!"

Sir Rogan returned to see what was delaying the others. He grunted at them as if to say, "Get moving, you slugs!"

Snarls came from behind and very close. "It is a pack, maybe two!" shouted Kaliam. "Go now, or we will be overrun!" Again, following Sir Rogan's lead, the knights of Alleble sprinted through the Blackwood. The wolvins, driven mad by the chase, were steadily gaining on them.

Even burdened with the full weight of their poisoned comrades, Sir Rogan and Mallik began to pull away from the rest.

To follow, Antoinette took to watching the movement of the tree branches that swayed from the passing of their leaders.

Their course through the trees began to rise steadily. Keeping the pace on the hill was grueling, but Antoinette managed. She struggled over a large root, stumbled once, and kept going. Hearing a great echoing yell from one of the other knights up ahead, she pushed herself to a speed she did not know she possessed, surging forward until the ground dropped out from under her, or at least it seemed to. She had run off the edge of a berm and tumbled down a ragged hill. The others who came behind met with the same fate, crashing awkwardly down the slope and landing in a heap at the bottom. Only Nock kept his balance, and that just barely. He raced down the hill and came to an abrupt stop just before he would have rammed into Sir Tobias.

Antoinette rose awkwardly to one knee and then stood. Her heart jackhammered and her breaths came out in a mist. She shuddered in the sudden cold. Lady Merewen was there beside her, blinking rapidly and absently brushing soil and dead leaves from her cloak. The rest of the team stood, and they found themselves in a large round hollow, ringed by the most immense trees they had yet seen. But these trees did not have the crown of crimson leaves like the others. These were barren and seemed dead. They reached up with twisted arms into the twilight sky. Tendrils of fog began to pour like a ghostly waterfall over the edge of the hill and down into the hollow.

"What is this place?" Mallik asked. He looked around, a stranglehold on his hammer. No one answered at first. They simply stared as the mist began to curl around their ankles. Kaliam alone seemed to possess the ability to move. He walked as if in a trance to the base of one of the huge black trees and looked down.

"There is a stone here," he said. "A rune is upon it, but it is ancient, beyond my knowledge."

Sir Gabriel went slowly to the base of another tree. "A marked stone lies beneath this tree as well," he said, shaking his head. "No scroll of Alleble records it meaning."

Antoinette looked from tree to tree, wondering if a stone lay at the base of each one. She noted that there were seven massive trees in the hollow. *Seven?*

"Do you not see?" Nock asked. "Seven trees! And beneath them, seven stones! We have come to the place I feared the most. We have come to the Sepulcher of the Seven Sleepers. We would have been better off facing a dozen packs of wolvin. We must leave this place! Sir Gabriel, do you believe now?"

Sir Gabriel did not answer.

"I fear you are right in this judgment," Kaliam said. "There is a foul presence in this hollow—an unknown malice all around us."

"But what if it is that place?" Mallik asked. "Do not the roots of the blackwood trees hold the sleepers beneath the ground?"

"Yes, or so it is told," Nock said with little certainty. "But look, the trees are dying. Once they were tall and secure. The kings of trees. If now they wither and perish, who can say?"

"You said they were just wolvins, right?" Antoinette asked. "If they did come up, we could take out seven wolvins, couldn't we?"

No one answered. The mist continued to swirl as it rose, grasping at their knees.

"Well, couldn't we?"

"The seven were of the first generation of wolvins," Nock explained. "They would be larger, swifter, and more powerful than any wolvin that yet lives. And they were endowed with the power to change form—perhaps to the likeness of any living thing. There is no telling what other dark powers the Wyrm Lord gave them!"

Kaliam nodded and said, "We need to depart from this place with all haste. Sir Oswyn, you possess something in your pouches that would cure our two sleeping warriors?"

"Verily," he replied, fishing two brown packets from his jerkin. "The spice I will use to revive them is so pungent it would indeed wake the Seven Sleepers!"

"Do not say such things!" Kaliam barked. "And make haste. I do not like it here."

Sir Oswyn mixed together a series of herbs and managed to wake Aelic and Tal more or less unharmed.

"My head aches as if Mallik swings his hammer within my very skull," groaned Tal.

"I feel the same," replied Aelic.

"Be glad you are alive," Kaliam said. "Aelic, from what Sir Rogan tells me, you owe Lady Antoinette a debt of gratitude for defending you when you fell. Had she not, the illgrets would have picked you clean."

Aelic looked at Antoinette with wonder. "I will repay you," he said.

"That's not necessary," Antoinette said. "You would have done the same for me."

Antoinette looked away only to see Lady Merewen staring at her. But before Lady Merewen could speak, a piercing howl came from over the edge of the hollow, and dark shapes began to appear. One after another, until wolvins were all around the rim—jostling and clawing for space. They stared down with pale eyes and snarled.

Antoinette heard a strange noise, turned, and saw Farix a few yards behind her. He cracked his knuckles again, looked up at her grimly, and said, "Stay close to me, Lady Antoinette. I give you my word. Not one of them will touch you while I breathe. But if we are all to die, then let us die well."

Antoinette swallowed, furrowed her brow fiercely, and nodded. "Never alone!" she said. Aelic stood as steadily as he could manage, drew Fury, and nodded.

Mallik hefted his hammer. "Let them come!" he growled. Tal and Sir Rogan stood beside him. The rest of the team made ready their weapons. They stood in the swirling mist and waited for the wolvins to charge.

They heard another howl—this one very different in pitch and punctuated by brief pauses. But where the sound had come from, no one would say. They were afraid to entertain the possibility that the howl had come from under the ground beneath their feet.

Antoinette thought that it must be a signal, that the pack would then pounce, but it was not so. One by one, the creatures began to withdraw from the edge of the hollow. And soon, they were gone.

"What do you make of that?" Farix asked, turning to Kaliam.

"I have never heard of a pack of wolvins to abandon easy prey," Kaliam replied.

"It would not have been easy," muttered Sir Rogan.

"Be that as it may," Kaliam said, smiling, "we were outnumbered and surrounded with no easy escape from this dell. They ought to have attacked."

Sir Gabriel sheathed his long knives and looked around. "It is almost as if they were content to leave us here," he said.

"Or perhaps they were chasing us here all along," said Tobias.

Antoinette looked at the seven trees, tall and dark, brooding over the hollow as if from a long, miserable labor. And down at their massive roots, the mist churned, obscuring the pale stones that lay there like burial markers. She wondered what powers the Seven Sleepers could have that allowed them to live while buried over the long passage of time. And she thought of the hate they must bear toward all things that walk free in The Realm.

"My dagger is missing!" Sir Rogan grunted. "It broke free when I fell!"

"And I have lost two scrolls!" Sir Gabriel exclaimed while patting his sides and the pockets of his cloak.

"Search quickly beneath the mist," Kaliam said. "If our sacks opened when we fell, we may be missing more than we can afford to lose." The twelve began to scour the area. Antoinette lost a pouch of gold coins, and two of her waterskins had burst.

"Knights, you move too slowly!" Kaliam bellowed. "Finish your search, and let us depart from here!"

"What is your wretched hurry?" Sir Rogan yelled back from the base of one of the closest trees. "I cannot find my dagger in this accursed mist!"

Antoinette, who had been on her knees looking for her coins, stood up abruptly and stared at Sir Rogan.

"Serves you right!" Tobias said, and he spat on the ground. "A fine path you led us on. It is your fault we are in this ghastly place!"

Sir Rogan stood up stiffly and lowered his eyebrows. "I only led the way because you did not offer your pathfinding services at the time."

"And a fine job leading you did," Farix said, his words dripping with sarcasm. "I am quite sure Aelic appreciates your effort as much as the rest of us. Tell us, how many branches did you crack on his skull as you ran heedlessly through the trees?"

"I am bruised all over thanks to you, oaf!" Aelic said bitterly.

"Aelic!" Antoinette said, her eyes wide. "Sir Rogan saved your life!"

"Keep out of this!" he replied angrily. "I do not answer to the likes of you!" His eyes flashed angrily, and he turned back to Sir Rogan.

"No, she is right, you ungrateful imp!" Sir Rogan growled. "I am beginning to regret that I did not leave you for the teeth and talons of the illgrets!"

"Perhaps if Sir Rogan did not have to lug you around," Nock said, his voice high and agitated, "we might never have come to the Sepulcher! Now, it is too late! We are all going to die!"

"We will all be drawn under the earth," Lady Merewen cried. "Buried alive until the long sleep takes us!"

"Nonsense! You might die, you and the archer," Tobias yelled. "But I will find a way out!"

"Tell me again, Pathfinder," Sir Oswyn interjected, "have you found us any safe way to this point? Admit it. You are out of your reckoning here. You have not the skill to direct us on this mission, do you?"

"And what great role do you play?" Tobias asked. "The knights of Paragory will not be frightened by your lute—though your playing leaves much to be desired!"

Antoinette stared in disbelief from knight to knight.

"Miserable whelp," Sir Oswyn fired back. "You would miss my fire powder—you all would—for you would have breathed your last were it not for my skills!"

"Close your bickering mouths!" commanded Kaliam. "This is getting us nowhere! The wolvins may come back, and we cannot traipse about waiting!"

"Is this counsel like your last?" Farix asked. "What magnificent wisdom it was to enter the Blackwood. Now look at us!"

"Why, you disrespectful wraith!" Kaliam drew his great broadsword and stepped toward Farix.

"Come any closer, Sentinel, and I will wash this hollow in your cowardly blood!"

"Wait, stop!" Antoinette cried. "Have you all gone mad?!"

Aelic shrugged and brandished Fury.

"No you don't!" said Antoinette. She snapped the flat of her sword on Aelic's hand, and he dropped the blade.

"You cut me!" Aelic screamed. "You witless wretch! You have cut open my blade hand! I will throttle you for that offense!"

Antoinette looked at Aelic's hand. There was no blood at all. It was unblemished. "No, Sir Aelic! Look again at your hand! It is not even marked!"

"It bleeds!" Aidan shrieked.

"We are all going to die!" Nock exclaimed. "Whether by illgret or wolvin, we are lost in this horrid place!"

"Shut your mouth, I said!" Tobias yelled, and he brought his staff around sharply and struck Nock in the back. He flew forward and disappeared under the mist.

"Stop it, all of you!" Antoinette pleaded. "Fighting and quarreling? This is not how servants of King Eliam behave! Don't you see? You are doing the enemy's work! It's this place—it's the hate of the Seven Sleepers!"

The others lowered their weapons a little. Nock rose up from the swirling mist and shook his head.

"What a victory for Paragor this would be," Antoinette cried out, "if we slay each other while he suffers no loss himself! Don't you remember the slaughter at Mithegard? Sir Rogan, so many of your kinsmen were slain by Paragor's minions—are you so anxious to join them? And Nock, you lost your brother to the enemy. Will you now fight for his killer against his friends?"

Nock stared absently, but then his eyes widened with recognition. "Listen to her!" Nock yelled. "She is right! This place is cursed with malice. Kaliam, you said it yourself. The ill will of the Seven took hold of me as well! We are not in our right minds! I am sorry to those I have offended. Rouse yourselves from this evil fog! Turn aside from your fury and appeal to King Eliam for aid before it is too late!"

Kaliam jolted and stood as one awakened by cold water. "May the King forgive me," he cried, "for what I purposed in my heart to do!"

"Forgive us all!" bellowed Mallik. "No wonder that the wolvins left us here! They would return and feast upon the carnage we made of ourselves!"

"Has anyone lost anything so precious that it is worth our lives?" Sir Oswyn asked. "If nay, then let us be off!"

"Who needs a dagger?" Sir Rogan said. "I still have my axe!"

"Good, then," said Kaliam. "Tobias, what direction?"

"You know very well that it is south," Tobias answered. "But thank you for your confidence in my abilities."

"Mallik!" Kaliam called.

"Say no more," he replied. He swept up his hammer and went to work on the southern bank of the hollow. In a few moments, he had pounded out a steep stair from the hillside, and the twelve emerged from the Sepulcher.

"What will happen?" Antoinette asked Nock as she took a last look at the shrouded hollow. "Will they escape?"

"The roots of the blackwood are strong," Nock replied. "Even in death they rival the strongest blades made of murynstil! But, if the Seven *should* rise, then . . . there will be trouble."

"We must warn King Eliam as soon as we can," Sir Gabriel said as they emerged from the hollow and began walking. "This is a serious threat too near to our city. Nock, I feel a fool for not believing you."

"He is no fool who studies the word of King Eliam," said Nock. "Your knowledge of Alleble's lore is profound, but if the ancient legends are true, then we may be forced to confront evils beyond any of our wisdom. I believe the Seven Sleepers are stirring . . . slowly awakening. And I fear what that could mean."

"The Wyrm Lord," Oswyn whispered.

THE FIRSTBORN

Having given up hope of reaching the Forest Road before the massive army from Paragory, the twelve trekked south and west through the Blackwood. The terrain did not improve, and so their progress remained slow. Kaliam did not want to stop, but he felt and saw the weariness that they all bore. He allowed the team to halt—but only for enough time to catch their breaths or eat something quickly from their provisions. There was no time for fires.

Lady Merewen handed Antoinette a full waterskin. "Please, take this to replace your own."

"And one of mine," Aelic said.

Antoinette smiled warmly at her friends and took a long drink from one of the skins. "Thank you," she said to them. And they were off again, seeking the road at the best speed they could manage.

"Hold!" Nock suddenly yelled from the front of the team.

"Is it the Forest Road?" Mallik called out hopefully.

"Nay," answered the archer. "But it may be something of value to us. Come and look."

The rest of the twelve caught up and found Nock examining a broken blackwood sapling.

"How in The Realm did you see that in this ruinous forest of shadow?" Mallik asked.

"In Yewland, the finest archers train their eyes to hunt in the darkness," Nock replied. "I am in my element among the trees. Tobias, come tell me what you think."

They followed as Tobias and Nock slowly advanced. Branches of young trees had been roughly hewn, gouges had been cut into the base of the larger trees, and some saplings had been broken nearly in two.

Tobias bent very low to the ground and strained to see. "Look here," he said. "There are the imprints of a small band of warriors. No more than a hundred, I would guess."

"The Glimpses of Yewland would not dare to harm the trees in this forest," said Nock. "So I can only conclude that the enemy made this path."

"Nock, I do not believe it was the force we saw this morning," Tobias said. "Do you agree?"

The archer nodded. "Tobias is right. This path was made by a force numbering a hundred or less—rather smaller than the several legions observed before. It is also clear from the cuts in the wood and the coverage of the tracks that this path is far too old—made perhaps even as long ago as a full season."

"So what does that mean?" asked Sir Rogan.

"It means," said Lady Merewen, "that the enemy has been prowling the Blackwood without our knowledge for some time."

"Stealing this precious wood for their weapons, no doubt," said Nock with a sneer.

"I wonder," replied Kaliam, and he was quiet.

"Their trail heads in more or less the direction we wish to go," said Tobias. "Shall we follow and see what may be seen?"

"Yes," Kaliam said. "I think we should."

The twelve had little trouble following the winding path of their foes, for the Paragor Knights had left behind quite a trail of destruction. They had gone perhaps a mile when Nock said, "It could be that my memory is flawed or perhaps some trick the shadows play upon my eyes, but something about this way seems familiar to me."

"But you said this path was made by Paragor Knights, that your kin would not destroy the trees," said Antoinette.

"No, Lady Antoinette, we do not harm the trees. We collect the fallen, but only what the forest gives us. But there is something I remember, ah—I cannot be sure."

A little farther up the path, Kaliam stopped the group. "There is a strange smell in the air," he said, and his brows furrowed deeply. "It is very faint. Do any of you smell it also?"

"I have been running behind Sir Mallik," said Farix. "The only thing I have smelled is his great stench!"

"Ha! Very amusing, Master Farix." Mallik grinned. "Just be glad I have not been eating the spicy cuisine of my Blue Mountain kin. That would indeed be a rude aroma!"

Everyone shared a laugh, except Sir Oswyn. "No, Kaliam is right. There is a scent on the air. It smells of something burned . . . of charred wood."

For a moment Nock stopped and stood transfixed. Then he said cheerfully, "Now I know why this seemed so familiar! This is the way to the Arch of Reverence! The passage to the Ancient One!

Come, follow me, and prepare to see one of the great wonders of The Realm!" And he sprinted up the path.

The rest of the twelve followed swiftly. At last they came to a place where the trees lined up on both sides of the path, and their immense boughs arched in such a way as to form a natural tunnel. Nock stopped at the entrance, grinned broadly, and then raced into the forest tunnel. The others followed close behind.

Antoinette was in awe, staring at the tunnel as she ran. The smooth black trunks formed the sides of the tunnel, and the great boughs above intertwined so closely that no light illuminated their path. Soon, they walked in total darkness. "The smell of smoke grows stronger," Sir Oswyn whispered.

They emerged in a vast clearing, and the twelve found it easier to see compared to the profound darkness in the tunnel.

Nock doubled over and fell to his knees as if he had been punched hard in the stomach. "Nooo!" he cried. "Please, noooo!"

In the center of the clearing, a great tree had been felled. Such a tree, Antoinette had never seen. It was impossible to tell how tall it had been, for its treetop had crashed into the forest beyond the clearing. Its trunk was as thick as a house, and gigantic limbs sprawled away from it in every direction. But its limbs were bare, and it was now plain why the air reeked of smoke. The great tree had been burned, charred to a husk in many places. All that remained unburned was a vast circular stump.

"Why?" Nock cried. "Why do this thing? They could have taken all that they needed and more from the deadfall! Why slay *Sil Arnoth*, the Ancient One?!"

Mallik stood by Nock and put a hand on his shoulder. "Nock, my friend," he said in a very low voice. "There are many great trees among the blue sequoias of my homeland—magnificent, sturdy, and towering. But I have never seen an equal to this one. And something about it speaks to me of its history. I am sorry for your loss."

"He is the firstborn of all trees in The Realm, the grandest of all the great ones. When we were young, Bolt and I used to climb in his lowest branches while our parents collected fallen limbs. I do not understand . . . why lay him low for lumber when there was no need?"

Sir Gabriel strode along a stretch of the fallen giant. "I do not believe the enemy was after the wood of this great father of trees," he said. "For there are no signs of harvesting—only fire."

"They did this out of their own depravity, then," Mallik muttered. "I will lay low the one who took an axe to this great tree."

Nock stood up and smiled at his hammer-wielding friend. "That is only if you can get to him before one of my arrows finds him. But I wonder if either of us will want to face the warrior mighty enough to fell the Ancient One. And I wonder that there exists an axe blade so sharp as to cut through the King of Blackwoods."

"Nock, come and look at this!" Lady Merewen said. She stood by the enormous stump of the fallen tree.

Nock and the others joined her and gasped at what they saw. The stump was thirty feet across and yet the cut was not ragged. It was as if an enormous blade had swept through the tree's base, felling it in one stroke. "Verily, you are right about the warrior and the weapon," Lady Merewen said. "For no ordinary axe could have shorn through this mighty bark, leaving a cut so clean. Mark my words, Paragor's dark arts are behind this tragedy."

"I do mark them," said Sir Gabriel. "And I mark something else as well. Blackwood trees are not known to have a hollow in the center, are they, Nock?"

"No, they are not," Nock replied, and he sprang lightly up onto the stump. He tread carefully over the myriad of gray rings until he came to the center. There, he knelt and peered into a dark hole.

"I do not know how far down it goes," Nock said, reaching into the hole. "It may pass beneath the ground even. But this is most unusual. Blackwood trees are solid to the core. Why the Ancient One has this strange hollow, I cannot say."

"Could it have been done after the tree was felled?" asked Lady Merewen.

Kaliam sighed. "Too many questions, and far too few answers. I am afraid that we shall never know unless we capture those who felled this great tree."

"The Ancient One may yet bring us a few answers," Nock said. "For I kneel upon one of the most precious libraries in all The Realm."

"What do you mean?" Mallik asked.

"The rings," Kaliam whispered, staring at the huge stump with interest. "Nock, you read rings?"

Nock smiled proudly. "My family descends from a long line of readers, taught by King Eliam himself when Yewland was but a settlement. Bolt was better at it than I, but I may be able to glean something of value."

Nock lay on the stump and traced his finger along the tiny gray ring that encircled the hollow center. He mumbled something and frowned. "When the center was removed," Nock said, "many of the Ancient One's first years were lost. This ring speaks of the sprouting of his first saplings, the beginning of the Blackwood Forest. He was very proud."

"You mean this tree speaks?" Antoinette asked.

"Are you surprised?" Kaliam asked. "I believe you had a conversation with a mortiwraith in the chambers beneath the Castle of Alleble, did you not?"

"Yeah, but a tree?"

"The rings of most trees tell only the most general tales: those of fires, floods, or extremely cold winters," Nock explained. "But King Eliam gave the blackwood trees a different kind of awareness. They do not have eyes or ears, but through wind and soil, bark and leaf, they sense much more than ordinary trees. And for those who have the skill, their rings tell fantastic tales."

Antoinette looked down at the wood and ran her own finger along the sketchy gray circle nearest the edge. She wondered what the Ancient One said near the end of his very long life.

"He speaks of visits from the Master," Nock said, reading from the center rings. "'Long did the Master recline in my shade,' he says, 'and he spoke many kind things to me and told me of his plans.'"

"I can only guess how profoundly this history touches your heart, Nock," Kaliam said gently. "But we need to discover more recent events."

"You are right, of course, my Sentinel," he replied. "I will progress outward more rapidly. Ah, here—this ring is disturbed! Let me read."

Nock was quiet a moment. And then he began to read aloud. "'Horror! Sorrow! A dark one has destroyed Torin! Alas!' Let me skip a few circles now. 'The Master brings them to me, and yes, my children will hold them down, keep them deep forever more! Sleep, foul ones. Sleep.'"

"The Seven Sleepers," said Sir Oswyn.

"Yes," Nock replied. "Wait, there is more here. 'Will I keep it? The Master asks me to. I will. I will lock it in a place where no one will look. Though there are dark things now dwelling among my trees, they will not get it.'"

"What does that mean?" asked Aelic.

"I do not know," said Nock.

"Nor I," said Kaliam.

"Maybe that's why there's that hollow part in the center," Antoinette suggested. "Maybe King Eliam put something there for safekeeping."

"That makes sense." Kaliam nodded. "But what was it? Nock, read on. See if you can determine what 'it' is."

Nudging himself a few inches at a time, Nock followed the same ring around the massive stump. "Nothing so far. He tells of the arrival of Glimpses, the tree-dwellers, he calls them. He must mean my ancestors, the founders of Yewland! Remarkable! He speaks here of a terrible storm and of a fire started by lightning."

Antoinette suddenly felt very cold.

"Here, he tells of the invaders with weak roots. 'They hem my children in, but they cannot thrive among us. They will not drop seed here. This is the land given by the Master to the Firstborn. We will keep it pure.'"

"Nock, I am sorry," Kaliam said. "But we must press on."

"Wait, here, let me read far ahead. See, there is a break! I shall read. 'I am afraid,' says the Ancient One. 'Something wicked has come. He touches me, and he is cold. He cannot have it. He does not have the power to take it!'" Antoinette and the others hung on each of Nock's words.

"Here again," Nock continued. "'The dark one returns. He threatens to hew my children. He threatens fire. But I am loyal, Master. It remains safe.'"

"This is maddening!" Sir Rogan grunted.

"There is much here about his children," Nock went on, skipping many rings and dwelling only on those that were broken or disturbed. "He is sad because one of his sons fell near the river. And here, he loses a limb to the wind. Let me see, no broken lines until . . ."

Nock slid around until he came to the last ring. Then he stared, and his face contorted with sadness. He began to read aloud. "This is just before the end. 'The dark one has returned,' he says. 'He is not alone this time. There are many soldiers. They bring a burning blade. I am sorry, my Master. I withheld it as long as I could. Agony! Agony! I am fading. He is near to it. I am sorry, Master. He must not have it all. If I can, yes, I will try, but he is so close to it now. I try to keep some, but his reach is long. I am sorry.' And there is no more."

"The dark one?" Tal asked.

"Lady Merewen was right," said Kaliam. "It was Paragor. For who else in all The Realm is so bent on the destruction of noble things? But what was it that he stole? And how did he know that it was hidden there, within the Ancient One?"

"It must have been something of extraordinary power," Sir Gabriel said, thinking aloud. "But The Scrolls of Alleble speak of no such relic or heirloom."

"And what did Sil Arnoth mean by trying to keep some?" Nock asked, glancing back at the hollow in the center of the tree.

"That seems clear enough," Kaliam said. "The firstborn tried to keep Paragor from getting all of this powerful item, but in the end, he was overcome. Alas, if it is some perilous weapon, that he was not able to keep it hidden!"

Antoinette looked around the gray rings, spiraling round and round until they disappeared into the hollow. No one spoke.

Finally, Mallik broke the silence. "I do not know the answers to these questions, but we will not find them standing around here."

YEWLAND

The twelve trudged along the meandering path of the enemy through the night. Drained emotionally and near total exhaustion, they pressed on, fueled by loyalty to King Eliam and the urgency of their mission. By dawn the trail had led them to the Forest Road.

"Alas, it is as I feared!" Sir Tobias called to the group. "While we were delayed in the Blackwood, the enemy's convoy has passed us by!"

"How long ago?" asked Antoinette.

"Several hours, at least," answered Nock. He sighed and seemed relieved. "Well, at least they did not stop to conquer my homeland!"

"Yes, then where are they going?" Mallik asked.

"From the Forest Road?" Kaliam replied. "Acacia is possible, though I think Baen-Edge is most likely their destination. The Glimpses there are no friend to Alleble. And some claim that slave trade thrives there. Who can say? After that there is Clarion and a whole host of small provinces to the far east. Alas, that we may never know."

"What do you mean?" asked Antoinette.

"Our path now is to Yewland, young Antoinette," Kaliam said.

"But shouldn't we follow the enemy? You said yourself that he is up to something wicked, and that we must discover his plans."

"No one wishes to know more than I," Kaliam said. "But our charge is to travel to Yewland. There is still the matter of the false ambassador who is poisoning Queen Illaria's mind with contempt for Alleble. No, as much as I would like to know what else the enemy is doing, we must first see that his plans fail in Yewland."

There was nothing more to be said. Kaliam commanded their team, and he was not to be questioned a second time.

As they neared Yewland, Tobias asked Nock to lead. The twelve made their way several miles west along the Forest Road and then due south to the borders of Yewland. As they traveled the well-trodden path, the foliage around them became much more lush and green again. And now, far from the constricting roots of the Blackwood, a great variety of trees sprang up and thrived. Birds sang from the treetops. Squirrels, chipmunks, and other small woodland creatures chattered at each other and played under the wide ferns and among the tangled roots. The demeanor of the twelve had improved mightily. Only Kaliam was pensive.

"We must be wary," Kaliam said. "Of all the provinces of The Realm, Yewland of old has been our friend. But now we cannot be certain of a hospitable welcome. Keep your words humble and brandish not your weapons."

At last the trees funneled them to a place where the path seemed to end and a grove of tall bamboo rose up before them. "We have perfect timing," said Nock. "To arrive just as the morning sun begins to wax! For through this bamboo curtain is the Hall of Sun and Moon—a sight I have sorely missed!"

Nock led the way, finding a seam in the bamboo and easily parting the tall shoots to reveal a path that had been invisible. The twelve emerged from the bamboo and found themselves in a great open glade lined on all sides by tall silvery trees. Thick shrubs with deep green leaves and broad white flowers flourished everywhere and filled the glade with soft sweet smells. Birds of many colors soared from tree to tree, and large blue butterflies danced around the garlands of broad yellow flowers that hung in the treetops.

Nock stopped and inhaled deeply. "Moonblossom and Golden Tear," he said. "They grow in Yewland and nowhere else. It is good to be in the land of my kin."

"How . . . how is it that the high flowers glitter?" Mallik asked.

"Golden Tear, they are called." Nock smiled. "For each pale bloom brings forth a single large drop of nectar each morning. The sun's rays shine through it like a window into The Blessed Realm. In my city, Mallik, they prepare a drink from that nectar that will restore a Glimpse's energy with some to spare. Curl your beard, it will. But it is very costly. Perhaps we can all share—"

"Nay, I will buy each his or her own!" Mallik interrupted.

"But, Mallik, it is a month's wages for even a tiny glass!"

"A pittance to me," Mallik said, a sly grin forming. "Trading in the marble from the Blue Mountains has—"

"Shhh!" Kaliam warned. "Be silent. There are—"

But before the Sentinel could utter another word, tall Glimpse warriors surrounded them. They were clad in cloth armor that was many mingled colors, matching the trees, shrubs, and foliage all at once. It seemed to Antoinette that they had appeared out of thin air. One moment they were not, and the next moment, they were there. And each of them had a Blackwood bow raised, an arrow trained on one of the twelve. The tallest of the woodland warriors, a Glimpse with very long golden hair, stepped forward and addressed them.

"Hail, travelers from Alleble," he said, and his voice was deep and commanding. "You tread on hallowed ground in uncertain times. State your business in Yewland!"

"Why, Baldergrim, I ought to put a shaft in your foot!" Nock laughed as he came to the front. "Honestly, greeting your own kin as if you did not know any better! Tell your braves to stand down!"

"Master Nock!" the blond warrior exclaimed with sudden recognition, and Antoinette noticed that his eyes flickered blue. He slung his bow and embraced Nock fiercely. The other warriors lowered their bows. Some of them smiled; while others looked doubtful. But all of them were surprised. "Of all the unlooked-for blessings—seven summers it has been since I've laid my eyes on you!"

"Far too long!"

"And where is that rascal Bolt?" Baldergrim asked, craning his head to examine the twelve.

A shadow passed over Nock's face. "I have tidings concerning my brother, among other things. But I would gain an audience with Queen Illaria to share them. We have come from Alleble with vital news, and on our way have discovered news I deem even more grave."

"I see you choose your words carefully," Baldergrim said. "Come then, I will deliver you into Her Majesty's throne room, but do not look for favor. Your Ambassador Eogan has left Yewland a divided house!"

"Ambassador Eogan?" cried Sir Gabriel, stepping forward. "So, we now know the imposter's name!"

"Imposter?" Baldergrim replied.

"Yes," said Nock. "That is part of what we came to share, but come, bring us to the Queen, and you shall hear much."

Kaliam stepped forward, and Baldergrim looked upon him with awe. "This is Kaliam," Nock announced. "He is Sentinel over all Alleble and the leader of this team."

Baldergrim stared. "M'lord Sentinel, it is an honor to meet one so highly favored by King Eliam the Everlasting!"

Kaliam nodded to the Yewland Brave and said, "Baldergrim, what did you mean when you said Eogan left Yewland a divided house?"

Baldergrim glanced at Nock and continued. "Forgive me for not being immediately forthcoming, but I believe the information you seek must wait also. Come, and I shall bring you before the Queen!"

Baldergrim and his braves led the twelve into the green city of Yewland. Antoinette gawked to look upon it, for it was as if wooden castle turrets had sprouted from the trunks of great trees—alder, oak, beech, hemlock, ash, and pine. Long parapets and battlements had grown along their massive boughs. And everywhere there were stairs. Twisting, spiraling, stretching in all directions. Long stairways reached up from gabled cottages clustered at the trees' roots and disappeared into the massive green spread above. Others crisscrossed between the treetops, while still others wound in a serpentine fashion around the tree trunks.

Baldergrim dismissed his team of warrior braves, led the twelve from Alleble to a wide stairwell, and began to climb. They came to many forks in the stairs where one branch would descend while the other climbed, but Baldergrim did not pause.

"How do you find your way?" Antoinette blurted out. "These passages have me all mixed up!"

"Indeed, that is the aim," Baldergrim said. He looked over his shoulder at Antoinette and winked. "The stair network provides more defense for Yewland than would a dozen granite walls, for we braves always have the higher ground. Our best archers, like your comrade Nock, can simply pick off the enemy as he tries in vain to find his way!"

Baldergrim glanced from Antoinette to Lady Merewen. "There is one other advantage to having such a labyrinth of passages," he said with a wink. "It makes it difficult for such lovely visitors to escape!"

Antoinette and Lady Merewen blushed. Aelic and Kaliam frowned.

Baldergrim led them up a last great climb to a wide platform in the top of a towering hemlock. Their climb had led the twelve through so much foliage that they had no real sense of how high off the ground they actually were. Now they saw the dizzying height and shrank back from the edge. The hemlock overlooked a deep valley, where a massive knee of stone jutted skyward. Upon this mountainous rock was an enormous green castle. It had many turrets and bastions that spread out from the center keep like buds of some wild, flowering shrub. From the platform, an arrangement of cables traversed a wide, terrifying gulf to the castle's main gate. Suspended carriages moved back and forth along the cables. Aside from those, or perhaps a ride upon the backs of dragons, there seemed no other way to gain access to the castle of Yewland.

Just then, a very large carriage arrived, drawn up to the platform by dozens of Yewland Glimpses. On Baldergrim's command, two Yewland Braves with eyes glinting green opened the carriage doors. Baldergrim beckoned for the twelve to enter. Once the twelve were comfortably seated, he entered and sat beside Antoinette on the cushioned bench. Aelic, who sat to Antoinette's left, stared at Baldergrim strangely. On Baldergrim's command, the pair of Yewland Braves shut the door. They looked at Antoinette with expressions polite but not welcoming.

"Baldergrim," she asked, "you are a knight in the service of Yewland?"

"Yes, m'lady, an Argent Brave, commander of many in the Queen's Army."

"But you also serve King Eliam, right?" she asked. "Your eyes, I mean."

"Yes, they sparkle blue with the purity of my devotion to Alleble," he replied as he glanced at the two braves now busy securing the carriage. "Ah, I perceive your confusion! You wonder that one family can serve two masters! Yewland for a long, long time was an independent realm. When King Brand the Stern-hearted many seasons ago announced our alliance with Alleble, many entrusted their hearts to King Eliam . . . most, in fact. But some remained hesitant—though not fearful—and so Yewland remained at peace. Even after Queen Illaria—who is from a long line of those who wished to remain independent—ascended the throne, there has been little conflict between the green and blue eyes. That changed only recently, but I will say no more."

The carriage lurched forward, and Antoinette watched the platform slip away. They now hung suspended by a single cable over a wide, perilous gulf, and it seemed as the carriage inched along that they moved farther away from safety and into the dangerous unknown. Antoinette wondered how strong the bond holding the alliance between Yewland and Alleble was. For like their carriage, it seemed to hang on only a thread.

Queen Illaria

Welcome, pilgrims from Alleble," said Queen Illaria, entering the cavernous throne room from a passage on the left. She gracefully ascended several stairs and sat upon the throne to look upon the twelve. "I am grateful that you heeded my correspondence, though I expected you to come *sooner*."

The Queen's long fine hair, like black silk, hung across one shoulder in an elegant braid. Her Glimpse skin was so purely white that it seemed to glow. And her eyes were very large and dark. She wore a long violet gown with fluted sleeves, and sat like a rare orchid on the green throne. She was beautiful, stunning—but somehow inaccessible. Antoinette got the feeling that many Glimpse knights had called upon the Queen for her hand in marriage, only to be found wanting when measured against such elegant grandeur.

Kaliam stepped forward. "Your Majesty," he began, bowing. "I am Kaliam, the Sentinel of Alleble—"

"Sentinel?" The Queen's eyes widened and flashed green.

"Sentinel, you say? That speaks well of King Eliam that Yewland should merit one of such rank."

"King Eliam cherishes all the kingdoms of The Realm," Kaliam said. "But Yewland he prizes chief among them."

"As a footstool, you mean!" The Queen stood, and tension flashed into the throne room like a sudden storm. "I suppose King Eliam learned we have spurned your silver-tongued ambassador Count Eogan! He claimed he had business in Acacia and fled not two nights ago. So now King Eliam sends his chief knight and a band of no-doubt seasoned warriors to force us to meet his demands! Well, let me assure you, Sentinel, the Kingdom of Yewland will not pay tribute in gold, blackwood, or soldiers! And your so-called Alleb Creed, which has had so many of my Glimpses tied in knots, will never become for us the law you desire!"

"Your Majesty, you mis—"

"SILENCE!" the Queen commanded. Yewland Knights stepped out of the shadows on both sides of the throne room. "You are before MY throne now! And I will not be interrupted, not even by the Sentinel of Alleble!" Her face was twisted with anger, and she stared at Kaliam for many silent moments as if daring him to speak again. Finally, her expression softened, but her eyes still smoldered as she sat again on the throne.

"I have drafted a letter to King Eliam," she said, "formally declaring Yewland's return to an independent realm. And though I know that many in my homeland are devoted to King Eliam and would depart if this proclamation be ratified, I am no despot. I would allow them to leave. If that is what is required to secure Yewland's freedoms, then so be it!" Queen Illaria swallowed as if she had just tasted something unspeakably bitter. She turned away for a moment. When she looked back, her eyes were glassy.

"The letter waits only for my seal in wax," she said, almost in a whisper. "But tell me, Sentinel, how is it that your King wants to shackle the Glimpses of Yewland to Alleble when so many already come willingly? Has he so quickly forgotten the faithful service of Yewland's armies? And why would he demand such a price from us, a sum that—if it were paid—would stagger our place in the trade market of The Realm? Why ask us to pay when he must know there are other offers on the table . . . offers from suitors who would give, rather than take!"

After a short pause, Kaliam nodded and Sir Gabriel came forward. "Sovereign Queen Illaria, ruler of the Green City," he began. "I am Sir Gabriel, King Eliam's true emissary to Yewland. The answers you seek lie in one fact: the ambassador of which you speak, Eogan, was not from Alleble at all!" A collective startled gasp rose from the throne room. Queen Illaria stood.

"What is this you say?"

"King Eliam does not demand gold or any such tribute!" Sir Gabriel went on. "Nor does he wish to impose a harsh code of conduct on any, save that all should live in peace! Count Eogan is an imposter!"

"But he wore the armor of Alleble," the Queen said. "And his eyes, they shone forth blue even as yours do!"

Nock touched Kaliam on the arm. Kaliam nodded and Nock came forward. "Queen of my homeland," he said, "you have been deceived. Eogan's eyes were false. How he was able to do this, we are not certain, but we know who his true master is. This imposter was a servant of Paragor."

"Nock, as a Yewland Brave, your word is respected in this hall," she said. "But you level a serious charge. On what do you base your accusation?"

"There was another," Nock said. "He traveled among the Knights of Alleble as one of us. Acsriot was his name. He betrayed us, my Queen. Betrayed us in our moment of need. I saw myself his eyes flash blue in one moment, and then red the next. And when my team from Alleble clashed with Paragor's forces in Mithegard, it was by Acsriot's command that my brother Bolt was slain!"

The Queen seemed to sway and steadied herself with a hand on her throne. Baldergrim rushed to the Queen's side. The Yewland Braves lowered their weapons and murmured loudly. One of the guards slowly edged toward the door and disappeared from the throne room.

"Bolt," she whispered as she looked away, and Antoinette thought she struggled mightily to master her emotions. When Queen Illaria looked back, it was clear that she had lost the battle. Her face was drawn and her eyes were weary and without focus.

"I am stricken!" she cried. "Stricken!! Bolt has fallen? Alas, that Yewland should lose one so noble and I . . . one so beloved."

Nock's eyes widened.

"Yes, Nock," the Queen continued softly. "You knew he was my friend, even from our youth. But there was something more . . . a kindred spirit between us. And I thought—I hoped—ere he departed for Alleble that he might ask my hand. Hard was that parting on us both. Many sunlit days were dimmed as I sat upon my throne wondering if he would return. It is some comfort, Nock, to look upon you—his very likeness. I am sorry. Sorry for us both."

Once again, the room filled with murmurs.

She looked about and regained her composure. Her expression seemed to harden then, and her eyes narrowed. "Silence!" the Queen commanded, though her voice faltered. "There will be time for grief, but we must keep clear our minds if we are to decide rightly in this matter. You say that Paragor's forces were responsible—that Paragory is now at open war with Alleble?"

Sir Gabriel answered, "Your Majesty, Paragory is at open war with all in The Realm who will not surrender to their rule!"

"But they have sent emissaries here," she said. "And they have brought us much commerce and token gifts of friendship! Just recently, we allowed four legions of Paragor's forces to travel the Forest Road on the way to Baen-Edge! I believe there is even yet a rank of Paragor soldiers in the Kismet purchasing supplies."

"It is this force that delayed our arrival here," said Nock. "We diverted through the Blackwood to try to get here ahead of them. I at least feared that they would attempt to conquer Yewland!"

"Conquer us?" the Queen exclaimed. "Four legions are not nearly enough to defeat us in the wood."

"That may be so," said Nock. "But Paragor's armies are much more powerful now than in the past. And they grow bolder and more wanton in their arrogance. I reveal now with great regret Paragor's crime against Yewland! As we traveled through the Blackwood, we followed the trail of a rank of soldiers to the Arch of Reverence . . ." Nock's voice failed. He cleared his throat and continued. "We entered and alas, found Sil Arnoth, the Ancient One, has been laid low! He has been cut down and his trunk charred. I read his rings myself . . . Paragor was his murderer!"

"Outrage!" cried Baldergrim. The other Yewland Braves tore at their garments. Walking unsteadily, the Queen came down from her throne. She stood before the twelve and looked from Glimpse to Glimpse.

"Bolt was a noble knight. His death at the hands of Paragor is enough to turn me against Paragory forever," said Queen Illaria, her chest heaving as she spoke. "But with this greatest crime against the Ancient One, it is enough to turn all of Yewland against Paragor."

"I am afraid we must prepare for the worst. Baldergrim, send fifty of your band. Go into the Blackwood and search for clues. Return to me with word at all speed. And, Baldergrim, do not allow any of Paragor's legions into Yewland."

"Aye, my Queen!" he replied. Baldergrim put his hand briefly on Nock's shoulder and then was gone.

"Your Majesty," Kaliam said, "if there are soldiers from Paragory still within Yewland's borders . . ."

The Queen's eyes narrowed and she nodded. "King Eliam chose you well, Sentinel! Yes, something must be done about that. Boldoak!" she cried out, and suddenly, a Yewland Brave was at her side. He held a long Blackwood bow in a death grip and had a scar on his cheek.

"They will not leave Yewland alive," he said in a coarse, deep voice.

"By your leave," said Kaliam, "may I take some from my team to assist Boldoak? We have some experience in battling the Knights of Paragor."

"You may indeed," she replied. "Boldoak, see to it that Kaliam's warriors are equipped with anything they need. And give Nock enough Blackwood shafts to litter the streets of Kismet with the enemy. Be swift!"

Kaliam bowed to the Queen, then said, "Sir Gabriel, Lady Merewen, and Sir Tobias, remain with the Queen until Baldergrim returns."

TREETOP HOPPING

Minutes later, Boldoak and nine Knights of Alleble exited the sky carriage and raced across a long suspended bridge to a cluster of barracks nested in a vast elm. Boldoak loosed a blast on his war horn. In moments, they were surrounded by a host of archers.

"My braves!" Boldoak cried. "The Paragor Knights have outlived their welcome here!" The braves cheered. "We have the Queen's orders to capture any Paragor Knight who lingers, but we should begin with those in Kismet. And if they will not surrender . . . then we will do what must be done! Quickly, prepare yourselves and break out the glides! We need all speed!"

The braves scattered to the barracks and returned with supplies, weapons, and strange-looking devices. To each of the Knights of Alleble they gave one of the devices. Antoinette stared at the contraption in her hands. It was a large slotted wheel threaded onto an axle. There were handles on either end of the axle.

The archers raced off across a bridge to another platform on a neighboring elm tree. Kaliam and the others raced after them. At the end of the next platform a single cable of rope was fastened to an elm branch about head high. The rope gradually descended to another flat in the trees several hundred yards away. Boldoak slung his glide over the cable so that it fit in the slot of the wheel. He grabbed the other handle with his free hand, checked to make sure the wheel rolled atop the rope, and then he was gone, hurtling down the rope. One after another, the braves whooshed away. At last, the brave who had handed Antoinette her glide came over to her. "Get a tight fit, wheel to rope," he said. "Step off of the platform, and hold on tight!"

Then he too sped down the rope. Nock jumped on next, followed by Kaliam, Farix, and Tal. Antoinette turned to Aelic. "This is like a Zip Line!" she said.

"A Zip Line?" he echoed. But Antoinette didn't answer. She lobbed her glide over the cable, grabbed the handles, and stepped off the platform. She lifted her legs so that her body was in an "L" shape and flew down the rope. The angle of the cable became shallower at the bottom. Antoinette's momentum slowed, and she cruised to a soft stop on the platform below.

"That was fun!" she said to Aelic and Mallik when they arrived seconds later.

"Agreed," said Aelic. Mallik said nothing, but his pale face seemed rather green.

Nearby, a Yewland Brave was speaking to Boldoak and Kaliam. "Yes, surprised to see him, I was," he said. "The Queen's personal guards do not usually come 'ere themselves. They send squires, most times."

"How far ahead of us was he?" asked Boldoak.

"Perhaps five minutes," the brave replied. "No more 'n that."

Boldoak turned to the others. "That is disconcerting news," he said, absently rubbing the scar on his cheek. "One of Queen Illaria's personal guards arrived here moments ago. He was headed in the direction of Kismet."

"A spy of the enemy?" Kaliam asked.

"If he is, he will no doubt warn the Paragor Knights who remain in Kismet! Make haste!" Boldoak yelled to his braves. "There is something wicked afoot! I will lead us, braves! And to those from Alleble: Watch your step. It is a long way down!"

"How far is Kismet from here?" Antoinette asked Nock.

"About a league and a half," he replied. Then they were off. The journey to Kismet was the most complicated and harrowing venture Antoinette had experienced thus far. The nine from Alleble followed the Yewland Braves from platform to platform, from tree to tree. They climbed and descended stairs, glided across gaping chasms between skyscraping trees, and marched across dozens of bridges— all at top speed. At last they came to a wide-turreted platform, high in a wide oak that grew on the edge of a grassy cliff.

Boldoak led them to the eastern edge of the platform and pointed down. Carriages ran along the cables from the platform to the small town far below. "That is Kismet," he said. "The spy—if that is what he is—has already passed over the Allure." He pointed to a railed walkway that was attached to the side of the platform. It zigzagged between platforms until finally ending at a castle tower in Kismet.

"Hurry, now!" Boldoak said, and he cast his glide to the ground and sprinted to the walkway. "Follow me on the Allure! Be swift!"

"But wait!" Antoinette called. Boldoak and most of the others were already gone, but Aelic was with her, and a few of the Yewland Braves turned around. "Why do you delay?" one asked.

"That way," she said, pointing to the Allure. "That'll take too long! The Paragor Knights will get away!" She looked over to the cables running steeply down from the platform. "What if we use the glides on those?"

"Are you mad?" one of the braves asked, staring at Antoinette. "Those cables are for the heavy wheels of the carriages. And the angle is far too steep. You would smack into a carriage or crash at the bottom! Come on! We must go!"

The braves ran off, leaving Antoinette and Aelic on the platform. "They'll never get there in time," she said to Aelic.

"You are not thinking of—"

"I'm going!"

"But, m'lady! You heard what they said!"

Antoinette swung her glide over the cable, winked at Aelic, and plunged over the edge.

"I am going to regret this," Aelic said, and he followed her.

The glide worked well on the cable. Too well. She raced down the cable faster than she ever dreamed possible. The distant ground sped by beneath her in a blur, the wind blasted her face, and her arms strained to hold on to the handles of the glide. She stole a glance back over her shoulder and saw a dark blur that she took to be Aelic.

When Antoinette turned back, a carriage loomed on the cable ahead. It seemed to be flying toward her. She had to act fast or she would smash into the carriage at seventy miles an hour! She looked down, but the ground was still too far to simply let go. Then, as she sped toward the carriage, she had a thought. "Aelic!!" she yelled, hoping he could hear her. "Watch me!!"

There was no response. Antoinette dropped her legs out of the L position and let the air blow her now-vertical body backward so that she swung up toward the cable. Then she bent back into the L and pumped herself forward. *Not enough!*

The carriage zoomed closer. She repeated the swinging motion, pumping herself as fast as she could. The wind fought to still her speed. She swung back and then forward again—a little higher this time. *Maybe!* Again, she swung back and forth. *I need to get higher! King Eliam!* She swung back one more time and heaved herself forward with all of her might, all the while thinking it would not be enough. But she had no choice! The carriage sped toward her.

Antoinette swung forward and just as the momentum carried her body up, she let go of the glide with one hand. She felt the whoosh of the carriage go beneath her, and she started to fall. The cable rose up suddenly beside her. She grappled awkwardly and twisted the glide on to the cable and then barely managed to grab the other handle with her free hand. The wheel did not seat correctly at first on the cable, and Antoinette tugged and twisted it. And then, a strange thing happened.

As she twisted the glide, it created friction. The rubbing of the wheel's edges slowed her descent considerably and *WHAMMM!!*

Aelic slammed into her from behind. The impact knocked the wind out of both of them. Antoinette lost hold of her glide and started to fall. She grasped frantically. Her glide fell, smacked against her thigh, and disappeared. Aelic let go of one of his glide's handles and grabbed Antoinette's collar.

"Get the handle!" he yelled as he felt his glide begin to tilt to the side of the cable. Antoinette reached up, and with Aelic's boosting, grabbed the free handle of Aelic's glide.

Each holding on to one handle of the glide for dear life, they sailed down the cable the last three hundred yards. The platform at the bottom was coming up fast. Too fast.

"Twist the glide!" Antoinette yelled. "It'll slow us down!"

Antoinette and Aelic began swinging in opposite directions to twist the glide. They managed to turn it so that its rails burned against the cable. They slowed considerably, but not enough. Then, fifty yards from the platform, they heard the sharp sound of cracking wood. A quick glance up confirmed their fears: the glide's wooden wheel had split. As pieces of the wheel flew into the air, Antoinette and Aelic plummeted downward.

To Honor
Old Alliances

SPLASH!!! Antoinette and Aelic plunged into the large pond at the base of the Kismet platform. Antoinette surfaced first with a splutter. "Aelic! Aelic, where are you!"

"Right behind you!" he said. "And the next time you have a splendid idea like that one, remind me not to follow you!"

Antoinette laughed and swam to the shore. "Deal," she said. "Those glides weren't made from blackwood, were they?"

"No, unfortunately, they were not."

Emerging from the water, Aelic drew Fury from its sheath. "Let us see if your shortcut was worth the risk! Stay behind me, and keep your head down. We do not wish to draw any attention to your darker skin."

Antoinette and Aelic sloshed up the hill and found themselves behind a blacksmithy. A very large Glimpse with enormous forearms hammered away at a blade he had just pulled from his wood-burning furnace. He looked up, his bushy black eyebrows raised. "'Ere now, what are you doin' back 'ere?"

"We are sorry to intrude, sir," said Aelic. "But Her Majesty Queen Illaria sent us. Do you know if the Paragor Knights are still here in Kismet?"

"What, the red-eyes?" He snorted. "Yeah, they are here, unfortunately. Last I saw they were over at the Guild haggling over Blackwood bows." He pointed beyond his shop at a little path between two cottages. "Say, you interested in a shield? I have some fine bucklers here at a very reasonable price!"

"Maybe another time!" Aelic called over his shoulder and ran up the path. With Antoinette close behind, Aelic darted between the two cottages. He turned the corner and smacked right into the back of a tall knight in black armor.

"Watch where you are going!" the knight growled, turning around. He squinted at Aelic and Antoinette through long, oily locks of dark hair, and his eyes glinted red. Antoinette looked left and right. They had run right into the middle of the knights from Paragory—only there were a lot more of them than Antoinette had expected would be there. At least a hundred warriors in dark armor were gathered there in the square before the Guild. Some were mounted upon black horses. Some were still loading their packs. There was no sign of the Yewland Braves or the Knights of Alleble.

Okay, Antoinette thought. *Bad idea.*

"Here now," said the soldier they had slammed into. "Where might you be going in such a hurry?" Then his eyes narrowed. "You two are not Yewlanders. From Alleble by the design of your armor."

"See, Master Scaliant, I told you!" whined a high-pitched voice. A Glimpse wearing the green-and-brown livery of Yewland's Braves stepped out of the crowd. "I told you they was coming. She was with them. They both were! Please, let us depart for Baen-Edge!"

The tall warrior, the one called Scaliant, drew his sword and called, "Hoy, Lord Kearn, come take a look at what washed up on shore! A couple of wet rats—from Alleble, no less!"

A knight near the edge of the square leaped down from his horse and strode slowly toward them. Even from a distance, there was something much more menacing about this knight than any of the others. As he walked, only his flashing red eyes were visible from under the dark hood.

"Old Toby here says these are from Queen Illaria!" Scaliant said, laughing so that his armor rattled. "He says they were in Queen Illaria's court! Maybe these two have come to get us. What do you think of that, eh, m'lord?"

"That is not to be taken lightly, fool!" Kearn's voice had a strange quietness that resonated like a tuning fork. "Do you not know our peril here?"

"I just did not think these two could be—"

"Shut your mouth," said Kearn even more quietly, "or I will shut it for you so that it will not open again." It sounded almost like a hiss. He turned to Antoinette and lowered his hood. She gasped. He had long blond hair that fell savagely about his shoulders and penetrating green eyes. They flashed red, and Kearn drew a long double-wide–bladed sword.

"How many are coming?" Kearn asked.

"Drop your weapons and surrender!" Aelic shouted. "You are no longer guests in Yewland!"

And this time Kearn did laugh, but it was distant and cold, as if he knew a dangerous secret but would not tell. "Tell me how many are coming, or I will gut you like a stag!"

Antoinette stood very still. Her sword slowly lowered until the tip of the blade stabbed the turf. Aelic jumped in front of her brandishing Fury. "Let fly one stroke," said Aelic, "and it will be your last."

Kearn stared for a moment at Fury, and then his eyes bored into Aelic's. "Fool," he seethed. "Do you not know who I am? I am Lord Kearn, left hand of the Master! I have the power to take you beyond the gates from whence none return!"

"Your master is not here," Aelic said. He glanced back at Antoinette. She still did not move. "And Queen Illaria knows what Paragor did in the Blackwood. Your lives have been forfeited!"

"Liar," Kearn said. "Scaliant, get the last of the blackwood loaded. Make haste, for we shall soon have other visitors."

"What about these two?" Scaliant asked.

"See to the wood," Kearn whispered. And suddenly he slashed forward, wide blade humming in the air. Aelic had just enough time to block, but the force of the blow knocked him backward into Antoinette.

"Antoinette!" Aelic yelled. "Snap out of it!"

Kearn slashed again, and the strike would have taken Antoinette's head but for Fury and Aelic's lightning reflexes. The sound of the clash brought Antoinette around, but she was off balance. Kearn's next strike came at her side. She guarded, but Kearn's blade slid off her sword and cracked the armor on her thigh. She fell and Kearn raised his blade high, intending to drive it into her as she lay on the ground.

Fury again came to Antoinette's rescue. Aelic used both hands and wheeled his blade at his enemy's. Kearn's stabbing thrust was knocked wide and the point stabbed into the dirt near Antoinette's shoulder. Kearn growled and drove a fist into Aelic's jaw. Aelic staggered and fell to the ground next to Antoinette. They both rolled, stood, and raised their swords.

At that moment a black-shafted arrow whistled by and stuck deep into the mortar of the Guild. Then there was a gurgling scream, and one of the Paragor Knights fell from his steed. Antoinette and Aelic smiled, for they saw the Yewland Braves sprinting down the last few flights of stairs, firing as they ran. Two more Paragor Knights fell. Kearn saw this too, and he turned to run. Aelic seized the opportunity and charged forward with Fury. He struck with a heavy blow aimed right between Kearn's shoulder blades.

"Noooo!" Antoinette screamed. She lunged between Aelic and Kearn and batted Fury away. Kearn turned and looked at her. His eyes flashed red, and then he strode quickly away. In a moment, he was on his horse and gone.

"Antoinette, have you lost your mind?" Aelic asked. "I could have felled him, put an end to one of Paragor's chief warlords!"

Before Antoinette could answer, a group of Paragor Knights stormed around the corner of the Guild and attacked. There were five of them, reckless, swinging at them in a blind rage. Two went for Aelic, leaving the other three for Antoinette. She thought immediately of her first test and the urchin. *Kalium was right. The Paragor Knights will take any advantage. They will not fight fair. Focus on your objective,* he had said. Antoinette ducked the slashing blade of the first, leaped over the sweeping blade of the second, batted away the wild stroke of the third. And then she evened the odds. She slashed her sword upward with both hands, forcing the third knight's blade high. Then, with lightning speed, she slashed beneath his shoulder where there was no protection, no armor. The knight screamed, and his sword arm fell limp at his side. Antoinette swept her blade next behind his knees, and he crumpled to the ground. The second warrior fell next to him, thanks to a devastating stroke from Aelic.

The first knight was more skilled. He turned and came at Antoinette with a series of rapid thrusts and slashes. Antoinette backed up slowly, blocking with short compact strokes and watching his approach. When at last he paused, Antoinette unleashed her kakari-geiko attack. Her sword in continuous motion, she rained down blows upon him until he lost his balance and dropped his guard. It was all the advantage she needed. Her blade put a dent in the Paragor Knight's helmet, and he staggered backward. Aelic finished him off with a thrust into his side.

Just as quickly as the battle began, it ended. Many of the Paragor Knights had been slain. But more had escaped, including Kearn—and Aelic was not happy about it.

"Why did you block my attack, Antoinette?" he yelled at her. "You heard what he said. He is close to Paragor himself! Why?"

"That's him," Antoinette answered. "Don't you see? I had to save him!"

"What?" Aelic squinted at her.

"It's Robby's Glimpse!" Antoinette cried. "I had to save him!"

"They were fortunate to escape," said Queen Illaria. She had gathered her advisers and highest-ranking braves. They sat with the twelve around a massive diamond-shaped table in the castle's largest hall. Their voices echoed slightly in the cavernous room. A great fire crackled on the hearth behind the Queen. Antoinette had her *Book of Alleble* open on her lap. She stared at Robby's picture.

"It was not fortune that saved them," said Aelic. "One of your servants forewarned them. They called him Old Toby. They had already mounted most of their steeds when we arrived."

"Toby!" the Queen exclaimed. "I ought to have known! He seemed far too interested in my plans concerning the Paragor Knights. I wonder what his price was!"

"For whatever he was paid in gold, he has paid an even dearer price," said Kaliam. "His body was found among the slain."

"Boldoak?" said the Queen.

"It was not one of our braves," said the deep-voiced knight. "He was hewn with an axe cruelly from behind. That is not the way of a Yewland warrior."

"Nor was this deed done by one of my knights," said Kaliam. "It is my guess that Toby outlived his usefulness to his masters. That *is* the way of Paragor and his ilk."

"I fear that all of Yewland will be in mourning for the Ancient One after Baldergrim arrives," said Queen Illaria. "To think that we allowed Paragor free passage on the Forest Road and our other wooded paths! Alas, that I did not foresee this end. Paragor will pay for his treachery."

"Paragor may indeed attempt to return by the Forest Road," said Sir Tobias. "He has a formidable army."

"If he does," said the Queen, "he will find the forest choked with thorns, and few of his soldiers will ever emerge from the trees."

"There is something that troubles me," said Kaliam, "and I would advise caution, Queen Illaria, should Paragor's troops return this way. When Paragor slew the Ancient One, he took something from inside his great trunk."

The Queen leaned forward. "What is this thing? And what threat does it hold?"

"I do not know anything as certain," he replied. "Nock's reading of the Ancient One's rings fills me with a creeping dread. The rings record that King Eliam hid something within its trunk when The Realm was very young. It was something that no one, especially not Paragor, was meant to find. I can only conclude that it is a relic of horrible power. Paragor went to great lengths to get it. And now that he has it, there is no telling what he will do."

Nock suddenly sat up very straight. "With this thing," Nock said, "do you think Paragor will have the power to raise the Seven Sleepers?"

"Seven Sleepers!" Boldoak bellowed. Nervous conversation buzzed among the Yewland commanders gathered there. "That is fearsome even to the stout among us! Nock, why do you dredge that thought before us?"

"We found the Sepulcher," Nock replied.

"It is real then?" whispered the Queen, and she slumped in her chair.

"We found it, by chance or by design, we do not know," Nock explained. "But the Sleepers stir, and the great blackwood trees that keep them in the depths are perishing. There is a foul menacing power at work there, and great packs of wolvin roam the forest at will."

"This is grievous news," said the Queen, "if Paragor could release such a nightmare upon us! Kaliam, what do you propose we do? Do we launch an assault on Paragor's forces? They muster at Baen-Edge."

"Nay, to fly into that unfriendly place without first knowing your peril would be a reckless venture!" Kaliam said. "Instead, alert all of your forces and make ready for war. If Paragor does return by the Forest Road, I fear you will need every shaft and blade in Yewland to defeat him. And even then, it may not be enough."

"There is wisdom in what you say," Queen Illaria replied. "Yewland will prepare for war. But what of you and your team? Will you at least go to Baen-Edge to track the enemy's movements?"

"No, there is still the matter of the imposter, Count Eogan," he replied. Antoinette looked up sharply. "We must pursue him to Acacia. By your leave, Queen Illaria, I would take twelve of Yewland's fastest dragon steeds for my team. We will fly to Acacia and see what Count Eogan has to say to real servants of Alleble!"

"But Kaliam!" Antoinette objected. "The enemy and whatever it is that he stole from the tree are in Baen-Edge. We can't just let them go!"

"We must first capture the imposter," Kaliam said. "That still is our charge."

"But they'll get away!" she pleaded, looking down at Robby's picture. "He'll get away."

Kaliam glared at her. Lady Merewen caught Antoinette's eyes and motioned for her to be quiet.

"We must remember the objective, Antoinette," Kaliam said with finality. "Once we have the imposter, we will return to Alleble. King Eliam must be informed of all this, and we must learn the nature of this thing that Paragor has stolen."

"Your Majesty, Queen Illaria," Sir Gabriel said, standing. "We have discussed much, but we have not yet determined the standing of the allegiance between our two kingdoms. Have you not heard enough to soften your stance toward your true friends?"

"Baldergrim has not yet returned from the Blackwood," said Queen Illaria. "But I have always found Sir Nock to be trustworthy. And the confrontation in Kismet confirms what you claimed about Paragor's plans." The Queen stood and paced in front of the fireplace.

"Many years I ruled over a Yewland I thought divided by allegiance to your King. Count Eogan simply confirmed my private resentment, and I had an excuse to make Yewland independent once more. It was folly."

Sir Gabriel went to the Queen. "King Eliam does not wish to rob you of your position," he said. "Nor does he seek to force Yewland's allegiance. He asks for your trust, that you might willingly join Alleble to rid The Realm of fear and injustice. Queen Illaria, you and every Glimpse in Yewland are precious to King Eliam. Will you not honor our allegiance of old?"

The Queen reached into the folds of her gown and withdrew a long rolled parchment. "Here is my answer," she said and threw the parchment into the fireplace. "Never again, under my rule, will the alliance between Yewland and Alleble be shaken!"

"Kaliam, you shall have twelve dragons," said the Queen. "The swift White Wyrms, as are used only by my palace guards. In the morning, they will bear you to Acacia like a western wind! But tonight, while we await Baldergrim's return, stay and enjoy the hospitality of Yewland!"

Mallik turned to Nock and whispered, "The drink made from Golden Tear . . . I do not suppose we could come by any of that now, could we? I am weary and in need of refreshment."

"Yes, hammer-meister," the Queen said. "There will be Golden Tear to drink—an extra large goblet for you."

Mallik looked at Nock with eyebrows raised.

"Queen Illaria always did have the ears of a fox," he whispered.

"Yes, Nock, I have," said the Queen, and she grinned. "Now, go. Refresh yourselves. Be ready for a glad gathering. And not only that, but a merry feast as well!"

"Did someone mention food?" bellowed Sir Rogan.

"Yes, I believe I could eat an entire roasted blackhorne myself," added Farix.

And for the first time since the knights from Alleble had arrived in Yewland, Queen Illaria smiled out of gladness. "Hearty knights," she said, "I will see to it personally that the table is set for an army— though in truth it may only be for a few that feed like an army!"

The meeting was over. Much had been decided, and it seemed a weight had been lifted from the shoulders of the twelve.

"Come," said Lady Merewen. "I will show you to our chamber. There you may bathe before we are summoned to the meal."

Not even the idea of a much-needed bath could cheer Antoinette. She stood, clutching her *Book of Alleble*, and absently followed Lady Merewen.

In a few hours, a feast in the grandest sense was served—all the more satisfying when compared to the meager provisions the twelve had eaten during their long journey.

Yet Antoinette only picked at her food. She wanted to be loyal to the twelve, but she had promised Aidan to try to find Robby's Glimpse and then do what she could to convince him to turn to King Eliam. Now she had found Robby's Glimpse, Kearn, and he served at the side of Paragor himself. Even now he was returning to his evil master. Antoinette shook her head. She wanted to keep her promise to Aidan, but how could she without defying Kaliam's orders?

Caught in the Act

Aelic approached Antoinette on one of the more secluded balconies off the banquet hall. "What are you doing out here in the dark?" he asked.

"It's not really dark when your eyes get used to it," Antoinette replied. "Besides, the moon peeks out from the clouds every so often. It's really quite beautiful. Have you seen it?"

As if on cue, the clouds parted and a little moonlight fell upon the balcony. "Yes, very pretty." Aelic frowned. "I know you did not leave the feast to come gaze upon the moon."

"I needed to think," she said.

"And you could not think inside where it is warm and festive?"

"Are you kidding?" Antoinette asked. "With Mallik, Sir Rogan, and Boldoak having a belching contest, who could think in there?"

Aelic laughed. "I suppose you're right, m'lady. Still, there are many dark tasks ahead of us in the coming days. Why not be merry for just one night?"

Antoinette turned her back to Aelic and watched a carriage glide over the cable across the gulf from the castle to a platform. "I promised Aidan," she said.

"What? What did you—" Aelic squinted at her. "Oh, now I understand. This is about Kearn. Is it not?"

Antoinette nodded. "Aidan is counting on me! You said yourself that if King Eliam wanted me to reach Robby's Glimpse, I would find him. And now I have."

"But Antoinette, the fate of Robby's Glimpse is out of our hands," Aelic said. "Kearn has gone to Baen-Edge!"

"But we've got to do something!"

"Perhaps, m'lady," said Aelic. He moved forward to stand next to her at the balcony rail. "But it is not King Eliam's will for you to do anything about it now. Has it even occurred to you that once we return to Alleble, we may be sent out again—maybe to Baen-Edge—with an army?"

"But it could be too late by then!" Antoinette replied. "What if Paragor's forces return on the Forest Road? Kearn could be killed, and Robby would be lost!"

"That is true," Aelic replied. "And I sincerely hope that such a thing does not happen. My twin in your realm would be heartbroken—just as I have been heartbroken to see some of my friends in Mithegard and Clarion choose the wrong side." Antoinette looked away, avoiding his stare. She hadn't realized that Aelic too had seen friends join Paragor.

"But that does not change the fact that King Eliam has called you to be a part of this team on this mission. It is not his will for you to—"

"How do you know what King Eliam's will is for me?!" Antoinette asked, turning her back to him. "Did he tell you?"

Aelic ran his hands through his dark hair. "Nay, the King did not come to me personally. He did not have to. We were both chosen by the King to travel to Yewland and restore the alliance."

"And we've done that!" Antoinette spun around.

"But we have not captured the imposter," Aelic replied. "You heard Kaliam. We need to go to Acacia. That is our mission. Can you not see that?"

"Yes, I know what Kaliam said." Antoinette shook her head. "And he's a great leader, but I just can't sit here and do nothing."

Antoinette and Aelic stood in silence at the balcony rail. Antoinette's feelings were a train wreck. In truth, she had already decided what she was going to do long before Aelic came to the balcony. She had just hoped that Aelic would be more sympathetic. Now, she didn't know what to do. Should she still ask him? Would he give her away?

A bank of very dark clouds smothered the moon, and Antoinette stood in the shadows and trembled. "Come with me," she said quietly.

"What?" Aelic backed away from the rail.

"To Baen-Edge," she replied, staring at Aelic with pleading eyes. "Tobias let me look at one of his maps while I was at the feast. It's not that far. With two of the dragons Queen Illaria has provided, we could get there quickly—and maybe meet the others in Acacia later."

Aelic was speechless for a moment. His eyes narrowed, and he said, "And suppose we do what you suggest and we find Kearn in Baen-Edge, what then? Will you just command him to follow King Eliam? Do you think it will be that easy? There are four legions of enemy soldiers there—Paragor himself is there!"

"I don't know," she replied angrily, wishing she had not asked Aelic to join her. "I haven't really thought that far . . . maybe we can take him prisoner."

"You are right, m'lady," Aelic said. "You have not thought this through. I would go with you into the belly of a dragon—if I believed that King Eliam willed it to be so. I owe you my life, but, Antoinette, this is madness. To defy Kaliam's orders, to refuse to attempt the mission for which King Eliam has chosen us—that I cannot do."

Antoinette's shoulders fell. She had thought that Aelic would refuse, but hearing him say it still crushed her. They stared at each other for a long moment before Aelic turned to leave the balcony. "Aelic, wait," she said. "You won't—"

"I will not tell Kaliam," he replied. "Not tonight. I will wait and see what the morning brings. I am still hopeful that you will search your heart during the night and change your mind. But if the dawn finds you not among us, I will tell Kaliam everything."

Antoinette slowly closed her chamber door. Lady Merewen had not stirred for a long time, but still Antoinette did not want to risk waking her. She crept up the torchlit hall, padding barefoot on the cold stone floor. She passed Kaliam's chamber, Tal and Sir Oswyn's, the others'. But when she walked by the room where Aelic, Nock, and Mallik slept, she felt the tugging of guilt. Well, she did search her heart, she rationalized. But she had promised Aidan, and she refused to go back on her word.

Her first stop was a small anteroom near the balcony. She had left her boots there and stashed some waterskins, as well as food she had pilfered from the feast. She sat on a bench and looked into the satchel. Cheese, dried meat, a little bread—it was all there. She tugged on her boots and was off.

Earlier, she had scouted the castle and discovered the pens for the white dragons on the lower level. *Their pens are really set up like an airport,* Antoinette had thought. *The dragons step to the edge of the platform and,* whoosh, *they are gone.* Just like that. The pens had been busy too. Dragons were coming and going the whole time Antoinette watched, but she hoped that it would be quieter now in the wee hours of the morning. She wondered if there was a guard assigned to the pens all night long. She hoped not. There were other worries as well. For one, Antoinette had never ridden on the back of a dragon. She had no idea what she would do if they did not respond to the leg commands and reins like horses and unicorns. And supposing she did get a dragon off the ground and escape into the night, she wasn't altogether sure how to get to Baen-Edge. It was east of Yewland, and the Forest Road led to it more or less directly. If she could eyeball the road from the air, she reasoned, then she could find Baen-Edge. *Easy,* she thought. *Yeah, right.*

She trotted quickly down a spiral staircase and became a little disoriented for a moment. The door to the pens was supposed to be right at the bottom of the stairs. But no pens. Just a long hallway. She stared back up the steps and wondered how she could have gotten lost. At last, she realized what must have happened. She had missed the central stair in the upstairs hallway and wound up taking the stair at the end of the hall. She figured the door to the pens must be just farther up. And as she walked, the unmistakable scent of dragon pens made its presence known.

Antoinette found the pens and entered. No guards—so far, so good. She sat on a bench and started to double-check her satchel when—

"I thought I might find you here," came a voice from behind.

Antoinette jumped up, her hand going to the hilt of her sword. A tall, cloaked figure came out of the shadows. The figure lowered a dark burgundy hood, revealing long silver hair that rested upon her shoulders like layers of silk.

"Lady Merewen!" Antoinette gasped. "How did you—"

"How did I know you would come to the dragon pens in the middle of the night? Is that what you want to know?" Lady Merewen laughed.

Antoinette nodded. "Aelic didn't tell you, did he?"

"Nay," Lady Merewen replied. "He did not need to, for you gave yourself away. What else was I to think when you kept staring at that strange little picture—the one you pulled from the book—during our most recent visit with Queen Illaria? And the look in your eyes screamed of disappointment when Kaliam told you we would not go to Baen-Edge. Instead of enjoying the feast like the rest of us, you were out exploring the castle—at least I thought that was you I saw. But the decisive clue was that you wore your armor to bed! You have much to learn about being stealthy."

Antoinette sighed heavily. "So what will you do now? Turn me in?"

"That depends upon your reasons for wanting to go to Baen-Edge," Lady Merewen replied. She sat on the bench and motioned for Antoinette to sit next to her. A white dragon in the nearest pen woke up and peered with sleepy eyes over the gate at the late-night visitors. "Tell me now," said Lady Merewen, "what is so pressing in Baen-Edge that it cannot wait until we can return with the King's full armies?"

Antoinette reached into a leather satchel and removed the photo of Robby. She handed it to Lady Merewen. Then she explained everything about Robby's Glimpse and her promise to Aidan to help if she could. Lady Merewen nodded when Antoinette was finished.

"And so you fear any delay could have dire consequences for Aidan's friend?"

Antoinette nodded. "I have to do this," she said.

"Well, now that I have heard your tale," Lady Merewen said, "I will not stand in your way. But I will tell you what I think. In spite of your noble motives, I believe it is still a rash thing that you do. You will be flying into deadly peril, for Baen-Edge is a foul place, one of Paragor's chief trading partners. It is full of ruthless brigands. Villains from all over The Realm buy and sell illegal wares there. And Baen-Edge is notorious for its slave trade—I can only imagine what price you might bring since you are not Glimpse-kind."

Antoinette shuddered.

"If this Kearn is as close to Paragor as you say he is," Lady Merewen continued, "you will find it nearly impossible to gain an audience with him. And even if you do, he will not change allegiances easily. For he will not want to give up the power."

"What do you mean?"

"Glimpses serve Paragor for many reasons," Lady Merewen explained. "But chief among them are fear and power. Those who join the enemy out of fear can be turned. Fear of harm, fear of pain, fear of loss, fear of loneliness—all fade in the radiance of King Eliam's enduring love. They need only to learn that servants of Alleble are never alone!"

"Is that why you renounced Paragor and came to Alleble?"

Lady Merewen nodded. "It is, and I will never look back. But for those who crave power, the transition is far more difficult. If Kearn is one of these, he lives to control others—to rule over them. He finds meaning only if he is superior. And if he needs to enslave, torture, or kill Glimpses to establish his power, then he will do it. Powermongers of this kind have never been loved, and so love means nothing to them. If Kearn is one of these, then he feeds upon the fear of others."

"How can I reach him then?" Antoinette asked.

"You may not be able to," Lady Merewen answered. "That is why I urge you to reconsider your course of action. Do not go, Antoinette. Trust that King Eliam's plan for you is the right one. And wait to see what is in store."

"I'm going," she said.

"Very well," Lady Merewen replied. She handed a bundle to Antoinette. "Take this then. It is a fine hooded cloak, the finest from Alleble's market. It is light in weight, but sturdy against the wind—and prying eyes that would wonder about the color of your skin."

Antoinette stowed the bundle in her satchel and took a very deep breath.

Lady Merewen smiled sadly at Antoinette. "You are resolved, I see," she said. "I say this to you then. Seek a notch in Kearn's prideful armor. Find a way to make him trust you—even if that means you have to cut off one of his arms! Often those who use force will respect only force."

Antoinette nodded. "I will try," she said. "But, uh, there's one more thing. Do you know how to ride a dragon?"

Lady Merewen laughed. "Of course, and so do you! They will respond to your commands just like the unicorn. But remember to squeeze with your knees and feet. Do not kick."

"Why?"

"A sharp kick to a well-trained dragon means to loose a stream of fire!"

"Oh," Antoinette replied. "Good to know that."

BÆEN-EDGE

Antoinette sat upon the white dragon at the very edge of the platform. She leaned over, stared into the seemingly bottomless depths, and wondered how her choice might come back to haunt her.

"Well, dragon," Antoinette said, bending forward in the saddle and whispering, "do you have a name?" The beast emitted a timid growl that ended in something like a honk, and then it craned its long neck to look at Antoinette. Its eyes were large and golden-yellow. They were predator's eyes, keen and intelligent. They reminded Antoinette of owl eyes.

"Well, there's no way to know what your real name is, but I can't just call you dragon. You are truly beautiful and white. Maybe Snowflake or . . . Blizzard?"

The dragon honked again and shook its head. "No?" Antoinette asked. "Okay, how about something more fierce, like Raptor or Snowfire?"

The creature exhaled a puff of dark smoke. *Honk!*

"Oh," Antoinette said. "Okay, then. I'll call you Honk!" The creature nodded and flapped its wings. "Well, Honk, it's time to go!" She gave a slight flick to the reins and held her breath. The dragon folded back its wings, straightened its neck, stepped off the platform, and plunged at a terrifying speed. Antoinette felt light in the saddle, as if at any moment she might lift free. She pulled back on the reins, but still they gathered speed.

"Honk!" Antoinette screamed. "Pull up! Fly! Do something!"

And at last the white wings spread, and the dragon soared back up into the sky with one very relieved rider on its back. They sailed quietly over the treetops. Behind her, Antoinette could see Yewland's green castle outlined softly by torchlights. She aimed to get to the Forest Road, so she nudged Honk to go back the way she thought the twelve had arrived. It was hard to tell, for the trees were gray and featureless in the night.

The trees suddenly spread, revealing a great clearing. And there were pale lights shimmering in the foliage. Antoinette urged Honk down and saw that there were huge flowers there, glowing faintly in the fading moonlight.

Moonblossoms! Antoinette thought, and she knew it was the glade where Baldergrim had met them. It was not long after that she came to the Forest Road. Honk seemed to recognize the road, too, for the dragon began to follow its dark line from high above. Antoinette nibbled at dried meat and let her mind wander. The hours went by quickly. The sun rose red in the eastern sky, and the forest gave way at last to plains clothed in tall grasses and short, windswept trees. Harsh knees of stone poked up and then sparse foothills with cavelike crags. Here and there a river, like a ribbon, wound below, and the terrain began to change. The land rose up in folds and bulges. The river widened and cut a swath through the rolling hills. And Antoinette finally saw what she had been searching for. There was smoke far ahead in the gray sky. It was a dark shroud of smoke fed from many fires.

"That must be Baen-Edge," Antoinette said, patting Honk on the neck. "Good job getting me here in one piece!"

The land below became filled with irregular cottages, and twisted fences cordoned off the many plots of land that ran along the southern edge of the river. She knew the city of Baen-Edge was actually two towns, divided by the river, but she wasn't sure which side was Baen and which was Edge. A few Glimpses saw Antoinette as she flew overhead. They pointed and some waved. *Doesn't seem so bad of a place,* Antoinette thought. Then an arrow whizzed by her ear.

Okay, I spoke a little too soon! Antoinette steered quickly away, and whoever had shot at her gave no pursuit. Honk flew toward a hill crowned with a patch of trees. The dragon circled it once and then floated down. Antoinette dismounted and said, "I'll need to leave you someplace safe for a bit."

She rummaged around in the supplies she had packed around the creature's saddle, grabbed the cloak from her satchel, and put it on. Then she withdrew a half wheel of cheese and put it in the pouch that hung from her belt. She patted Honk on the head and said, "Stay here . . . and don't eat anyone unless you absolutely have to!"

The dragon rolled its eyes and crawled into a patch of feathery ferns. Antoinette tightened her sword belt, drew the hood close to her face, and set off on foot. She followed a dry and dusty road that snaked through patches of trees and stretched beyond the hills ahead. Around one bend, she came upon three Glimpse children who were gathering branches for firewood near the edge of the road.

The littlest one, a girl, Antoinette thought, dropped her stack of wood and pointed. The three stared at Antoinette as she approached. Antoinette stared back. These children were filthy, dressed in soiled rags, and dangerously thin. Their eyes twinkled green.

"Excuse me," Antoinette said, and they backed away. "No, it's okay. I won't hurt you."

"Yer not from around 'ere, are you?" asked one of the boys. He was sandy-haired and looked maybe six or seven years old. "Look at 'er skin!"

"Is it weel?" asked the girl, enunciating poorly.

Antoinette laughed. "Yes, it is. And you're right. I am from a very faraway place."

"Where is yer master?" asked the other boy, the tallest of the three.

"My master?" Antoinette stared.

"You know," said the first boy. "The one who brings you 'round the market."

"Everyone 'as a master. My da tole me so," said the girl, nodding continuously.

"Well," Antoinette replied, kneeling to look at the girl, "I don't have the kind of master you are talking about. But I do serve a very great King. He lives in the land of Alleble."

"Alleble?" The tall boy scrunched his face and looked at Antoinette. "I 'ave never 'eard a such a place. No masters, really?"

"It's true," Antoinette said. "Now, I need some help. I am following a group of soldiers in dark armor. Have you seen them?"

"I daresay we 'ave," said the sandy-haired boy. "Couple days ago, they came through 'ere. A whole bunch of knights, far as the eye could see!"

"Fousands and fousands," agreed the girl.

"But they went to the other side of the river," he said. "To the marketplace on Edge-side."

Antoinette smiled. "No, this would have been yesterday late in the afternoon. And there were probably only about fifty."

"Oh, them," replied the tall boy as he wiped his nose with his entire arm. "I saw 'em. They 're still 'ere I think. Down Whitchap Lane. Ferries come there, you know."

"Do you think you could tell me how to get there?" Antoinette asked.

"What is in it fer me?" he replied.

Antoinette looked into her pouch and realized with dismay that Kaliam had never replaced the coins she had lost in the Blackwood. Of course, Kaliam hadn't expected Antoinette to leave Yewland in the middle of the night either. "I, uh, don't have any gold," she said.

"Who does? . . . Well, I guess the masters do," said the boy.

"What else ya' got in there?" the girl asked, and the three of them stretched their necks to look into Antoinette's pouch.

"How about . . ." Antoinette fished around. "How about I give you each a wedge of cheese?"

"CHEESE?!!" the little girl screamed. "You mean real cheese like they 'ave in Edge?"

"Shhhh, yes, I suppose," said Antoinette. "I'll give you each a wedge if you'll tell me how to get to Whitchap."

"Done!" said the boy. And after he had given the directions, Antoinette drew her dagger and cut her half wheel into thirds. It left her only half the wheel, and she'd have to go back to the dragon to get it, but she knew they needed it more.

"Oh, fank you!" cried the little girl, holding up the hunk of cheese and spinning in happy circles. The boys greedily tore at their hunks. Antoinette donned her hood and started to leave, but the tall boy put a grimy hand out.

"Lady?" he said. "Careful at Whitchap. Bad folk, there are. It is no place fer a lady like you."

Antoinette followed the boy's directions. But the trip was cheerless, for everywhere she looked there was squalor. Glimpses lived in roof-less homes and toiled away at fields where very little seemed to be growing. Rubbish fires burned at every corner. And a foul stench was in the air. In an hour she came to a post on the side of the road. It leaned and the sign upon it was cracked. Antoinette brushed the grime away and read the sign. Whitchap.

Homes gave way to taverns and wretched shops where discol-ored meats hung from thatched rafters. Slovenly, weather-beaten Glimpses stood in shadowed doorways and stared at Antoinette as she passed. One of them, a crooked-looking fellow with wrinkled slits for eyes and a mustache that reached down to his belt, fingered the edge of a dagger and spat on the ground. He shifted a bit and leered at Antoinette. Uncomfortable, Antoinette walked with one hand always on the hilt of her sword, and kept her cloak and hood drawn close to conceal that she was not Glimpse-kind.

The sun, which had been high in the sky, disappeared behind low gray clouds. *Rain*, Antoinette thought. *And soon.*

She followed the curving road until it came to a river. Long, shallow craft moved back and forth across it, bearing passengers. *The ferries!* Antoinette thought.

The ground sloped gradually, and as Antoinette looked toward the bottom of the hill, she noticed that some of the shops and dwellings there were built on stilts. The river, it seemed, would swell and flood, and the Glimpses of Baen had learned to build with that in mind. A long blockhouse sat at the edge of a wide apron of boardwalk, and a tall turret stood guard beside it. Gathered at the base of the tower, like swarming insects, were soldiers in black armor. They had already begun boarding the ferries. Having no idea what she would do when she caught up to them, Antoinette dashed down the hill.

Just fifty yards from the dock, Antoinette suddenly tripped. When she looked up, the crooked Glimpse with the long mustache was there. He grinned at her and held his dagger in one hand, a notched sword in the other. "Where you goin', pretty thing?" he asked, his voice phlegmy and coarse. He stared all the more now that her hood had fallen.

Antoinette stood up, brushed herself off, and looked over at the dock. The last of the Paragor Knights were boarding the ferry! If she didn't hurry, they would be gone. She turned back to the crooked man. "Leave me alone," she said.

"Oh, deary me," he replied, shuffling closer. "I hope I haven't gone an scared ye'. Don't ye be worried 'bout ole Paddock. I mean ye' no harm."

Antoinette drew the Daughter of Light from its sheath. Thunder rumbled, echoing from across the river, and rain began to fall. Antoinette turned away from Paddock and saw a heavy, bearded man closing a gate on the ferry. She sensed Paddock moving at her side. She slashed her sword in a vertical arc toward him. He stepped back, easily avoiding the stroke. "Do not come any closer!" Antoinette warned. "You'll regret it if you do."

Paddock spat on the ground. "Oh, so a sword in your hand and some plate armor are to scare me, now, are they? Nay, strange, dark-skinned beauty with hair aflame, you don't frighten me. Let us have a bit of fun, eh?" He lunged at her with the notched sword. Antoinette batted it away, but his dagger clipped her shoulder and dragged across the mail. He was faster than he looked. Antoinette needed to be more careful, but she could not wait. If the ferry left and Kearn met up with the other four legions of Paragor's soldiers, all hope of reaching him would be lost.

She charged forward, the Daughter of Light slashing right to left and then chopping high to low. Paddock stumbled backward, righted himself, and slashed back. His blows were becoming weaker. He was tiring, but she was always mindful of the dagger.

"Wait!" cried Paddock. "You're one a them from Alleble! I can see it on yer armor. Yeah, you are." He spat. "I bet I'd fetch a pretty price fer you over the water."

Water! Antoinette looked back at the dock. The wind had picked up and whitecaps appeared on the river. The ferry had started to pull away from the dock. But just then, someone leaped off the back of the boat. He wore a dark hood and his cape sailed behind him as he charged ashore toward Antoinette. The wind gusted, pulling his hood away and revealing the knight's long blond hair. *Kearn*, Antoinette realized, and he had drawn his sword.

Something made Antoinette turn around just in time. Paddock tried clumsily to grab her shoulders, but Antoinette whipped her blade inside out and opened a huge gash on Paddock's hand.

He dropped his dagger and cursed. "Arghh! My hand! You filthy maid! No price is worth this trouble. I'll cut you in half!" He swung wildly. Antoinette blocked with her sword and shoved his blade away such that it spun Paddock around. She put her foot on his back and pushed. He sprawled face-first onto the muddy ground. He did not stir.

"Turn to me, swordmaiden from Alleble!" a voice demanded from behind. "I would not slay a woman when her back is turned!"

Her blade vertical in front of her, Antoinette spun around to face Kearn. And for a moment, Antoinette's will quailed. Kearn was menacing, a living shadow, garbed all in black with his wide cape floating behind him on the wind. He seemed much taller than he had in Yewland. His green eyes smoldered, and when they flashed red, it was like torches kindling. His long hair hung in wet locks like tarnished gold upon the brow of a dead king. And kingly he looked, but dreadful. Not to be adored, but always to be followed. He slowly raised his sword—a doublewide blade, black at the hilt but gradually brightening to silver and tapering to a cruel point.

"The upper hand was yours by chance in Yewland," he said. "But you find yourself alone now."

"I am never alone!" Antoinette replied, but her mind flickered with doubt. She had, after all, ignored Kaliam's orders and abandoned the mission for which the King had called her.

"Oh, but you are," Kearn hissed, circling slowly to Antoinette's right. "You are alone. I see it in your countenance, and your eyes tell a sad story. For you are not of this world. You . . . do not belong here."

Suddenly, he lashed out—two strokes, swift and heavy. Antoinette blocked them, barely, and a numbing shiver crawled over her hands. She had the feeling that he was measuring her, testing her strength and, possibly, her resolve.

"You have some skill with a sword," Kearn said, and he smiled. "I am glad. For I would feel cheated if I missed the ferry for only a quick kill." Antoinette looked over his shoulder, and indeed the ferryboat full of knights was already far from shore.

He came at her again, horizontal strokes this time. One at her ankles; the other near her shoulder. Antoinette darted backward, parried the strikes. She had never defended against such strength before. His blade carried the weight of a hammer. Again, only two strokes, and then he backed away.

"I wonder," Kearn said, "why it is that you have come this way, so far from safety, and legions of my master's army so near."

"I came for you," Antoinette said. For a split second, Kearn's sneer vanished. His sword dropped an inch. But then he mastered himself.

"Then you came for death," he said, but he nodded knowingly. "Ah, I understand now. They do not know that you are here, do they? Or, better, you defied them to come to me? Hmmm, is that it?" Antoinette looked down for a moment, away from his eyes. He seemed to look right through her. "That was a bold venture," Kearn said. "I see now! That is why you defended me from that coward who meant to strike me in the back! You heard that I am the master's left hand, and you sought to gain my favor. Very well, then. You shall have it. My Prince would welcome such bravery, especially with my blessing."

Antoinette shook her head. How had things gotten so backward? She had come there to turn him to Alleble! And here Kearn was recruiting her! Something had to be done. What was it Lady Merewen had said? Even if it means cutting off one of his arms, make him respect you. *Okay.*

Antoinette feigned a thrust at Kearn's stomach and swept her blade up at his face. He dodged only just in time. Antoinette held her blade above her head, the tip pointed at Kearn. She crouched low, like a tiger ready to pounce. "You misunderstand me," she said, "if you think for one moment that I could join you. You are on the wrong side."

"Hasty words spoken by one who has already come half the way," Kearn replied. Thunder rumbled, and the rain came harder. "You have already betrayed those you once served, have you not? It is merely the next step you seek. And why not? There is much to be gained. I have legions at my command, vaults of precious things. So could you, m'lady."

"Antoinette," she said. "My name is Antoinette." As soon as the words were out, she regretted them. Why had she told him her name? She was about to say something, but that wasn't it. It just came out.

"Antoinette?" Kearn echoed, grinning. "There, you see? I have power, magnificent power—given to me by the Prince. What has your so-called King given you? Come, the next ferry nears. Let it bear us both hence to power and glory. Will you not consider what I offer you?"

Antoinette felt a strange feathery sensation all around her. It was not peaceful, but more like gentle coaxing from unseen hands. There was something attractive about being powerful. Lightning flashed overhead. Thunder cracked and rolled ominously. She felt for a moment that if she joined Paragor, she would never have to be afraid again. She would never have to fear what could happen to her or the ones she loved. With that kind of power, she could put down all threats. She would have control. . . .

NO!! The thought crashed into her mind. Antoinette convulsed as if startled from sleep. Kearn was so close to her that she could feel his breath on her face. She recklessly slashed her sword at him and backed quickly away. "No! I will never join you!" she said.

"Pity," was his only reply. He leaped into the air and brought his sword crashing down on top of her. Antoinette's block was not firm enough. He knocked her backward, and she stumbled. Her arms throbbed with fresh pain. He pressed the attack with sharp measured strikes, hacking at both sides. Antoinette backed away. Suddenly, she felt a stair behind her. She turned and leaped up onto the porch of the blockhouse. But Kearn followed. He swung for her neck, but Antoinette blocked it. His blade came back too fast. She ducked and his sword crashed through a wooden beam. The roof caved about a foot and scraps of rotting wood fell from above.

"So much could have been yours, Antoinette," he said, stalking her along the porch. "It might still be. Put down your sword. Come with me."

"No!" Antoinette screamed. "What you call power is only cruelty! You control through fear, but you do not have love!"

Then she realized what he had done to her. He had made her doubt. Made her uncertain about herself—uncertain even of King Eliam. She had not been focused. She had forgotten her own skill in awe of Kearn's. Antoinette heard again the echo of Lady Merewen's words: *Make him respect you.* And Antoinette remembered her skills. The years of practicing kendo forms and sparring—it all came back.

She raised her sword, the tip straight up at the sky. She bent at the knees, one foot slightly forward. Her upper body was straight and very still. She felt coiled and ready to spring. Antoinette waited, and Kearn did exactly what she expected him to do.

He lunged at her, bent on running her through. Antoinette swerved to the side more quickly than Kearn ever dreamed she could. She loosed a back kick into his side as he passed. Kearn crashed down the stairs. He landed in a heap. His sword stabbed into the mud a couple of yards from where he fell. He was up quickly, though. He yanked his sword out of the muck and turned. Antoinette was already there. The Daughter of Light slashed at him again and again. And then his broad, heavy blade, for the moment, was no longer an advantage. It was slow. Kearn backpedaled.

Antoinette had to be careful. If she killed him, she failed. Robby would be lost. No, she had come to reach him, to turn him from evil. Antoinette chased him out into the road. "I came after you, Kearn," she said. "Not to join you, but to rescue you!"

"Rescue me?" he spat. "From what, pray? I have thousands of knights at my call. The mighty Prince of Paragory himself defends me. There is nothing in The Realm that can harm me!" He lunged at her. The great blade knocked her off balance, and she was forced to retreat. He pursued, striking with renewed fury. Antoinette defended and struck back. Their struggle ranged all over the road. Lightning flashes reflected in their swords, and the rain became a deluge. Still they fought. And it seemed that their skills were nearly equal, for neither could gain an advantage for long. They dueled at last up onto the dock. And, more than once, they came perilously close to driving each other into the river.

Then Kearn took his sword in his left hand and thrust it at Antoinette's right shoulder. Antoinette swept it away with a two-handed slash, but Kearn struck her in the face with the full fist of his free hand. The blow was mighty. The steel of his gauntlet drove into Antoinette's jaw and she staggered backward. Her ears rang, and she swayed for a moment. *King Eliam, help me!* she cried out in her mind.

Kearn came at Antoinette again, seeking to finish her, but she shook her head and stood. He rained down blows—but her sword answered, and she parried each attack. Kearn became enraged, for she simply would not relent and perish.

Suddenly, a shadow appeared in Antoinette's peripheral vision. Someone was behind her and held up a dark blade, ready to strike. Antoinette whipped her sword around and thrust it backward, under her arm. She heard a hoarse groan and turned in time to see Paddock's eyes. He groped at his wounded stomach and fell away into the river.

When she turned back, it was too late. Kearn wheeled his sword around and hacked into Antoinette's side. The armor she wore was good armor, and it absorbed most of the force of the blow. But the sword was also sharp. It cleaved the breastplate right along her ribs and opened a gash there. Antoinette fell to the dock and clutched at her side. Lightning flashed, and Antoinette heard deep, throaty cheers. She looked out on the river. Not far from shore, a ferryboat drifted among the whitecaps and the spray. Within the boat were at least twenty of Paragor's soldiers. They had come back to retrieve their commander.

"You see!" shouted Kearn triumphantly. "You are utterly alone, and you will die utterly alone! Your King is powerless to stop me, for this is the fate that is ordained for all who oppose my master. You will fall. Alleble will fall. It has been foretold!"

Foretold? Antoinette winced. Pain throbbed and blood ran warm down her side. *What did he mean?* She looked up at Kearn and to the river. The enemy knights were almost there. Finally, she jabbed her sword into the dock and dragged herself to her feet. And suddenly, she was not there anymore. She was in the dark chamber below the Castle of Alleble. There were two white pedestals before her. On one, a scroll. On the other, a sword. And she heard the mortiwraith scratching to get in. And she remembered . . . the sword did not save her then.

And the sword would not save her now. *I trust you, King Eliam.*

And there she was again, back on the dock. She looked Kearn in the eye and sheathed her sword. His eyes flashed and he rushed her. Antoinette swayed, lowered her head a little as if resigned to her fate.

Kearn had the pommel of his sword tucked into his side and directed the tip of the blade at her chest. He charged at her as if jousting with a lance. The knights in the boat exulted, awaiting the kill.

Kearn thrust his blade into Antoinette up to the hilt. But Antoinette had twisted slightly to the side. Kearn's sword did not penetrate, but instead raked across the left side of her breastplate under her arm. Antoinette clutched her arm to her side and at the same time turned inward, pinning Kearn's sword to her side for a moment. Then, she drove the sharpest part of her right elbow as hard as she could under Kearn's chin.

Kearn reeled backward, blood streaking down the sides of his mouth. He still held his sword, but weakly. Antoinette loosed the Daughter of Light and hacked away at the wide blade of her enemy. He blocked, but his guard went lower and lower.

Finally, Antoinette hammered high at his right shoulder, and he was not fast enough to block it. The armor split. Kearn screamed. His blade tumbled out of his hand. Antoinette planted a sidekick into the center of his chest. He crashed to the ground and lay still on his back. Antoinette pounced. She pressed her sword to the neck of her fallen enemy. But she did not kill him.

"I do not understand," Kearn said, his eyes staring beyond Antoinette for a moment. "He promised me."

And then he focused and stared at Antoinette. "Do it then," he said. His eyes flashed defiantly, but there was fear there also. "Get it over with."

Antoinette lifted her sword away from Kearn's neck and sheathed it. She said, "The reason I defended you back in Yewland is the same as the reason I spare you now. I will not slay one who would go into forever not knowing his true peril."

Kearn opened his mouth but found no words. He lifted a hand

and pointed to Antoinette. She looked down at her right side and saw dark red blood. She felt lightheaded and her vision began to gray at the fringes. Suddenly, an arrow whooshed by her ear. Another struck her shoulder but sprang back.

She looked up and saw the Paragor Knights scrambling up onto the dock from the ferryboat. She tried to run but felt dizzy. It was no good. They would catch her or put her down with a shaft. She knew they would. So Antoinette did the only thing her clouded mind could think of. She dove into the river.

As she slipped beneath the surface into the cold embrace of the current, she thought she heard voices. They were faint as if in a dream.

"You three, get downriver," one voice said. "Finish her off."

"No," answered a commanding voice. "She is gone already."

And Antoinette knew no more.

ONE GOOD TURN

Antoinette awoke and found herself staring into gigantic golden-yellow eyes. Something coarse and wet lapped at her cheek, and she heard a purring growl, followed by, *Honk!*

She turned her head, and there was the snow-white dragon that had borne her from Yewland. "Honk!" Antoinette cried, and she tried to sit up. Pain streaked up her side.

"Easy there, lass," came a deep, folksy voice. "Now, you lay yerself back down thar and give that wound time to seal." Antoinette turned her head the other way and saw a tall Glimpse with a wide brown beard and kind blue eyes. And standing beside him were three children. Two boys and one small girl.

"I thought you was dead," said the little girl, and she stepped to Antoinette's side and grabbed her hand. "Da, she's the one who gave us the cheese this morning!"

"Is she now?" said the father, patting the girl on the head.

244

"Well, Alyth, one good turn calls another, or so it is said." He turned to Antoinette. "Your dragon brought you 'ere just before sundown. You were sopping with a mortal wound on yer side."

"The river," Antoinette mumbled.

"I thought as much," he replied, and he lifted a cloth that lay across Antoinette's side. "You can thank the stars that the water is cold this time of the season. The only thing that kept you from bleeding away to nought."

Antoinette smiled. She did not thank the stars, but voiced a silent thank you to the one true King.

"Smart dragon, that!" said the Glimpse. "Bringin' you here, that is."

Antoinette turned and smiled weakly at Honk. "I'm glad you didn't stay in your hiding spot," she whispered. The white dragon ducked its head shyly.

"Y'know there are folk in Baen who would just as soon cook you in a stew . . . or leave you fer dead. Myself, I was not sure what to make of you, dressed in fine armor like you are. The littlins here said you are a kindheart, so I took you in."

"Thank you, sir," Antoinette said weakly, but she tried again to get up. "My name is Antoinette."

"Now, then, Lady Antoinette, you just lay back down! I told you, yer wound must seal. I put a fair amount of ruddy wet clay on the gash. The bleedin's stopped, and it'll mend fine—if you let it be for a bit." He went to another room and brought back a waterskin. "'Ere now, drink a bit of this," he said, putting it to her lips. "It'll be a wee bit tart, but that's the dormer herb. Then you'll rest a bit."

"But Kearn," Antoinette mumbled. "And the other knights . . . they'll get away."

"Rest now, Lady Antoinette."

"Maybe just a little while," she replied, but soon she was fast asleep.

———

"'Ello!" said the tall boy. He smiled broadly at Antoinette. "Da! She's awake!"

The bearded man came back into the room. "So she is! There now, that was a good nap. I'll wager you feel a bit better!"

Antoinette found that she could sit up. There was dull pain in her side, and her jaw still ached, but it was nothing like before. "That's amazing," she said. "The pain is almost gone. Thank you again."

"Yer color's changed," he replied. "You were looking a lot like us for a while there."

"Yer a right regular healer, Da!" said the boy.

"Thank ye, boy," he replied. "I can't take much of the credit. The sleep was what she needed. Now, you git out with Alyth and Gregg. Fetch the wood, hear?"

"Yes, Da!" the boy called over his shoulder and was gone.

"I slept how long?"

"The sun has just come up on the second day since yer dragon brought you here."

"Two days . . . ," Antoinette muttered to herself.

"What brings you to this bad corner of The Realm?" the father asked. "You are not Glimpse-kind, yet you wear the armor of Alleble, and the littlins say you've got no master."

Antoinette swung slowly around to face him. "I am from the Mirror Realm," she said. "I am not a slave to any master, but I willingly serve King Eliam of Alleble."

"It is not safe for you here—nor for us—if you stay. If the Watchman come by, he will take you away, and no mistake."

"I will leave," she said. "I do not wish for any of you to be harmed on my account."

"I am sorry, m'lady. I would like to do more." The father looked down. "It is not like me to put a lady out in the street, but the littlins . . . I cannot see them hurt."

"You have saved my life. I do not wish to endanger your lives. I feel well enough to ride. I will be fine," she said gently. "Is there anything I can do to repay you?"

He shook his head, but Antoinette had an idea. "Where is Honk?"

"The dragon?" he asked. "Behind the cottage, under the gable."

He led Antoinette outside, and Honk was there. Sound asleep. "Wake up, sleepy beast!" Antoinette said. The dragon opened its jaws in a great yawn. The creature wandered drowsily out from under the gable and stretched its vast wings. Antoinette climbed into the saddle and reached into her satchel for a small loaf of black bread and the half of the cheese wheel, which was almost all the food she had left.

"Please take these," she said, and she put them into his hands.

The bearded Glimpse stared. "Why, this is three months' wages," he said. "Even if I could save it. But, no, it is too rich a gift."

"I want you to have it," Antoinette said. "You have three little ones to feed."

"That I do," he said. "And they do eat something fierce."

"I'd better go," Antoinette said. "I was pursuing a soldier—a Paragor Knight. He and his men took the ferry."

"They've gone to Edge, no doubt," he said. "To join the others. A fair army came through here not three days ago, tramplin' as they went. Never seen so many knights. You know your own business, but I'd steer clear a' them if I was you."

Antoinette smiled grimly. She knew he was right. She should stay away from Kearn and his armies. She knew she should fly immediately back to Yewland or to Acacia to meet up with the rest of the twelve.

"And, Lady Antoinette," Da said, "be careful in Edge. It is a different sort that lives there. You will stand out in the town proper, and no mistake. Keep your hood up." He looked down at his feet. "I wish there was something more I could do for you."

"I'll be all right," she replied. "Tell the little ones I said good-bye. They are brave, and I owe them much more than I will ever repay."

He nodded and smiled proudly. Antoinette pulled on the reins, and the dragon stretched its wings and leaped into the air. The ground fell away, and Antoinette looked west. She knew that was the way she should go, but she also knew that she wouldn't.

THE REDEMPTION
OF TRENNA

Antoinette steered Honk north and crossed the great river far from populated areas. The city of Edge appeared on the horizon, tall towers and grand castles. It was a stark contrast to the weather-beaten village to the south of the river. Antoinette brought the dragon down just outside of town. She found an old abandoned farmhouse in the hills that she thought would hide a white dragon with ease.

"Now, stay here!" Antoinette said. "Unless I need you!" She nuzzled her forehead against the cheek of her steed. "I'm not sure how you knew to come fish me out of the river, but I'm grateful. Just stay here. Stay hidden, okay?"

The dragon emitted a rumbling growl and honked twice. Antoinette left the farmhouse and clambered down a grass hill. Her side was still tender. She looked at the wound. It had healed amazingly fast, but it would leave another scar. *Again with the side! I need to work on my defense,* she thought. Antoinette quickly brushed off

Lady Merewen's cloak, which she had been wearing when she fell into the river. Now it looked rather dull and dirty.

From the farmhouse, it looked about a mile to the road leading into Edge, so Antoinette began to jog. As she ran, Antoinette wondered what she would do if she met Kearn there in the city. And what if the massive armies from Paragory were there with him? She remembered as well that Sir Gabriel thought Paragor himself was with his troops. What could she do against such forces? Antoinette hadn't the first clue. She only knew she had to try.

She wondered also what Aidan was doing back in the world she had left behind. *He better be trying to get Robby to believe!* Antoinette thought. *Wait until I tell Aidan what trouble he got me into.* She laughed, but then she thought, *No, I can't blame anyone but myself for the choices I've made. And I certainly deserve the consequences.* She felt the dull throb in her side. She had a strange feeling that her bruised jaw and a scar would not be the only consequences for abandoning the mission King Eliam had given her.

Antoinette pulled her hood and cinched it tightly to hide her flaming red hair. Since entering The Realm she had seen very few Glimpses with red hair, and she did not wish to risk drawing attention to herself. When she entered the town of Edge, she found it to be a bustling city of commerce. Everywhere she looked there were shops and stands where Glimpses were hawking everything from spiced muffins to magnificent coats of armor! She passed a small shop where gold rings of intricate design were displayed on burgundy velvet. A Glimpse craftsman withdrew a long pair of tongs from a nearby hearth and poured molten metal into an ivory mold. He set the mold down and stared up at Antoinette.

"Rarely have I seen such a dark-skinned beauty," he said. "You are not Glimpse-kind—that I can see." Antoinette felt very conspicuous, and she pulled her hood even tighter.

"No need to worry, m'lady," said the craftsman. "We get all kinds here. But there is a problem." Antoinette tensed. "Your lovely pink hand has no ring upon any of those remarkable slender fingers. I have just the thing."

Before she could say a word, he was already sliding an exquisite ring onto her finger. It was gold and silver interlaced in a serpentine fashion. A single blue onyx was set upon it and glistened in the sunlight. "There, now!" he said. "A riddle ring, more to it than meets the eye, there is—like you, I'll wager."

"A riddle ring? Why, it's beautiful," Antoinette said, turning her hand, but remembering she had no gold. "But I . . . I'll have to think about it. Did you make all of these?" She quickly changed the subject, slipping off the ring and handing it to him. "They are the finest I have ever seen."

The Glimpse turned pink in the cheeks, and his eyes glinted green. "Why, thank you, m'lady. But I think, then, that you have not seen much of what Edge has to offer. I am considered one of lesser skill. That is why I'm so far from the center of town. The town masters only allow the truly gifted ones to work the town proper."

"Well, I don't care what they say," Antoinette said. "Your work is marvelous."

The craftsman smiled broadly and bowed. Antoinette thought for a minute and asked, "I was told that a great army of soldiers from Paragory had come here for provisions. Do you know if they are still in town?"

"They were here as recently as yesterday," he replied. "But they do not spend much time on the Outskirts as they call us. Try the town proper." He pointed far up the avenue. "See those flags? That is where the finest weapons in The Realm can be bought. There are other things there too for those who can afford them."

"Thank you," Antoinette replied with a brief curtsy. "Good luck with the rest of your business. With your talent, I'm sure you'll make out well."

The craftsman grinned, hurriedly stepped around his stand, and pressed something into Antoinette's hand. She looked down and saw the gold-and-silver ring. "I couldn't," she protested.

"No, I insist," the craftsman replied. "You had no need to say such kind words to me. Few ever have. I do not care if I sell another thing this day, for I have met a pretty lady!" And just like that, he hopped happily behind his stand and went back to work, whistling while he did.

Antoinette slipped the ring onto her finger and smiled at the craftsman. He did not look up again. Antoinette hurried up the road, ignoring calls from other shopkeeps to come and look at their wares. She had the information she needed and forged ahead toward the flags. As she neared the town proper, there were fewer shops. But those that were there were much larger and offered many precious things. Antoinette saw brilliant tapestries for sale and throne-sized chairs carved from rich dark wood. The streets became more and more crowded as well. And those who milled about shopping looked like royalty. Glimpse men with embroidered surcoats and leggings strolled along with tall Glimpse ladies in elegant long gowns.

But still, there was no sign of Kearn. No sign of the Paragor Knights. Finally, she came to the place where the flags were. It was a wide square, lined with more magnificent shops and jam-packed with Glimpses. She could hear cheering and loud conversation from the center of the square, but she could not see what was going on. As she pushed her way through the crowd, Glimpses stared at her. Antoinette thought she heard a bit of conversation as a princely looking fellow and his wife wandered by.

"Did you see?" he said.

"How deplorable," she replied. "That cloak, so besmirched, really."

"She ought to stay in the Outskirts."

Antoinette shrugged. She was not there to win a popularity contest. She made her way over to a large shop that backed up to a castle wall. Again she heard cheers from the center of the square, and a loud voice called out, "Sold!"

Antoinette saw a Glimpse in ornate gold armor standing in front of a gated stairway. He looked like a guard or an official of some kind. Antoinette figured perhaps he would be able to help. "Sir," she said. He did not respond. "Excuse me, sir."

Still there was no reply. He seemed to be staring out over the heads of the crowd into the center of the square. "Hello, sir!"

"Yes, what is it?" he finally said. He glared angrily down his long nose at Antoinette. "Make it fast! I hear they have a live one today!"

"I was wondering if you have seen the Knights of Paragory. I was told they would be here."

"They were here," the guard replied gruffly, craning his neck to see over the crowd. He said nothing more.

"They *were* here?" Antoinette pressed on.

He looked down at her, annoyed that she was still there. "Yes, they were. A whole army. They left, what . . . four days ago? A smaller group came after them, left last night. Now, if you'll excuse me."

"Well, where did the smaller group go?" Antoinette asked.

"North," the guard replied.

Antoinette expelled an angry sigh. "Well, where did they go up north?"

"Look, m'lady," he said. "The Knights of Paragory are good customers. They buy a lot. They sell a lot. They do not meddle in my affairs. I do not meddle in theirs. I will tell you this, and then please go away. The whole lot of them, even their icy commander, went north. I daresay it wouldn't be to Clarion. Those folk will not parley with the red eyes, no, not on your life. Where else they might be going, I don't know. Now, move along, m'lady, or buy something." And with that, he turned, unlocked the nearby gate, and disappeared up the stairs.

Antoinette looked up at the sky. "Now what?!" she said aloud. Kearn and his troops were at least twelve hours ahead now. How was she supposed to find them? She figured she could take Honk and crisscross the wilderness until she caught sight of them, but who knew how long that would take. She had given away most of her food. What little provision she had left would not be enough for a long search. It seemed more and more likely that she would have to turn back.

From the center of the square, a sharp crack followed by an anguished scream pierced the air. Antoinette could not see what was happening over the thickening crowd. She heard a loud voice but couldn't quite make out the words. Cheers erupted from the crowd. She heard another crack and another scream. Then with a glance back the way she had come, Antoinette plunged into the crowd.

With numerous "Excuse me's" and "Pardon me's," Antoinette pushed through the masses of Glimpses. Some ignored Antoinette altogether, so focused were they on whatever was going on in the center of the square. Others looked at her darkly. Some shoved back. Still, Antoinette finally pushed through. She emerged between two extremely wide Glimpses wearing long fur robes. They looked down at her with disdain, but not for long.

"Who will open the bidding?" came a thunderous voice. And Antoinette looked into the center. There stood a huge Glimpse wearing a full coat of chain mail draped in a long fur. At his side was a broadsword. In one hand he held a whip. In the other, he gripped the end of a long chain. At the other end of the chain, shackled hand, foot, and neck was a young female Glimpse. She sat, splayed on the dusty ground, and clutched at her chains. Her extremely long dark hair covered her face and hung all about her.

"Come now, do not be shy!" called the warrior. "You will not find a better breed than this!"

"She doesn't look very tame to me, Ebenezer!" called someone from the crowd.

"Yeah," someone agreed. "She looks likely to bite the hand that feeds her!"

The crowd cheered and laughed.

"Nay, she is tame!" said the one called Ebenezer. "Watch and see for yourselves. Stand up!" he commanded her. "Let them have a look at you!" He cracked the whip near her ear.

Slowly, she stood. She wore a patched leather jerkin that stretched just below her knees. She shook her hair out of her face, and it fell down her shoulders to her waist. She had gleaming dark eyes that smoldered defiantly at the crowd. The master cracked the whip again, and she stared at the ground.

Antoinette was horrified. This girl looked to be about her age, and they were going to sell her!

"She's strong, and can be put to good use in your fields," Ebenezer roared. "Come now, I'll open the bidding at a modest price of two gold!"

"I'll give you one!" someone cried out.

"Nay, two is the starting bid, and it is a marvelous bargain. This lass is from Yewland. She is of the hunter breed."

She struggled against her chains. Ebenezer's whip clipped her shoulder, and she screamed. "Two gold! Who will make the offer?"

"Two! I'll give you two!" This from a balding Glimpse wearing a dark green gown. Ebenezer grinned. It had begun.

"Four, then!" said another.

"Excellent," Ebenezer bellowed. "You will not regret it. Just look at her. She is a rare mix of beauty and strength—a fine addition to your slave holdings!"

The girl looked up with pleading eyes, as if anwering Antoinette's stare. Antoinette had to help her. But how? Antoinette had no gold. And she couldn't rush out there and take on Ebenezer. If she did, she'd never escape. The other guards would pen her in.

"Ten gold!" called out a portly Glimpse wearing a red satiny tunic. He gestured with a hamlike fist with rings on every finger.

"That is more like it!" Ebenezer yelled. "Ten gold. Do I hear fifteen?"

"Fifteen!" said a thin older man with a mossy white beard and small shining eyes.

"Twenty-five!" thundered Hamfist. He looked at the thin old man and sneered.

"Twenty-five!" yelled Ebenezer. "That is a fair wage for property so worthy. But it is not unreasonable to think one might offer more. Do I hear a higher offer?"

The crowd muttered. The Glimpses turned this way and that,

wondering if any would bid. Antoinette felt sick to her stomach. She couldn't let this happen!

"Going once!" Ebenezer bellowed.

Antoinette stared into the slave girl's pleading eyes.

"Going twice!"

Antoinette drew her sword.

"Going—"

"Fifty!" the thin man interrupted.

The crowd uttered a collective gasp. The hamfisted Glimpse scowled, looked into a leather pouch at his waist, and scowled some more. The thin, bearded man shuffled forward to claim his prize.

"A moment, m'lord. I must still make the offer," said Ebenezer. "We have a daring bid of fifty gold! This from one who knows the value of a diamond in the rough. Is there not one among you all who would see it raised?" He pointed out into the crowd and turned to look eye to eye.

"Fifty gold, going once . . . twice . . . so—"

"Wait!" Antoinette cried. She rushed out into the center. "I would like to make a bid!" Ebenezer looked at her with great mirth.

"You are not one of the usual patrons," he said. "And by the look of you, I doubt very much that you can afford to bid."

"I do not have any gold," Antoinette said. Ebenezer laughed. The slave girl hung her head. "But I do have this!" Antoinette held out the Daughter of Light so that all could see the intricacy of its bird-wing crossguard, the detail in the engravings, and shining silver of blade and pommel.

Ebenezer reached for the sword, held it aloft, and stared. "Now, this . . . this is a worthy offer," he muttered. "Never in all my years have I seen—wait! Yes, I have seen craftsmanship like this before.

Naysmithe was the name. Naysmithe, once Sentinel of Alleble. It was he and none other who forged this blade!"

The thin beady-eyed Glimpse frowned, hands on his hips.

Ebenezer swallowed and stared at Antoinette. "You would part with this priceless blade?"

Antoinette felt suddenly guilty, for it was not really her sword at all. It belonged to Gwenne. *But then again,* she thought, *Gwenne is noble. If she were here in my place, she would do it. The girl's life is worth far more than a piece of metal!* The crowd muttered.

"Done, then!" Ebenezer said, and he handed Antoinette the end of the chain.

"Seventy-five!" yelled the old Glimpse. Ebenezer shook his head.

"One hundred gold!" He tried again.

"Did you not hear me?" Ebenezer yelled. "This blade is priceless! Take your gold and go home. This market is closed!" And with that, Ebenezer started to leave.

"Wait," Antoinette said, tugging on his robe. "You gave me her chains, but you did not give me a key to unlock them." The slave girl looked up suddenly.

"Here it is," he replied, handing her a long gray key. "But I would not release her until you have trained her well."

Ebenezer walked away, still marveling at the sword. The crowd began to disperse, except the old Glimpse. He stood there glaring at Antoinette as if he could cause her great bodily injury with his eyes. At last, he shook a cane at her and shuffled away.

Antoinette turned to the slave girl. "Follow me," she said. "As soon as we get out of town, I'll get these ridiculous chains off you." The slave girl nodded. Her eyes were so dark, like polished coal. But they glinted green.

Antoinette carried as much of the chain as she could manage. The two of them moved quickly through Edge-town-proper and finally into the Outskirts. Once beyond the city, Antoinette and the girl ducked behind a grassy hillock. Immediately, Antoinette took the key and began to unlock the shackles. "What is your name?" Antoinette asked.

"I am Trenna," she replied. "Trenna Swiftfoot."

"I'm Antoinette," she announced as she turned the key in the last lock. The heavy chains fell away to the grass. "Well, Trenna, you are free!"

Trenna fell at Antoinette's feet and wept openly. She began to kiss the tops of Antoinette's boots. "Hey," Antoinette said, kneeling and lifting her chin. "Don't do that! You don't know where my boots have been."

"You do not understand," Trenna replied, tears streaking her face. "Three years of my life I bore those chains! I had given up hope of ever being free. Then I saw you in the crowd. There was hope in your eyes, and behold! You paid a great price to redeem me! Why did you do this?"

"I was angry," Antoinette replied. "No one should be enslaved! We were all made to be free. In a way, that's what I've been fighting for since I've been in The Realm."

"You are a warrior then?"

"Yeah." Antoinette laughed. "I guess I am. I serve as a knight under King Eliam the noble ruler of Alleble."

"I know of Alleble," Trenna said. "The famous twin archers from my homeland went there and won great glory!"

"Nock and Bolt," Antoinette confirmed. "That's right, you're from Yewland. Did you know them?"

"How could I not? I made it my business to know every brave

or huntress who possessed such skill. I learned from the masters whenever I could."

Antoinette nodded and asked, "Trenna, Yewland is a free land. How did you end up in those chains?"

"I was distracted while hunting a clever wolvin in the forest on Yewland's southern border," Trenna replied, rubbing her wrists. "A dozen spearmen lay in wait for me. The hunter became the prey. But, Lady Antoinette, may I ask you something? You said that all must be free, so why do you then serve King Eliam?"

"All who follow King Eliam do so willingly," Antoinette said. "There was a time when King Eliam gave up something precious to save his people, and they have not forgotten it. I serve King Eliam because he loves me and wishes only to bring peace to The Realm."

"Then I will serve him too," Trenna said.

"What?" Antoinette stared.

Trenna's eyebrows arched high, reminding Antoinette of Nock. She looked at Antoinette quizzically. "You have set me free, Lady Antoinette!" Trenna said. "I deem that you did this in keeping with the precepts of your homeland. You follow the example of King Eliam, so I will follow him too. Just tell me how."

Trenna stood there, waiting. Antoinette wasn't sure what to say. She tried to remember how she first believed in Alleble. It wasn't really a specific memory though. Her parents had taught her, and she just accepted it. Then she thought about the ceremony where Kaliam invited her to make the good confession. *Yes, that's what we'll do!* she thought.

"Trenna," she said, "I think following King Eliam is the work of a lifetime—at least that's what my parents told me. But, it has to begin somewhere. So, let it begin here, now.

"Trenna Swiftfoot, do you give your service to King Eliam? Even if you are threatened by enemies who want to kill you, even then will you trust King Eliam? Answer aye only if it really shows what's in your heart."

Without a moment's hesitation, Trenna answered, "Aye!"

Antoinette grinned. "Then, Trenna, kneel before me." Trenna knelt on the grass and looked up expectantly. Antoinette reached down to her side, but then she remembered her sword was not there. She loosened her belt, removed the sheath, and laid it on Trenna's shoulder. "Trenna Swiftfoot, by your making the good confession, I now dub thee a willing servant of King Eliam the Everlasting!"

Then Antoinette watched as something wonderful happened—something she would never forget as long as she lived. Trenna's dark eyes gleamed green, but the color began to change. And suddenly the purest blue shone forth.

Antoinette embraced Trenna. "Welcome to the Kingdom of Alleble!" Antoinette said, and it was her turn to cry.

Back in the farmhouse, the white dragon sniffed Trenna from head to toe and honked twice.

"I think that means it likes you!" Antoinette said.

"You mean *she* likes me," Trenna replied. "Do not forget. I was raised in Yewland where beautiful steeds like this one abound."

"She, huh?" Antoinette laughed. "Will *she* bear the two of us?"

"With little trouble. We are both light, and she is a powerful creature, grander than many I have known."

"Good," Antoinette said. "Then we can go to Yewland together, and I can drop you off."

"What do you mean by 'drop me off'?" Trenna asked, her eyebrows arching again. "You will not drop me from the sky?"

"No! Of course not." Antoinette felt very awkward. How could she explain that she had left Yewland in secret to pursue a mission of her own—outside King Eliam's plan for her? How could she explain that to Trenna, who had just chosen to serve King Eliam? And Antoinette simply would not lie to her.

"Trenna, I can't stay with you in Yewland," Antoinette said. "I am chasing a soldier of Paragory, and his trail is already growing cold."

"One of the many who came through Edge?" Trenna asked.

"Yes," Antoinette replied. "He is one of their commanders. His name is Kearn."

"Has this Kearn harmed you?" Trenna asked. "Are you seeking revenge?"

Antoinette felt the dull throb in her side. "He has harmed me," she said. "But I don't want revenge. Oh, it's really hard to explain."

"Then you shall have to explain it to me as we seek Kearn together!"

"What?"

"I will not be *dropped off* at Yewland and allow you to fly into peril alone!" Trenna said.

"But don't you have family in Yewland?"

Trenna nodded gravely. "Yes, they are dear to me, and I will return to them as soon as may be, but . . . Lady Antoinette, you are family now as well. You bought me and gave me back my freedom. I am coming with you."

Antoinette was speechless.

"Besides," Trenna said, smiling mischievously, "you said yourself that the trail of the Paragor Knights has grown cold. My tracking skills will be of good use, will they not? Let us depart, for the sun is waning. And though I will easily follow the trail in the dark, I prefer not to."

Antoinette couldn't argue with that. She had no idea how she would find Kearn and the Paragor Army in the wilderness.

Trenna led Honk and the still-speechless Antoinette out of the farmhouse and into the golden light of the evening sun. Antoinette climbed into the saddle, and Trenna sat in front of her. "Now, while we search for the trail, tell me two things," Trenna said. "First, tell me why this Kearn is worth our pursuit. Then, explain to me how you came to Alleble, for you are not Glimpse-kind."

As Antoinette began to explain her adventure to Trenna, Honk took flight—effortlessly bearing her two passengers into the sky.

LEGEND OF
THE WYRM

Many Glimpses in Yewland are faithful to King Eliam," Trenna said, winding her long dark hair into braids. "Some of them told stories of the Mirror Realm. I always thought they were myths, clever tales to entrance the little ones. And yet, here you are, proof that they are true."

"People in my world find it hard to believe too," Antoinette said as they flew north of Baen-Edge, following the trail of the enemy.

"So I have a twin," Trenna said. "Only she wears skin like yours and lives on—"

"On earth," Antoinette explained. "And yes, your twin is out there somewhere."

"Amazing!" Trenna said. "And this Kearn?"

"He is a Glimpse of a young man named Robby, who happens to be very important to a friend of mine."

"I am amazed at you, Lady Antoinette!" Trenna said.

"Why?"

"You came all this way alone, risking your life for a friend!"

Antoinette sighed and ran a hand through her hair. It was time to tell Trenna the rest of the story. "I didn't come alone. There were eleven others. We set out from Alleble to come to Yewland, for Queen Illaria had been threatening to break up the alliance."

"What? Why?" Trenna asked.

"Well, that's what we wanted to know. We discovered that Paragor had sent an imposter to Yewland posing as an official from Alleble. This imposter, Count Eogan, made horrendous claims and nearly destroyed the alliance."

"What happened?"

"The imposter fled Yewland just before my team arrived. He apparently went to Acacia."

"Did you pursue him there?"

"No," Antoinette replied. She took a deep breath. "We were supposed to, but while I was in Kismet, I saw Kearn. I realized who he was, but he escaped. I wanted to go after him, but my commander insisted we follow the imposter to Acacia. I . . . I went against his orders, took this dragon, and, well . . . that's why I'm here instead of in Acacia with my team."

Antoinette wished she could see the expression on Trenna's face, but she could not. Trenna sat in front. Finally, Trenna nodded and said, "You should not have defied your commander. And it pains me to hear that you forsook the mission King Eliam assigned to you. And yet, I understand the division that strove in your heart. Growing up in Yewland, I lived with such division every day. One of my very closest friends could not understand why I would not follow King Eliam. I am not sure myself, really. I suppose I liked the idea of Yewland being an independent power in The Realm. How strange it is that now, when I finally acknowledge him as my King . . . it is due to your disobedience. I find it heartening in some ways."

"What do you mean?" Antoinette asked.

"It is good to know that King Eliam can make noble use of imperfect servants, that good can be made—even from mistakes."

They flew in silence for some time, each busy with her own thoughts as gradually a starry darkness claimed the sky.

Honk! The white dragon bobbed her head.

"She smells something!" Trenna said. "Smoke it is. Lady Antoinette, take her down."

With the heels of her boots, Antoinette applied gentle pressure to the dragon's sides. They circled quietly down into a grove of pines.

"The enemy's camp will not be far ahead," Trenna explained as they slipped off the dragon's back. "It will be better for us to go on foot."

"I feel naked without a sword," Antoinette said as they crept slowly through the trees.

"I cannot claim to be sorry you are without one," said Trenna, "for that blade paid my price. Surely slaying all of them was not your plan, was it?"

Antoinette was silent.

Trenna stared at her. "You do have a plan, do you not?"

"I haven't thought that far ahead," Antoinette admitted.

"Well, you may wish to begin thinking," Trenna whispered. "I see the flicker of a campfire ahead."

Antoinette crouched lower to the ground, for she saw the light ahead as well. Most of the trees were evergreens—for that she was thankful. Walking upon their needles made little sound. Still she was cautious. Whatever plan she decided on, it surely did not include being captured because she stepped on a dead branch. At least she didn't have to worry about Trenna. Apparently her experiences hunting had taught her to use great stealth, for she made no sound at all.

Antoinette and Trenna passed a clearing where a group of not less than forty dark horses grazed on ferns and tall grasses. The horses seemed not to mind the strangers who were crawling through their midst. Antoinette and Trenna followed a wandering path through more pines and came as close as they dared to a second clearing where the Paragor Knights were seated around a crackling fire.

Then, behind a hollow fallen tree, the two spies lay motionless and silent. Antoinette still did not have a plan, so she decided it was best to wait and listen.

"I am not one to question the master," said a gravelly voice. "But I still do not think it is true."

"Yeah, Grimmet is right. Why 're we botherin' with all this Wyrm Lord superstition anyway," answered another knight who obviously had his mouth half full of something tough and chewy. "We have enough troops to take Alleble down ourselves!"

"What, 'ave you got rocks in yer 'ead, Savadrel?" came a third voice, deep and throaty, full of contempt for the others. "Yeah, we might be able to knock down the enemy's front gate with what we've got. But should the plan fail, Yewland, the big chaps from the Blue Mountains, and all the rest a' the stinkin' allies will come chargin' in and run us down. We need an edge, I say." There was muttering among the many knights sitting near.

"Well, the plan's already failed in Yewland," said the knight called Grimmet. "I daresay we'll contend with those cursed bow-hawkers before we're done!"

"The plan in Yewland did not fail," came a new voice, low, confident, and menacing. Antoinette recognized it as Kearn's. "The master did not expect Yewland to change sides like so many of the weaker kingdoms have. Eogan's work there was simply to plant seeds of doubt—to purchase time and stay their hand until we have achieved our goal."

"That's just grand for now," said Grimmet. "But what about when we return? The trees along the Forest Road will be ripe with archers! What will we do then?" A dozen other knights grumbled in agreement.

"Faithless, you are!" Kearn hissed, and the other knights fell silent. "When our mighty Prince at last frees the Wyrm Lord from his tomb in the Shattered Lands, all will flee before us! It is no legend! King Eliam himself knows this. That is why he hid the scroll away in the old tree, where he thought no one would ever find it. And, as for the Braves of Yewland, there will be few enough of them when we return. For as the prophetic scroll decrees, the Wyrm Lord will call forth his allies of old. And the Seven Sleepers will again prowl the woods of Yewland!"

There were cheers and raucous laughter around the fire. Antoinette's eyes met with Trenna's, and what she saw there mirrored her own fear.

CAPTURED

Antoinette risked peering over the fallen tree and saw Kearn stand up and face his men. "Feast a little longer, recover your strength!" he said. "We have a hard ride still before us. Put all thought of fear and doubt out of your minds. Tomorrow we begin a season of victory."

Kearn leaned over and whispered something to one of his lieutenants and then stepped out of the firelight into the trees on the other side of the clearing. *Where's he going?* Antoinette wanted to know. She ducked down and turned to Trenna.

"I'm going to follow him," she whispered. "Maybe if I corner him one on one, he'll listen."

"And maybe he will put a dagger in your back!" Trenna replied. "That is your plan?"

Antoinette frowned. "Have you a better one?"

"Yes," Trenna said. "How about we both get out of here, right now? I do not know anything about this Wyrm Lord they spoke of, but I know enough of the Seven Sleepers to convince me there is great danger on the horizon. There are many in The Realm who must be warned!"

"I know, but I can't just leave without trying," Antoinette said. "Go back to the dragon. If I don't come back in twenty minutes, or if you hear them coming for you, fly out of here. Go to Acacia. Find my team from Alleble. A tall knight named Kaliam leads them. Tell him all that we heard. He'll know what to do."

"I will not leave without you," Trenna said indignantly.

"If I don't come back, you have to. Remember, you are not bound to me. You are a servant of King Eliam. This news must get to Kaliam." Trenna nodded grimly. She embraced Antoinette quickly and was gone.

What have I gotten myself into? Antoinette asked herself. She shook her head and crept away from the fallen tree. Careful to stay out of sight, she made her way around the clearing and into the darkness under the pines. She followed as best she could the direction Kearn had taken moments before. She moved slowly, placing each foot deliberately upon the carpet of needles. All the while, she scanned the trees.

The tension made her heart race, and her side throbbed in rhythm. Finally, she saw him. Antoinette crouched behind a wide pine trunk and stopped moving. He was standing at the edge of a fold in the land where perhaps a creek or rivulet flowed. His back was to her, and he gazed up into the western sky, seemingly at the moon.

"Come out of the shadows, Antoinette," he said without turning. Antoinette's heart hammered.

"How did you know?" she asked, and she stepped slowly out from behind the trees.

"I heard something among the horses," he replied. "There was a sense of disquiet with them, but not much. You were quite stealthy by the campfire. I heard only the rustle of a branch, the snapping of a twig." He turned around and faced Antoinette. His eyes flashed red.

"It was very brave of you to follow me alone," Kearn said. Antoinette sighed inwardly, for he did not seem to know anything about Trenna.

"I must confess," Kearn said, "it relieves me to discover that you survived the wound I dealt you. But it vexes me to wish anything other than your swift demise. I ought to kill you now."

There is something different in his tone. It might be humility, Antoinette thought. *Respect? Maybe.*

"I am unarmed," Antoinette said, lifting the edge of her cloak so that Kearn could see the empty sheath. "I sold it in Baen-Edge."

"Pity, that was a marvelous sword," he replied. "But that explains how you were able to follow me. Those greedy fools in Baen-Edge will do anything or tell anything . . . if the price is right. And any price is right."

Kearn circled slowly around Antoinette as he spoke. "You should have killed me when you had the chance," he said angrily. "Twice now, you have delivered me—your sworn enemy!"

"Does that bother you?" Antoinette asked.

"Yessss!" And he was practically in her face. "I bear the shame of being at the mercy of *my* enemy not once but twice!"

"It's more than that, Kearn, isn't it?" Antoinette asked. She tried to take his arm, but he shrugged her off.

"Do not touch me," he hissed and drew his sword. "It is harsh enough that I cannot get your face out of my mind. And I fear that killing you would do nothing but make your words ring in my head all the louder." He slashed his sword in the air. "Tell me, what did you mean when you said that I would go into forever not knowing my own peril?"

"I believe," said Antoinette, and she took a deep breath. "I believe that there is still time for you to change. If I had killed you, that time would have ended."

"Change?" Kearn scoffed. "What? To follow the weak ways of Alleble? I am Kearn, the left hand of Paragor!"

"You don't think I'm weak, do you?" Antoinette asked. Kearn rubbed his jaw and was silent for a moment.

"Yes, you are weak," he said finally. He began to march again, gesturing in the air with his sword. "You should have taken my life. And you are weak-minded if you think that I would renounce the power that I have, and the glory! In Paragory, I can snap my fingers and ten thousand knights are at my disposal. I am hailed a victorious champion, and they bow when I pass."

"But that's not all there is," Antoinette said quietly.

"What?" Kearn stopped suddenly. "What did you say?"

Antoinette stared into Kearn's eyes and felt an intense conviction growing in her heart. "I said, the power and the glory—that's not all there is."

Kearn laughed. "What is this nonsense you speak? Power and glory—and the riches they bring—that is everything!"

"No, no it's not, and when you die, you'll lose all of it. And then you'll know; only it will be too late."

"Nay," Kearn argued, growing angry. "Paragor has foreseen it—when he looked into the first scroll and saw our destiny. Our victory will be final, and death will not rob us of anything. We who have served the master well will be remembered in the world to come, and we will rule it!"

"But King Eliam wrote the first scroll," Antoinette quietly said, hoping the others would not hear her. "Don't you get it? King Eliam was here before Paragor was even born. It is King Eliam who holds the future in his hand. King Eliam offers peace, unyielding love, and the promise that we never have to be alone again! But if you refuse his offer, your death will bring you just what you asked for: an eternity of discord, hatred, and isolation. That's what I meant! That's what I came here to rescue you from!"

Kearn sheathed his sword, and his mouth hung agape. He clutched his hair as if he might rip patches of it from his scalp. "Why me?" he asked finally. "That first moment in Kismet, you looked at me like you knew me, but I have never seen you before in my life. Why did you pick me?"

"I didn't pick you," Antoinette replied, reaching into a pocket. "But someone from my world did. He's a hero of Alleble, and at least in my world, he's a good friend of yours."

Kearn looked up. His eyes narrowed. "That is not possible," he whispered.

"Here," Antoinette said as she handed him the photo of Robby.

Kearn clutched the photo with both hands and stared. He looked up, and for a moment, Antoinette saw something flicker in his eyes. But it was quickly gone.

Kearn straightened, and his eyes darted right. "Lies!" he hissed. "Sorcery! Guards, bind her!" And suddenly, Paragor Knights had her by the arms. They roughly clasped manacles upon her wrists, manacles with heavy chains. Antoinette struggled, but it was no use.

Kearn stood before her and his eyes flashed red. "You will come with us to the Shattered Lands," he said. "And tomorrow, you will see just how wrong you are!" He tore the photo of Robby in half and let it fall to the ground. He laughed and walked away. The soldiers dragged Antoinette along behind him.

Trenna stroked the white dragon's neck and feared for Antoinette. She had been gone for much longer than twenty minutes. Much longer than an hour. Still, Trenna could not bring herself to leave. She paced by the white dragon, wishing she had a good bow and a quiver full of Blackwood shafts. *Then I might be of some use!* she thought. But she had nothing. To go charging alone into the enemy camp, she knew, would just give the enemy another prisoner. And the longer she waited, the more she thought about the legend of the Seven Sleepers and what it could mean for her homeland—what it could mean for The Realm—if it was true. Trenna leaped onto Honk's back and flicked the reins.

"I am sorry, Lady Antoinette," she said, and the white dragon soared away into the night sky.

ACACIA

The sun was already high when Trenna first caught sight of *Pennath Kirin*, the mountains just to the east of Acacia. They were small peaks compared to some, draped completely by a thick blanket of fir trees. Nonetheless, it was all the white dragon could do to fly over them. Trenna knew the beast was spent from the torrid pace, but she had to get to Acacia. "Just a little farther, Honk," she called. "Just a little farther, and then you shall rest!"

The first homesteads of Acacia appeared: cottages, fenced parcels of land, and grazing livestock. Next, there were cottages surrounded by crumbling stone walls, and at last, there came the castle of Acacia. It was built on a wide hill and had three towers and many rows of arched windows. At last, Trenna spotted a wide ledge of stone to the rear of the castle. Honk glided down and landed softly. Other dragons of various colors were there, sunning themselves or eating, but they stared at the white newcomer.

Trenna dismounted quickly. Honk made her way over to one of the feeding troughs and helped herself.

Two knights ran to greet Trenna. Their gray armor was inlaid with designs of a silver tree whose trunk and limbs were curvaceous and heavily laden with long bunches of white flowers. "Welcome to Acacia," the knights said together, and both their eyes glinted blue.

"Are either of you Kaliam?" Trenna asked.

"No," they both replied. "You speak of Kaliam from Alleble?"

"Yes!" Trenna said. "Is he here?"

"He is here," said one of the knights.

The other guard explained, "Kaliam and the other Knights of Alleble are holding court with Lord Sternhilt in the castle library."

"Take me to them, now!" Trenna exclaimed. "I am on an urgent errand!"

They led Trenna to the back of the ledge and under an arched overhang, then down a long torchlit tunnel, and finally up a spiraling staircase to a wide set of doors. The guards opened the doors, and Trenna ran into a huge room with a high, vaulted ceiling. The walls from floor to ceiling were laden with books. In the center of the library was a table surrounded by the most lordly warriors Trenna had ever seen. Nock she knew, but he looked older and stronger, and in some ways more solemn than she remembered. At the head of the table sat a Glimpse with a long gray staff that split at the end and spread like a silver blossom. He was large in girth and had a thick brown mustache that quivered when he spoke. "What is the meaning of this?" he demanded.

"I am sorry, Lord Sternhilt!" said one of the guards. "This lady just arrived upon the back of a white dragon. She seemed in peril, so I brought her to you." At the mention of a white dragon, several of the knights stood up.

"Which of you is Kaliam?" Trenna asked.

A tall knight came forward. He was dressed all in silver armor except for his massive bare forearms. His head also was uncovered and long black hair fell about his shoulders. "I am Kaliam," he said. "I am Sentinel of Alleble."

"Sir, I have come with urgent news. Lady Antoinette is in great danger! We all are in great danger!"

"What do you know of Lady Antoinette? She was our companion, and she left us four nights ago."

Trenna revealed all she knew of the events that led to Antoinette's disappearance, and how she had met Antoinette. When she had finished, Kaliam fell backward into his chair.

"This is grievous news!" he said.

"It is all true, then," said Sir Gabriel. "The Wyrm Lord—"

"Is it that hard to be believed?" Nock asked. "We saw for ourselves the Sepulcher!"

"Lady Antoinette is killed or captive," recounted Kaliam, staring from Glimpse to Glimpse. "Paragor goes to the Shattered Lands of the Wyrm Lord, an ancient horror from our darkest dreams. And from what Trenna has said, the Wyrm Lord will awaken the Seven Sleepers to wreak havoc upon Yewland. It is a many-faceted evil, and I do not know how we can hope to face it all or even solve any part of it."

"Yewland must be warned!" cried Nock.

"And we must send word to King Eliam!" said Tal.

"But there is a chance that Antoinette still lives," said Aelic.

"I agree," said Lady Merewen. "We must go to her aid!"

Kaliam turned to Lord Sternhilt. "M'lord, by your leave, we will need your swiftest dragon steeds and many of your most able riders."

The big Glimpse's mustache quivered, and he banged his staff on the stone floor like a gavel. "Sir Wahlion! Sir Danebass!" he bellowed, and the two guards who had escorted Trenna into the castle bowed, awaiting their lord's commands. "Alert the Castle Guard! Give Kaliam whatever he asks for!"

And then Lord Sternhilt turned back to Kaliam. "Our dragons have not the speed of the white beasts from Yewland, but you shall have the best of all our breeds. And the two guards who left are among the finest riders in my kingdom. They and all that they muster are at your service."

Kaliam bowed. "Lord Sternhilt, your friendship to Alleble shall never be forgotten."

"Know that it is only a token payment, Sentinel of Alleble," said Lord Sternhilt. "King Eliam restored Acacia from a burned-out husk, as it was left by Paragor and his brood. Acacia stands ready to strike a blow, however small, against the enemy of The Realm." Kaliam bowed respectfully and then turned to his team.

"This, then, is my judgment," Kaliam said. "And may King Eliam forgive me if my decisions now go awry. Nock, you, Mallik, and Rogan go to Yewland, and make haste! Queen Illaria will need to muster every band of braves. The young and the old, the ones who do not fight, must be moved to a place of safety!

"Sir Gabriel, fly with Trenna back to Alleble! Let there be a dozen Acacian riders to escort you safely there. Trenna must tell her story before the King and the remaining Elder Guard. Find out what was written in the scroll that Paragor took from the Ancient One. All of our hopes may hinge on what you discover.

"For the rest, we fly into the worst danger! To the Shattered Lands we go to do what we may to stop Paragor from releasing the Wyrm Lord. And if Lady Antoinette is still alive, then we will rescue her or die in the attempt."

"But what of Clarion?" asked Lord Sternhilt, and they all turned to look at the ruler of Acacia. "Clarion is the nearest kingdom to the Shattered Lands. If the threat is what you make it out to be, then Clarion ought to be warned."

"Alas, you are right!" Kaliam exclaimed. "Clarion's defenses are formidable, their walls ever fortified, but against the threat which looms to their north . . . they must be warned. Ever the enemy seeks to divide us, and it seems now we have no choice. Tobias and Tal, lead a flight of Acacian riders to Clarion and prepare them for sudden war. The hammer of Paragory may fall there first!"

Lord Sternhilt was as good as his word. He sent an entire flight of dragon riders with Tobias and Tal to Clarion. A dozen more followed Nock, Mallik, and Rogan to Yewland. The same he sent with Sir Gabriel and Trenna to prepare Alleble for the coming storm. But his swiftest dragons and his most skilled riders he placed at Kaliam's disposal. The Acacian riders, Kaliam, Farix, Lady Merewen, Aelic, and Oswyn left within the hour to try to save a friend and stop an ancient nightmare from coming to life.

THE SHATTERED LANDS

The dragons of Acacia were not as fast as the white steeds of Yewland, but they were tough and quick to recover. Kaliam had stopped their journey only once to feed and water the dragons and to allow the team a brief rest. No one except Kaliam knew what to expect from the Shattered Lands. Glimpses from Alleble rarely ventured there, and most only remembered its name from childhood tales told around the fire during the harvest season. In fact, most of the newer maps of Alleble did not even depict the Shattered Lands at all.

And so the dragon riders were filled with great dread when they saw the red glow on the horizon. It was not from the sun, for it had set far to the west hours earlier and would not rise again for many hours more.

"Do not despair," Kaliam said as he rode the swiftest dragon. "We will find Antoinette."

"I should have gone with her," Aelic said, riding his dragon near Kaliam. He reached for the hilt of Fury. "I would have kept her safe."

"I am sure you would have tried, Aelic. But you cannot blame yourself for this. Antoinette erred by leaving us that night. She was caught between two paths and would not see the right way. You tried to talk her out of it. Lady Merewen did also. Antoinette made the choice—not you."

"Still, I knew she would go," argued Aelic. "And I am her friend. I should have gone with her."

"Friendship is the foundation of much that is good," Kaliam said. "But using it to justify an evil decision does not bring good to anyone. If you had gone with Antoinette, there is no telling what wickedness might have befallen you! Be content that you have done the King's will in this. And though Antoinette abandoned King Eliam when she left us that night, King Eliam has not abandoned her."

"You are starting to sound like my grandfather," said Aelic.

"Captain Valithor?" Kaliam smiled. "Ha! Yes, I learned much from him! His wisdom and courage will never be forgotten. How I wish he was here with us now."

Just then, they heard a series of low rumbles in the distance.

"Is that thunder?" Aelic asked.

"Nay, it is *Pennath Ruin*," Kaliam replied. "Or one of the other volcanoes in that miserable place."

"The Wyrm Lord was entombed within a volcano?"

"I am not certain, Aelic," Kaliam said. "No one but perhaps the King himself knows for sure. The legend, as I have heard it, says that the Wyrm Lord is locked in a vault beneath a lake of fire. How a creature could survive in such a place for these many long years, I do not know. He is said to be the firstborn dragon. And firstborns

have queer powers, it is said. Ah! It seems so strange to speak suddenly of this as real when it was for the longest time only legend."

"How will we find the tomb?" Aelic asked.

"We search for the lake of fire," Kaliam answered. "And there
may be other things that lead us to it."

"What do you mean?"

Kaliam sighed and smiled grimly. "Paragor is seeking the tomb
also," he said. "Four legions of knights are easy to find . . . even in
the dark."

The landscape beneath the riders changed markedly. Just a few
leagues before, there had been thickets of firs and pines and tufts
of long grass. Now there was nothing but harsh rock. Shattered
gray shale lay everywhere, cratered by missiles spewed from the
volcanoes or punctured from below by thrusts of jagged black
volcanic rock. Smoky gray wisps of ash floated about on stifling
hot breezes. Ahead lay clusters of active volcanoes with their reds
and fiery oranges. But none were larger or more volatile than
Pennath Ruin. That giant stood in the center of the landscape like
a shadowy guardian wreathed in smoke and ash. Only trickles of
molten rock veined down its slopes, but there were deep rum-
blings from within.

The riders came to rest on a broad but uneven shelf of rock,
fenced in almost entirely by rows of sharp black stalagmites. "Where
do we start our search?" asked the Acacian rider, Sir Danebass.

"We are looking for a lake of fire," Kaliam replied. "Either that
or any sign of Paragor and his legions. Spread out in teams of three.
Circle above the mounts, but be wary of them. Your dragons can

withstand more heat than you can, so keep a safe distance. If you find the enemy, do not engage. Stay out of sight, see what you may, and return here so that we may plan a course of action."

Kaliam waited anxiously for Sir Wahlion, Farix, and Oswyn to return, wondering what had become of them. At last, three winged shapes appeared high in the red vaporous sky. The dragons floated lightly down to join the others.

"We have found signs!" Sir Oswyn said. "But they are not encouraging."

"Signs of what?" Aelic blurted out.

Sir Oswyn looked at Aelic with sympathy and said, "Signs that the enemy has been here. Culverts, dams, and channels—all on the backside of Pennath Ruin. To what end it was built, I do not know. But all of it was abandoned. There was nothing living abroad."

Aelic hung his head at the news.

"Take us there," Kaliam commanded. "There may yet be enemies about, for they are dark like this landscape."

Deep thunder growled within Pennath Ruin as riders soared around its base. They gave the volcano a wide berth, for it bubbled tempestuously as if it might rain fire down on top of them at any moment. They came at last to the backside and found the scene as Oswyn had described it. Structures of iron stood, wheeled engines and shafts made for delving in rock. Rails had been laid and toppled carts lay in many places. There were canals cut into the side of the mountain. Some led away from the base of the volcano and were half filled with cooled magma. Others were blocked with dams or had channels diverting flows elsewhere. One great culvert was still full and flowing with white-hot lava that oozed continuously from the volcano's mouth. And everywhere there were tracks and trails and the prints of uncountable boots.

"I should have thought to bring Mallik!" Kaliam said. "He would certainly guess the work of the enemy. His folk know all things concerning rock and iron."

"I am puzzled by this riddle," said Farix. "These structures, the equipment, and the channels—they appear to me to be the work of many strong Glimpses. An army of four legions like the one we saw near the Blackwood could do this, yes. But this does not appear to me to be a recent endeavor."

"Lady Merewen, do you know anything of this?" Kaliam asked.

"If I did," she replied indignantly, "I would have told you long ago. The Prince's armies were constantly on the move while I served the wrong lord, but no rumor of labor in the Shattered Lands reached my ears."

"I am sorry, Lady Merewen," Kaliam said. "I did not mean it as an accusation. I am simply at a loss."

"Could the heat and soot make this look old when it is actually new?" Aelic asked.

"Maybe," replied Farix.

"Captain, come up here!" called Sir Wahlion. He had scaled a twisted rocky outcropping and now stood high upon it. Kaliam and the others followed.

"What is it?" Kaliam asked. "What do you see?"

"Well, sir, from down there I did not see much of anything," said Sir Wahlion, pointing out into the wasteland that stretched between the base of Pennath Ruin and the next volcanic mount. "But it takes on a different look up here."

Aelic stared out into the wasteland, and indeed it did look different. It was somewhat concave like a shallow valley or . . . "It is the lake of fire!"

"What?" Kaliam asked.

"Sir, look!" Aelic pointed. "Do you see the way the channels at the base of the volcano all curl away? Think of how the lava would flow if the channels were not there!"

"Yes, yes! I see it now!" Kaliam said excitedly. "Pennath Ruin would fill this crater over time, and it would become a lake of fire! Riders, to your steeds! If we are right, we must search this blackened valley for the tomb!"

They took to the air and soared out above the empty lake, but as they circled and began to search, there came an ominous rumbling from Pennath Ruin. Smoke issued forth from unseen vents and swirled into the sky. The mouth of the volcano went dim, and it became strangely quiet.

A blinding flash of orange lit the sky, and with the sound of cannon fire, Pennath Ruin erupted. Hot ash rained down upon the riders, and large hunks of rock began to fall.

"Take cover!" Kaliam bellowed. But it was too late. A jagged rock, streaked red and glowing like an ember, hit Sir Wahlion as he tried to race away. He and his steed fell still burning to the shattered ground. Another piece of smoking debris struck Lady Merewen's dragon just as she left the ground. But Farix upon his dragon dove down hard and fast. The dragon reached for Lady Merewen's limp form, gathered her gently, and flew swiftly away. The riders who survived gathered on a ledge at the other side of the crater.

"Lady Merewen!" Kaliam cried when he saw that Farix carried her in his arms.

"She lives!" Farix yelled. "The stone struck her steed, but she is only unconscious from the shock." Kaliam took her from Farix and laid her gently on the ground. He brushed her silver hair with his hand, and her eyes opened.

Suddenly, another explosion rocked the landscape. They turned and watched in horror as it seemed that the entire backside of Pennath Ruin was turned to molten red and began a long, slow slide into the basin.

"The lava has overflowed the channels!" Kaliam yelled.

Lady Merewen looked up at him. "Go," she said. "If you do not act now, we may never know."

Kaliam started to argue.

"I will be fine," she assured him. And with a slight sway, she stood. "Now, go! Find the tomb!"

Kaliam leaped into the saddle and urged the dragon into the air. The lava flowed steadily into the valley. Steam issued forth like geysers and great clouds of ash and soot swirled. Kaliam guided the dragon below the mist and just above the broken ground. Close behind him Aelic steered his dragon steed low, while scanning the wasteland. They circled round and round, and all the while, streams of molten rock poured into the basin.

"Kaliam!" Aelic yelled. "There! I saw something! Turn!" Aelic wasn't sure if Kaliam had heard, but then he saw Kaliam's dragon wheel about.

"Yes, I see it!" Kaliam said. "Some excavation! We'll land there!" As the dragons floated to a stop, they saw more clearly the large rectangular cut into the rocky terrain. They dismounted and came to the edge and looked down. Stairs were cut into the rock and led steeply down beneath the surface.

"I will go," Aelic said.

Kaliam looked back to Pennath Ruin. It continued to vomit a fiery stream of orange into the valley. "No! The lava is too close!" Kaliam said.

"We have to know!" Aelic said, and he leaped down the stairs. He disappeared from sight, and Kaliam waited. He waited for what seemed an eternity, and then he felt a rumble beneath his feet. He looked up at Pennath Ruin, but it was engulfed in a billowing cloud of ash. He felt a surge of hot air, fell to his knees, and coughed violently. Aidan's dragon screeched, then raced away. Kaliam grabbed the reins of his own dragon just in time. He looked up at the lava flow. It was only twenty yards away.

"Aelic!" Kaliam screamed down the stairs. "Aelic, you must come now! Aelic, the lava is nearly here!"

And then he saw Aelic's hand grasping out of the darkness for the bottom steps. The lava crept slowly over the edge and began to trickle down the first step. Kaliam went to the opposite side and reached down. "Aelic!" he screamed. "Grab my hand!" But it was no use. Aelic was too far down the steps—he could not reach him! Kaliam looked desperately about. Then he had an idea. He leaped on his dragon and snapped the reins. He brought the creature to hover so that its tail hung down into the opening. Kaliam leaned over, craning his neck to see. Aelic's hand was no longer moving. The lava descended another step.

"Aelic, wake up!" Kaliam yelled. "Grab the beast's tail!"

But Aelic did not stir. The lava surged down another step. Then another. Kaliam watched helplessly as the lava edged forward. He knew he must do something or it would become Aelic's tomb as well.

"ON YOUR FEET, THOU LUMPISH, TARDY-GAITED CANKER-BLOSSOM!!!" Kaliam yelled in his best imitation of Captain Valithor.

Suddenly, Aelic's hand stirred. And there he was, standing in the orange light cast by the lava.

"DON'T JUST STAND THERE, YOU EARTH-VEXING CLOT POLE! GRAB THE BEAST'S TAIL!!"

Aelic's hand shot out and clutched the dragon's tail. Kaliam snapped the reins. The dragon lifted off, and Aelic flew out of the opening just as the molten rock reached the bottom step. The ground fell away, and the dragon swung Aelic up onto its back behind Kaliam.

"You really are starting to sound like . . . my grandfather," Aelic said, hacking and coughing. Kaliam grinned over his shoulder at Aelic.

"Well, it got you moving!" Kaliam laughed. "Could you see in the tomb?"

Aelic turned to Kaliam. "Yes, the tomb is empty!"

Kaliam sat suddenly rigid. "Then it is as we feared, the Wyrm Lord has been set free."

FLIGHT TO CLARION

Kaliam, Aelic! The King be praised! You made it!" Lady Merewen cried, practically dragging them both from the saddle. "When Aelic's dragon came back wounded and riderless . . . we feared the worst."

Aelic's knees buckled and he almost fell, but Farix was there. "Got you, lad," he said as he helped Aelic over to a seat on a nearby boulder.

"You cut it a little close for comfort," Farix said. "What did you find?"

"We are too late," Kaliam whispered. The Glimpses stood as if in shock. Pennath Ruin rumbled ominously in the distance.

Aelic stood slowly and leaned against the boulder. The air was still acrid to him, and he continued to cough as he spoke. "A steep stairway was cut down into the stone at the bottom of the basin. It seemed ancient, and I felt as if I were stepping backward in time as I descended. It was dark at first, but when my eyes adjusted to the half-light, I saw the remnants of an enormous door of stone. It had been ripped free from its hinges, and it lay in shards on the ground. There was a vast chamber beyond. The moment I entered it, I was overwhelmed by something. There was a smell . . . a stench, foul beyond the words I have to describe it, but it was not that. Within that chamber was a presence, a dark and brooding hatred that clamped down upon my heart. I could feel it willing me to die, and I almost succumbed to it. As I turned to lunge free of the chamber, I saw upon the walls within, upon the frame of the door, and finally upon the stairs—long gouges. I am convinced they were scratched into the stone by the talons of the Wyrm Lord."

No one spoke. It seemed that fear and menace permeated the air like the swirling ash from the volcano.

"I feared it would be so," Farix said finally. "From the moment we entered this desolate land, I sensed something too."

Oswyn came up and handed a full skin to Aelic. "Drink some of this, Aelic. It is Golden Tear. Queen Illaria gave it to me, for I wanted to know what gives it its recuperative powers. I deem you need it now."

Aelic took a long drink, swallowed, and seemed to stand a little straighter.

"We have not been idle while you were away!" Sir Oswyn said to Kaliam. The Acacian riders gathered round. "It is more confirmation than news, I deem. We found a trail, well trodden by many soldiers and creased with ruts from heavy wheels."

"Paragor's legions," Kaliam said absently.

"They are not more than a day old," said Sir Oswyn.

"We followed the trail to the outskirts of the Shattered Lands," said Farix.

"Where do they lead?" Aelic asked.

Oswyn stared at the ground and said, "They lead due south . . . to Clarion."

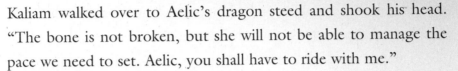

Kaliam walked over to Aelic's dragon steed and shook his head. "The bone is not broken, but she will not be able to manage the pace we need to set. Aelic, you shall have to ride with me."

Aelic drew near and saw the singed flesh and the gaping tear in the webbing of the dragon's left wing. He patted the creature on its knobby brow and looked questioningly back to Kaliam.

"Fear not. She will survive," Kaliam replied to Aelic's unspoken question. "With that wing, she will need to leisurely make her way back to her roost in Acacia. She will be far safer there than where we are going."

The riders pushed their steeds to labor past exhaustion. On they flew, driven by fear. Fear of failure. Fear of the unknown power of the evil that had been unleashed. Fear of what they might find in Clarion. The sun rose red in the hazy eastern sky, but it was soon devoured by a curtain of smoldering dark clouds.

"Why would the enemy go to Clarion?" Aelic asked, shouting to be heard over the swoosh of the dragon's wings.

"Clarion was ever sought by Paragor from long ago," Kaliam said. "It is a beautiful white city, hewn from rich granite and marble. The Glimpses there do not delve like Mallik's folk, but they are artists: shapers, sculptors, and engravers. The bright walls, fitted cunningly around the city, do not seem meant for military use. For in every panel there is carved an intricate design. But do not be fooled! Those walls are as strong as the bones of a mountain, and there is some hope in that!

"A round castle with many tall towers sits on a hill within the ramparts, and there are great halls as well, supported by long columns! It was an old Clarion master craftsman named Halberad who carved the throne on which King Eliam now sits.

"Paragor requested such a throne for himself. Offers of gold and priceless riches he made, but he was rebuffed. Alvisbrand was king in Clarion of old, and he was as true a friend to Alleble as The Realm has ever seen. His son, Alvisbrand the Younger, will not listen to Paragor's entreaties either. Not only has Clarion turned away Paragor's many offers of alliance, but they refuse even to trade with them.

"The most direct course for the enemy to take back to his dark realm would bypass Clarion altogether. I fear for Clarion, for there can be only one reason why Paragor would choose that direction: revenge."

Suddenly, Kaliam straightened in his saddle. "Loose Fury from that sheath, Sir Aelic," he said. "There is smoke on the horizon. Clarion is burning."

The dragon riders came upon a scene of utter destruction. The white walls of Clarion were thrown down. Many of the great buildings had been collapsed, their columns of strong stone snapped like young trees. Smoke from smoldering cottages curled in dark tendrils into the gray sky.

"The walls of Clarion were mighty and they had two legions of spearmen to defend them!" Oswyn cried as they dismounted and entered the city. "They should have been able to resist Paragor longer than this!"

"Do you see those stones?" Lady Merewen said, pointing to a ruined turret. "They are not just broken—they . . . they are melted! What sort of fire can melt cold stone?"

Kaliam drew his broadsword and said, "It is the dragonfire of the firstborn Wyrm in all The Realm. I fear Clarion could have boasted ten thousand spearmen, and yet the result would have been the same."

Aelic quickly surveyed the wreckage and turned to Kaliam. "Sir, where are the Glimpses?"

Kaliam looked sadly down at Aelic. "I do not believe there are any survivors."

"No, I mean, where are the bodies?" Aelic said, shaking his head.

Kaliam, Oswyn, Farix, Lady Merewen, and all the riders from Acacia looked hopelessly about. "The ground ought to be littered with the dead!" Farix said. "And yet there are none!"

"Could Paragor have taken them all prisoner?" Aelic asked.

"In the face of the Wyrm Lord, could they have all surrendered?" asked Lady Merewen.

Kaliam shook his head. "If I know Alvisbrand, he would not surrender," he said, concerned. "And the folk of Clarion would have fought to the last, but where are they?"

The riders dismounted their dragons and spread out into the wreckage. It was grim work, searching through the rubble and charred wood. They feared the death they would find, but feared worse to find none at all.

At last, Farix reported back that he had found two knights

crushed under fallen columns in a collapsed building. Oswyn made similar discoveries. Everyone but Lady Merewen had returned to the front gate, but after all the searching, the count was only twelve dead.

"Help!" Lady Merewen cried out from atop the roof of a fallen cottage. The others sprinted to her aid, and there on the other side of the roof was their friend Tal, his legs tangled in wreckage. "He is alive!" Lady Merewen said.

Oswyn and Kaliam knelt at the fallen knight's side. "Tal!" Kaliam cried. "Brother in arms! Praise to King Eliam, we have found you!" Then he saw the wound in Tal's side, and he gasped. With pleading eyes, he looked to Oswyn, but their herb-meister shook his head. He had no salve or medicine for such a mortal wound.

Tal's head turned toward his friends. His eyes blinked open and slowly focused. Tal's voice was thin and dry. "Kaliam, you are here—and you, Aelic."

Kaliam took out a waterskin and poured some over Tal's cracked lips. "Thank you, Captain," Tal said, his eyes roaming. "But where is Matthias?"

"Matthias?" Aelic echoed.

Farix leaned close to Aelic and whispered, "He calls for his old friend who fell in Mithegard. Alas, Tal is fading—" Kaliam held up a hand, and Farix went silent.

"I have not seen Matthias," said Kaliam, brushing aside locks of hair from Tal's face.

"Pity," Tal said. "I wanted to show him the notches in my blade!"

Kaliam looked about and saw Tal's sword. And though it was forged from *murynstil*, Alleble's strongest metal, the blade lay broken in three pieces a few feet away. "We have seen your sword," Kaliam said. "You fought bravely, Knight of Alleble."

"Not bravely enough," Tal said quietly. His eyes started to close.

"What happened here?" asked Kaliam.

Tal's body shook. He coughed and took in a breath. "They came in the night," Tal said. "Paragor himself led them to the gates of Clarion. But there was an unseen malice behind him, and the spearmen in the frontguard fled their posts. Only Alvisbrand stood on the battlement and defied the dark Prince.

"Paragor uttered one word, 'Surrender,' and that was all. Alvisbrand drew his sword, but before his refusal had even left his lips . . . something took him. A great carriage opened behind Paragor, and darkness took wing!" Tal looked up, terrified, as if he saw something in the sky.

"Tal, what did you see?" Kaliam asked.

"No," he cried. "It is not possible! It was blacker than the night sky and had vast wings like a dragon's. It was more swift than thought, and it leaped from the carriage to the battlement. And Alvisbrand . . . he was slain so quickly that he had not the time to cry out. It was as if he had never been at all.

"The dark thing flew back into the carriage. Before the carriage door shut, I saw a twisted, shriveled thing . . . like something unearthed from a grave. Then Paragor unleashed a mace, a great black spiked thing! It burst into flames. He whirled it about him, wreathing himself in flames, and then he smashed it against the main gate of Clarion . . . and it burst asunder and the flames spread.

"Everyone within, even children, fled in terror toward the safety of the castle, but they were struck down without mercy! At any resistance, the monster from the carriage emerged, spraying fire out of the darkness and kindling everything to char—even some of the stone itself melted! It was over in minutes. Tobias fell before the creature. I do not know what became of him because I was sent sprawling by Paragor's mace. I do not even think Paragor knew he had hit me." Tal laughed, a tired, hacking laugh.

"What about the survivors, Tal?" Farix asked. "Did Paragor take prisoners away?"

Tears slipped from the corners of Tal's eyes. He stared at Farix, but before Tal could answer, his eyes became still, fixed.

"You fought well, Tal!" Kaliam proclaimed, gently closing Tal's eyes. "Matthias himself may now tell you it is so. And your King will greet you in the Blessed Realm and say to you, 'Well done, Servant of Alleble! Well done.'"

Quickly but with great care, they raised a cairn of rocks over Tal. They stood in silence around it until one of the Acacian riders called out, "Look! The smoke clears! And the castle of Clarion still stands!"

They all turned and, beyond all hope, the white castle of Clarion was intact, resting upon the highest hill in the small kingdom. But Kaliam did not rejoice, for it seemed to him that the castle was surrounded by a gray shroud—a vaporous swirling mist that issued from its gatehouse.

They mounted their dragon steeds and soared up the hill to the wide stair before the castle's main gate. They all started to climb the stair, but Kaliam raised his hand and stopped them. "I will go," he said. He turned, walked slowly up the white steps, and disappeared within the hanging mist.

A moment passed, and then those gathered on the stair heard a haunting moan from within the castle. Kaliam emerged, shrieking, and fell to his knees on the steps.

"The stone alone survived!" he cried, covering his face with his gauntlets. "The rest . . . they are all burned."

And that was all they could get from him for a long while. Farix and Oswyn carried him down the steps and laid him flat by his dragon. They stayed near to Kaliam, but they could not comfort him. No one else went back into the castle.

Finally, Kaliam sat up and took a drink of water. Aelic came to him and sat down. He put a trembling hand on Kaliam's shoulder. "Kaliam," he said, a deep-seated tremor in his voice, "was Antoinette among the dead?"

Kaliam looked away. "It is impossible to tell," he said.

THE NAME
ABOVE ALL NAMES

Look!" Oswyn shouted. "In the sky to the northwest!"

They all turned and looked to the sky above the ruin of Clarion. And there, just as the sun broke through the clouds, the sky filled with dragons!

"At last we have a strand of hope!" Kaliam announced. "It is our own force of dragons! Gird yourselves, warriors! For the Dragon Guard of Alleble has come!"

Dragons bearing knights in gleaming armor swooped into Clarion. Banners they flew but all with the same emblem: twin mountain peaks with the sun rising between them!

Sir Gabriel, the lead dragon rider, rode a magnificent gray dragon with a vast wingspan. Its scales glistened in the sun as it landed softly at the foot of the stairs. Next, Trenna's dragon landed. They quickly dismounted their dragons and ran to Kaliam.

"Sir Gabriel, you are a sight for weary eyes!" Kaliam shouted, and he embraced him.

"My Sentinel, I bring you three thousand mounted knights!" he said. "But I fear we are too late!"

"For Clarion, yes." Kaliam nodded sadly. "Our worst fears are realized, my old friend. Paragor has set free the Wyrm Lord. Clarion fell in minutes before the onslaught of Paragor and his fell beast. It is a loss beyond words." Kaliam looked over his shoulder at the castle of Clarion. "But mourning must wait. Even now, Paragor turns homeward and approaches Yewland. Alas, I wish that you and the Dragon Guard had gone there instead of here!"

"Then know this!" Sir Gabriel said, and his eyes flashed blue. "The force that you see here is only a fraction of the army King Eliam has sent to Yewland. As we speak, twenty thousand knights march and ride to Yewland with haste!"

"Bless you, Sir Gabriel," said Kaliam, and he kissed him upon the cheek. "You encourage me! And I think now the pieces are in place to cast Paragor down once and for all!"

"But how?" Sir Gabriel asked. "How can you be sure now that the ancient wyrm has been called out of dark legend to life?"

Kaliam took Sir Gabriel by the shoulders and gently said, "Tal and Tobias were among those killed in the battle here." Sir Gabriel gritted his teeth, but he did not look away.

"But Tal saw the Wyrm Lord," Kaliam went on. "And what he told me leads me to believe that the old dragon has not yet recovered his full strength. Paragor keeps him in a large carriage, and he only entered the battle for short spans. Granted, even in his diminished form, the Wyrm Lord is a dreadful force. But if we could assail him now, before Paragor cloisters him away in his dark land, then we might have a chance!"

Kaliam held up a fist and a broad, lustful grin broke out on his face. "Paragor does not know this, but he is heading right into the jaws of a trap!"

"What do you mean?" Sir Gabriel asked. Aelic, Trenna, and the knights gathered close around.

Kaliam held up both hands and gestured vigorously as he spoke. "Paragor thinks he will march through Yewland as quickly as he did Clarion. But if Mallik, Sir Rogan, and Nock reached Queen Illaria as I think they must have, then she will have the Forest Road swarming with her braves! The massive force of our countrymen from Alleble, twenty thousand strong, will pour into the western exit of the Forest Road. Then we will swoop in from the east and we will crush the enemy from all sides!"

"Yes!" shouted Sir Gabriel.

Kaliam turned to the dragon riders and bellowed, "Dragon Guard of Alleble! Knights of all lands who have come to our aid! Paragor has much to answer for, and finally he has come out into the open! You must make one more flight, one more journey, and you must race to the Forest Road to face the enemy and defeat him!"

Thousands of voices cheered as one. Kaliam raised a hand to quiet them. "But servants of King Eliam, gird yourselves! Paragor has a weapon of dread, and old tales you have heard spoke more truth than many of you believed. The Wyrm Lord has been released from his tomb!"

Fear swept over the knights, and they began to clamor. Kaliam raised his hands, but they did not quiet. Finally, he raised his sword, and little by little, their anxieties ceased to be voiced. Kaliam kept the sword in the air and yelled, "I fear that name just as you do! It is a terror magnified by the years and yet still worse now that it is real. He is the firstborn dragon, the Wyrm Lord, and he is endowed with fearsome power. His name ought to make us all tremble. But I for one will not tremble, and do you know why?" A great hush fell over the knights and dragons that filled the streets of Clarion as they waited on Kaliam, their Sentinel.

"I will not tremble at the name of the wyrm!" yelled Kaliam. His eyes flashed, and his voice grew more powerful and assured. "No! Because I know another name . . . a greater name than his! A name that strikes terror in the heart of Paragor and the ilk who serve him! A name the Wyrm Lord himself will remember! And this name is on our side and wields a power none can overcome! I will not be afraid. Nay, we will not be afraid because the name we serve is King Eliam the Everlasting. And he will put down the enemy once and for all by our hands!!" Cheers erupted, and three thousand swords stabbed up into the air. And one by one, the Dragon Guards took to the air for the urgent journey to Yewland.

THE BATTLE
AT YEWLAND

The moon painted the Dragon Guard of Alleble silver as they surged across the night sky en route to Yewland. Kaliam commanded the guard from the lead dragon. On Kaliam's left flank, Aelic rode upon Gabby, Gwenne's dragon steed, sent from Alleble. Oswyn, Sir Gabriel, Trenna, and Lady Merewen's dragons flew in formation on either side.

Aelic was thinking of Antoinette. He didn't know why he felt so sure, but he truly believed she was still alive. *But in the midst of the fight? How long?* Aelic silently appealed to King Eliam for strength— strength to win the battle and deliver Antoinette from her bonds.

Kaliam's dragon steed swooped low. Aelic looked down. The trail of the Paragor Knights was becoming very clear on the land below. They were heading right for the forests of Yewland, and because they were on foot, they were not far ahead of the Dragon Guard.

A deep horn sounded. That was the signal from Kaliam to ride the dragons just above the ground for the last few leagues. *There it is*, Aelic thought. Just ahead was the large hill Kaliam had told them all to expect. They were to stay low until that hill, and then, as if the hill were a ramp, they would soar up over it and swoop down upon the enemy at the Forest Road. *They will not know what hit them,* Aelic thought as he turned and looked over his shoulder at the thousands of knights on their dragon steeds. The eyes of the riders flashed blue in the darkness.

"This is it, Gabby!" Aelic called to his dragon. Aelic pulled back on the reins of his steed, and Gabby climbed high from the base of the hill. Up they all went, dragon after dragon. With their trajectory straight up, none of them could even see the trees that rose up on both sides of the Forest Road.

But as they arced down, the forest—glowing with the fires of battle—rose up to meet them. Clashing warriors—some wearing the black and crimson of Paragory, and others the green and brown of Yewland—filled the Forest Road. Kaliam raced ahead and rode his steed into the wide gap between the trees. Aelic and the others glided in behind their Sentinel, weapons drawn.

A hail of arrows, glistening briefly in the moonlight, sprayed from the trees on both sides of the road, adding to the fallen enemies that littered the ground. Kaliam, Aelic, and company raced west and did not worry about being slain by the arrows from their allies. For Yewland's archers were born to wield a bow and raised to hunt in the dark. They picked off the enemy as fast as they could draw and fire.

Nock, Mallik, and Sir Rogan must have reached Yewland in time to warn Queen Illaria! Aelic thought as the Dragon Guard rode into the fray.

A warrior rose up ahead of Aelic and raised his sword menacingly, but before Aelic could thrust Fury forward, his dragon grabbed the enemy in her jaws and flung him cartwheeling into the air.

The ranks of the enemy thickened as the Dragon Guard swept up the road. Aelic brought Fury down on the helmet of one soldier and swept the legs out from another. A sudden flash of orange flame to Aelic's left distracted him, and he heard someone sing out, "Oh-ho!" Apparently, Oswyn had given the enemy a taste of his fire powder.

Suddenly, Aelic sensed movement to his right and pulled the reins. Gabby's wing bowled over a huge axe-wielding warrior. The enemy knight went down in a heap, but the axe struck the dragon's wing at the joint. Gabby roared in agony, tried to stay above the ground, but tilted and crashed into the Blackwood side of the Forest Road.

Aelic flew out of the saddle and hit the ground. His head barely missed the base of an enormous tree. Aelic jumped to his feet, shook the disorientation away, and began searching for Fury. Then he saw it, the blade shining blue in the moonlight that shone down between the gaps in the foliage. He ran for the blade, grabbed the grip, but it would not move. Aelic looked up and saw a heavy Paragor Knight standing upon the blade. His eyes flashed red as he raised his axe.

The axe never fell. Gabby made sure of that. She severed the knight's arm at the shoulder and spit it—axe and all—into the trees. The warrior howled, clutched his shoulder, and ran into the woods after his arm.

Aelic looked at Gabby's ruined right wing. It was a clean break, so she would not fly. He smiled reverently at Gwenne's dragon and patted her on the nose. "You have fought well, Gabby," he said. "Now, stay under the tree. Keep out of sight! I will return for you when I can." He grabbed Fury and hurried to search for Antoinette.

Most of the dragon-riders that left from Clarion were engaged in battle, but farther up the Forest Road, Kaliam and Lady Merewen were on foot. As they made their way around roaring fires, it became clear that the Wyrm Lord was not far away.

"This way!" Kaliam yelled, and he ran to help a Yewland Brave, who was struggling with a dark warrior wearing a sharp helmet and a long scarlet cape. But the warrior struck before Kaliam could get there, and the brave fell to the ground.

The warrior turned and raised two swords to greet Kaliam and Lady Merewen.

"Rucifel!" Kaliam yelled.

"Yes!" snarled the warrior. "It is fitting that you should know the name of your executioner. You, sir, are one of those whelps we fought at Mithegard! And, unless my eyes have failed, before me is Lady Merewen, traitor to Paragor's cause! How fortunate that I should have the privilege of dispatching you both!"

He leaped at them, both swords flying, striking with precision. And it was all Kaliam and Lady Merewen could do to fend off the initial onslaught. Kaliam quickly ducked one slash and drove his broadsword forward at Rucifel's chest. Deflecting Kaliam's thrust, Rucifel brought his other sword down hard, missing Kaliam by a fraction of an inch. Rucifel sidestepped a slash from Lady Merewen, and flung both blades at her midsection.

She staggered backward to avoid his strike, and Kaliam advanced. Their battle raged out into the middle of the road. Yewland Braves loosed arrows from the heights of the trees, but the quick-moving Rucifel dodged them and kept coming. Kaliam defended, but like an uncoiling snake, Rucifel spun back the other way. Lady Merewen missed him with a high thrust, and Rucifel slammed a backfist into Kaliam's chest. Kaliam sprawled on the road.

Rucifel pounced, but Lady Merewen threw herself shoulder-first into her enemy's back. Rucifel stumbled forward and drove one of his blades into the ground. Kaliam rolled to his feet and slammed his broadsword into the center of his enemy's trapped blade. The sword cracked and split. Shards fell to the ground. Rucifel was left with one sword and two opponents.

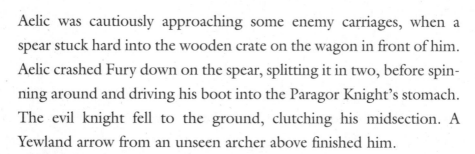

Aelic was cautiously approaching some enemy carriages, when a spear stuck hard into the wooden crate on the wagon in front of him. Aelic crashed Fury down on the spear, splitting it in two, before spinning around and driving his boot into the Paragor Knight's stomach. The evil knight fell to the ground, clutching his midsection. A Yewland arrow from an unseen archer above finished him.

Aelic began to search the wagons and carriages. *Antoinette has to be in one of them!* The battle was heavy around him, and he grew weary as he ran from wagon to wagon looking for, but not finding, Antoinette.

Then ahead, he spotted a wagon pulled to the side of the Forest Road. A tall Paragor Knight stood at the rear of the wagon. He had long blond hair and a gray cloak around his shoulders. In his hand was a wide-bladed sword. *It's Kearn! What is he guarding*? Aelic wondered.

Cautiously, Aelic approached him.

The Paragor Knight turned, and his green eyes met Aelic's. "You!" Kearn screamed.

"Where is Antoinette?" Aelic demanded. He let the tip of Fury drift down, preparing a moulinet.

"Aelic!" came a voice from inside the wagon.

Kearn laughed. "Does that answer your question?"

"Let her go!" Aelic yelled.

"What fun would that be? You come and get her!" Kearn said quietly, and he slashed his heavy blade in front of Aelic.

"Aelic, no!" came Antoinette's muffled voice. "Aelic, no! Don't kill him!"

"That's right, Aelic!" Kearn sneered. "You cannot kill me, or— what was his name—Aidan, yes, that was it. Aidan will lose his best friend."

Aelic looked to the wagon and back to Kearn. He had to get Antoinette out. He had to save her. But in order to do it, he had to get past Kearn.

Kearn lashed out with a two-fisted blow. Aelic blocked it at his waist. The strike was so hard that Aelic's ears rung and his hands tingled.

"You cannot kill me, Aelic!" Kearn mocked. "But I can kill you! And here is the marvelous thing about this arrangement. If I kill you, then I slay Aidan also!"

Aelic stood for a moment very still, but his eyes darted as if he was engaged in some silent, desperate debate. Then, suddenly, he sprang at Kearn, unleashing a sweeping backhanded slash. Kearn blocked but had been caught off guard. Before he could duck completely out of the way, Aelic whipped Fury up and opened a gash in Kearn's cheek. Kearn wiped at the blood with his hand and stared wide-eyed at Aelic.

Aelic held Fury in one hand and stretched out his arm so that the sword's point was at Kearn's eye level. "Antoinette and Aidan might not kill you," he said. "But I have no problem with it."

THE WYRM LORD

Far ahead on the Forest Road, Mallik and Sir Rogan leaped from the trees into a mass of Paragor Knights. Nock remained high on a limb and covered them with arrow fire. Mallik came up swinging his massive hammer, crushing two enemies against the trunk of a Blackwood. Sir Rogan's broadaxe felled three enemies as if they were saplings. The two Alleb warriors, with steely, grim purpose, marched side by side plowing up the Forest Road, and none withstood them. Nock leaped from tree to tree, keeping a watchful eye.

"Is your axe full yet?" Mallik joked. "Shall we go home now?"

Sir Rogan stroked his beard, glared at his friend, and thundered up the road.

"I guess not," Mallik said and raced to keep up with him.

Since the battle began, the three of them had fought their way through more than a hundred Paragor Knights, and Nock had to climb down to scavenge for more arrows. They walked along unopposed for a time, but something about the quiet of the wood was unnerving. And the absence of the enemy, the absence of an attack, was more troubling still.

Sir Rogan stopped unexpectedly and held up his large fist. "There is something on the air," he said. His voice was low, gravelly, and full of anger. "It is like the burning of many things." And soon, they all smelled it. With each step up the Forest Road, the odor became more acrid—and the sickening stench was almost too much to bear.

They proceeded cautiously, taking slow, even breaths and straining to hear. Nock noticed that foliage along the road began to appear wilted, and many of the trees had an odd lean. Soon, the smell became stifling, and the smoldering trees on both sides were toppled and charred as if an intense fire had come upon them suddenly. Small fires crackled deep into the woods. The road rolled out ahead, gray and shadowy, but crisscrossed with strange twisting patterns.

"Ah!" Nock exclaimed, pointing to their feet. "The road! Look at the road!"

Mallik and Sir Rogan strained to see, but at first they could not tell what had terrified Nock. Then Mallik leaped to the side. "They are bodies!" he bellowed.

"Shapes of bodies . . . ," Nock said.

"King Eliam, save us!" Sir Rogan exclaimed. "They have been burned into the ground . . . reduced to an ashen imprint upon the road!"

". . . and bows," Nock said as he recognized the distinctive shape of the Yewland Braves' Blackwood bows burned into the road. "My kin!"

"I am sorry, my friend," said Mallik.

"What has laid low so many braves?" Nock asked, his bow hanging limp at his side.

Sir Rogan knelt by one of the bodies and stared. "It is near," he said.

"What do you mean by that?" Mallik demanded.

"The Wyrm Lord," growled Sir Rogan. "It would take more than a regular dragon's fire to bring down the trees and burn hundreds of warriors into the ground."

Suddenly, Sir Rogan clutched his axe, looked skyward, and screamed with pent-up rage for the fallen at Mithegard, and delivered an unmistakable message: The enemy had better beware.

Sir Rogan charged up the road. Mallik and Nock followed.

The trail suddenly widened. The knights stopped and stood very still, their eyes locked on a huge, black, iron-framed carriage that sat upon eight enormous spoked wheels and was drawn by large horses. The top of the carriage was crowned with a dozen torches. A tendril of smoke escaped the roof and snaked up into the night sky.

"We should not have come here!" whispered Nock urgently.

"I feel the marrow in my bones beginning to freeze," said Mallik.

Sir Rogan did not reply.

And then there was movement at the front of the carriage. Someone very tall stepped down. They heard the dull clink of metal and the heavy thud of his boots as he walked slowly toward the back. Hidden by shadow, they could not see his face, only that he had a weapon of some kind hanging at his side—and his eyes flashed red.

He reached up and worked at something on the side of the carriage—metal sliding against metal. A voice came out of the shadows. It seemed to those who listened that the words were spoken from a grave. "Ancient One, how fortunate, three knights—a meal to enchance your strength. Go now and feast upon them. A taste of Alleble's fall!"

Though they knew they should flee, Mallik, Nock, and Sir Rogan stood rooted in the road as the huge doors atop the carriage swung open. A long, sharp gasp escaped the carriage as if something very large had drawn a breath. It was followed by a low growl that rose like the moaning of a haunted wind until it peaked with a hideous shriek. The sound rattled the Alleble Knights' armor and chilled their skin.

Nock stared at the top of the carriage, and what looked like a dark tentacle, blacker than the night shadows around it, began to creep out. Then another. And a third—twisting, grasping, reaching. They were not fleshly things, but rather tendrils of dark mist. More began to spill out of the carriage as if it were a cauldron that could not contain its horrid brew. The mist came more steadily, and the road became darker where it swirled.

The tall figure standing beside the carriage laughed. His eyes flashed red, and he seemed to fade into the shadows as something rose out of the carriage and perched heavily upon it. It was a great winged beast, wreathed in shrouds of the swirling mist. The creature was most like to a dragon—wide wings, long neck and tail, and sharp scales armoring the length of its body. But the black mist that swirled all around the creature issued from its jaws and trailed out from its nostrils. Its eyes, smoldering, red, reptilian eyes, stared back with cunning beyond that of other wyrms. In its gaze a deep history lurked, a knowledge of time that no Glimpse could boast. And there was also murderous hatred—malice born out of the creature's own evil but nursed in the never-ending night of a stone cell beneath the lake of fire while centuries passed.

Its eyes turned on the three knights of Alleble—first almost in curiosity, then in recognition and hatred. Craning its neck back, it drew in a great breath.

"Beware its fire!" Mallik bellowed, breaking their paralysis. Nock leaped off the road and clambered up the charred trunk of a large tree. Mallik had flung himself into a ditch near the bend in the road. Sir Rogan stood behind one of the blackened trees that remained standing.

The Wyrm Lord spewed a molten stream onto the road where a second before they had stood.

Nock let fly six arrows in rapid succession. But one by one they bounced away from the creature's scales. "Weak shafts!" Nock muttered, feeling around the quiver frantically for a Blackwood shaft.

The Wyrm Lord hissed and turned toward the archer's perch. It discharged a burst of flames at Nock's tree, and it gave way beneath him. Nock was far too agile to be caught so easily. He jumped from the tree where it fell and rolled to the side of the road. He stood to fire again. Finally, he found his last Blackwood shaft from among the other arrows. In a flash, he fitted it to the string and aimed for the beast's right eye. But the creature's fire streamed forth again. Nock's shot was rushed. He loosed it and dove for cover behind a low berm. For the first time in many years, Nock missed.

The Blackwood shaft disappeared harmlessly into the shadowy woods. The Wyrm Lord unleashed its flames once more, and kept Nock pinned down. Try as he might to sink into the ground, Nock was still too close to the heat. He felt his armor grow hot, and his bowstring frayed and snapped. Nock could not breathe, and his thoughts began to swim in feverish mire.

Seeing Nock's plight, Mallik climbed out of the ditch and ran into the road. He hefted his great hammer and yelled as he rushed toward the creature. "Turn to me, foul-smelling beast!" he bellowed. "And bring your broad face within reach of this hammer!"

But the Wyrm Lord was no dumb serpent, and it understood

full well the speech of Glimpse-kind. It leaped down from the carriage to meet Mallik's charge, but it kept its head away from the lethal hammer. Instead, it opened its jaws and prepared to loose an incinerating blast.

Were it not for Sir Rogan's quick thinking, Mallik would have perished there. Sir Rogan swept his axe across the tree he had hidden behind, and it crashed down upon the Wyrm Lord's back. The blow stifled the creature's fire, and it shrieked so loud and long that Mallik almost collapsed from the sound.

The beast reached up with one of its taloned forelegs and threw the massive tree trunk back at Sir Rogan. Sir Rogan tried to avoid it, but the great tree hit the ground in front of him, bounced, and smashed into him as he fled. Sir Rogan fell like a stone, but the blackened trunk did not come to rest on his sprawled body.

The beast turned back to Mallik, who suddenly realized how foolish and rash his attack had been. He may have saved Nock, but in so doing, he had forced Sir Rogan to expose himself. Now Sir Rogan and Nock were down, and Mallik was left alone before the Wyrm Lord. He turned to flee, but the creature's tail whipped around and took Mallik's legs out from under him. He rolled and stood and found himself staring into huge red eyes and gaping jaws full of ivory daggers. Mallik tried to run to his right, but the creature blocked him with one enormous claw. Mallik swerved aside and sprinted back only to find another claw waiting. Mallik—a massive Glimpse even among his large kin in the Blue Mountains—felt like a mouse being toyed with and taunted by a great cat so far superior in strength that it sought entertainment rather than a quick kill.

"I will not die like a common rodent!" Mallik roared. And this time, when the Wyrm Lord's claw barred his way, Mallik brought his hammer down upon it with every ounce of his strength. The immense pulverizing head of Mallik's hammer crunched down on the creature's claw, but only for a second. It sprang away as if Mallik had struck a granite boulder. The shiver of the blow shook the hammer free from Mallik's hands, and he stood as one thunderstruck. The Wyrm Lord drew back the uninjured claw and smacked Mallik across the road. Mallik shook his head and looked up just as the creature started inhaling a deep breath, but then it stopped as a baleful howl rang out from somewhere deep in the forest.

The Wyrm Lord craned its neck high and, with an odd tilt to its head, seemed to be listening.

Mallik stood, saw his hammer at the feet of the creature, and ran for it. Before Mallik could reach his weapon, the great cry from the forest rose in pitch and intensity until it blotted out all other sounds. Mallik could not bear it and fell to one knee. He covered his ears and looked up at the creature.

When the howling noise finally came to an end, the Wyrm Lord seemed to nod as if in agreement. Then, to Mallik's surprise, it appeared to have lost interest in the three knights.

Suddenly, the beast spread its great wings, and its body began to convulse. The Wyrm Lord roared, gnashed its teeth, and reared up on its hind limbs. It seemed to be gathering strength—drawing on some hidden reserve of power—preparing to unleash some horrific power. Mallik watched in horror as the rigid pattern of scales on the creature's armored chest and the folds of cracked skin on its stomach began to change. There appeared faces, anguished faces, as if beings were captive beneath the creature's flesh and, in great torment, were struggling to be released. The Wyrm Lord shrieked, began to moan, and vomited out a shroud of darkness. Like a dense black tide, it poured out of the creature's jaws and filled the road.

It swept over Mallik, and all went black.

ONSLAUGHT OF THE SLEEPERS

Rucifel slashed back and forth with his remaining blade, deftly keeping Kaliam and Lady Merewen from using their advantage. Kaliam hammered away with his broadsword, but always Rucifel ducked out of reach. And still more maddening was the way that Rucifel maneuvered his attackers into each other's way. Several times Lady Merewen thought she had an opening in Rucifel's defenses, only to stay her strike at the last moment when he lured Kaliam right into her path.

Their battle ranged all over the road, in and out of the trees, and among the other combatants of both sides, but still Rucifel eluded the two warriors from Alleble.

Then, Lady Merewen thrust her sword at his midsection. He parried it away, but rather than retreating immediately as he had been doing, he stepped forward and struck out at Lady Merewen with a series of quick stabs. It was enough time for Kaliam to circle round so that Rucifel stood between him and Lady Merewen. They pressed in on Rucifel like a vise. Kaliam swept his broadsword at the enemy's head. Lady Merewen raked her blade at his legs. Rucifel could not evade both strikes. He ducked Kaliam's long blade and tried to dive. But Lady Merewen's sword caught him on the back of his leg where there was no armor. Rucifel did not yell, but he rolled to a crouch, stood, and hopped back a pace favoring his left leg.

Sensing victory over their foe, Kaliam and Lady Merewen came on. They drove him backward. Rucifel seemed to give up any notion of offense and used his blade to block and defend. After every swipe, he turned and ran a few paces, always favoring his left leg.

"You run away!" Kaliam exclaimed as he pursued. "You are tiring, Rucifel!"

"No," Rucifel replied, and he stopped and glared at his attackers with such a strange expression that they pulled up short. It seemed to Kaliam and Lady Merewen that Rucifel had suddenly gone mad, for he was beaten and yet he began to laugh. "Not tiring," he said and grinned smugly. "Waiting. . . ."

At that moment, a howl rose up as if a sudden storm had come upon the forest of Yewland. But no wind of The Realm any living Glimpse had ever heard made such a hideous sound. Kaliam and Lady Merewen grimaced and covered their ears. Finally, the haunting noise ceased. All noise ceased. No arrows whistled. No blades clashed upon shields. The combatants all around had lowered their swords. It was utterly still and silent . . . until something advanced toward them on the road behind Rucifel.

Kaliam reflexively stepped backward. *A creeping mist?* he wondered, but it was inky black and reflected none of the moon's light.

Whatever it was, it began to quicken, devouring trees and road as it came. Suddenly, it washed over Rucifel, and he was gone.

Kaliam and Lady Merewen turned to flee, but it was too late.

Kearn came at Aelic, dealing out blow after blow. Back and forth they dueled. Aelic wanted to avoid killing Kearn if he could, but the way his enemy fought, it seemed there would be no other way.

Kearn lunged. Aelic brought Fury up hard, but their blades locked together. Pressing in toward each other, Aelic and Kearn came eye to eye.

"You cannot win," Kearn said, his eyes flashing red. "And when you are dead, I will take Lady Antoinette behind the Gate of Despair. If she will not become one of us, I will feed her to my master's new pet!"

"Don't listen to him, Aelic!" Antoinette yelled from the locked wagon.

Just then their blades slid apart, but Kearn's sword came down on Aelic's forearm. The leather vambrace split, and the sword left a deep gash. "Arghhh!" Aelic yelled. In a rage, Aelic slashed Fury against Kearn's blade and pinned it against the wagon. Then, he reached around and punched Kearn twice in the side where there was no armor.

"Curse you, whelp!" Kearn coughed and spat. He wrenched his blade away from the wagon, and Aelic leaped back. "Think your skill with that blade is enough to contend with, Kearn?"

Tired, Kearn sprang from the wagon, intending to drive his blade at Aelic's chest for a kill. But his angle was too low coming in. Aelic swept the wide blade away, and hacked at it again and again, growing stronger with rage as Kearn grew weaker. Finally, Kearn's guard became sloppy and Aelic's sword drifted into position. Aelic drew Fury back so that the pommel rested near his chest. He prepared to throw a moulinet to kill.

But before he could move, a frightening cry rose above the clamor of battle. At first it sounded as if it was coming out of the Blackwood. It rose in pitch to a great mournful howl, and Aelic felt his skull would split from the sound. Kearn too was affected, but not as much. He swayed for a moment but seized the opportunity and ran to the huge black horse that was hitched to the wagon. He leaped upon it and spurred it forward. Aelic whirled around and saw the wagon moving. He tried to pursue, but the sound had a crippling effect on him. He dropped his sword, fell to his knees, and clutched his ears.

When the sound finally ended, Aelic grabbed Fury and sprinted up the road after the wagon. But it was already rounding a corner far ahead. Aelic watched helplessly as Kearn's wagon took Antoinette away.

Suddenly, another howl rang out—this time Aelic was sure it was from the Blackwood side of the forest. Other howls answered—Aelic counted: five, six, seven! And then the ground began to tremble.

Then something dark was upon him. Aelic swung Fury recklessly like a child fighting off a nightmare. But the darkness had a texture like a spider's web, and it clung to his skin, his hair, and his armor. Aelic calmed himself and realized that he was not bound— he could move through it.

Aelic ran in the direction he thought Kearn had gone. Someone was up ahead. *Kearn?* he wondered. He could just tell it was a warrior with long hair, a long mustache, and beard. The mist seemed to swirl around him. Aelic slowed a little and blinked. *No, it could not be*

Kearn. The warrior was enormous—far taller even than Kaliam. He had no weapon, but he marched with deadly purpose. The warrior's eyes were strangely fixed. Aelic stopped and stared as a mist washed past the warrior, clouding the warrior from sight. The mist vanished, and there in the warrior's place stood a wolvin three times the creature's normal size. The hair on its back bristled. Its jaws fell open, and it growled menacingly. Aelic realized with dismay that before him stood one of the Seven Sleepers.

Aelic clutched Fury in front with both hands, and though he had little hope of outrunning the giant beast, he took a slow step backward. The wolvin's yellow eyes narrowed and it charged. Aelic dove out of its path but was slowed by the grasping mist. He avoided the wolvin's jaws, but it barreled into him with its shoulder and knocked Aelic aside like a rag doll. Heart pounding and breathless, Aelic leaped to his feet. The wolvin came again, but when Aelic tried to get out of the way, the creature reached out with its foreleg and slashed Aelic's right shoulder. Its claws tore the armor off and gouged deep into Aelic's arm. But even as it did so, Aelic slammed Fury down upon the creature's back. The wolvin howled in pain and began to scratch at its back as if something were still stuck there.

Blood streaming from his wounded arm, Aelic sprinted into the shrouded trees. He had no idea which direction to go. Aelic stumbled up a long hill and heard muffled snaps and cracks behind him. He pushed himself harder, straining against the incline. He toppled over the crest of the hill, and rolled down the other side. Jabbed and buffeted as he rolled, he clutched Fury in his left hand with all his might. When at last he stopped rolling, Aelic gasped for breath.

Using Fury as a crutch, he pulled himself to his feet. But just as he stood, the wolvin crashed into him. Aelic flew backward, the creature on top of him. They hit the ground with a crunch and

Aelic's legs went numb. The wolvin's teeth came at his neck, but Aelic wedged Fury up into its jaws. It bit down on the blade, yelped in surprised agony, but did not relent. It clamped down on Fury even harder and tore it from Aelic's hands.

The wolvin tossed the blade aside, and snarled. A mixture of saliva and blood trickled over its jaw onto Aelic's neck. "King Eliam!" Aelic whispered urgently. "Help me."

Just as the wolvin went for Aelic's throat, he heard a high-pitched roar. A shape appeared and smashed into the creature with such force that it was thrown free from Aelic. The wolvin howled in pain. Aelic turned and saw a dragon on top of the wolvin, tearing at it with taloned feet. "Gabby!!" Aelic screamed.

The two creatures grappled and bit, clawed and scratched. Gabby had only one good wing, but she held her own against the Sleeper. Aelic struggled to his knees and began to crawl toward his sword. Again using Fury for leverage, he pulled himself to his feet. Determined to help Gabby, he began to limp back toward the fight.

But the ground went out from under him, and Aelic was falling, falling, falling.

THE AFTERMATH

Kaliam had not slept for three days since returning from the battle in the forest, and still he waited at the main gate of the city of Alleble. Heralds sounded their trumpets as survivors arrived or were carried in, but there were too few and not often. Lady Merewen was safe, her wounds being tended to by Sir Oswyn in the castle. Farix had made it back as well.

Scouts had come back late on the second day to report that Nock was found still alive. He was to remain in Yewland with his kin until he recovered his strength. And Trenna, reunited with her family, remained in Yewland as well. All told, nearly twenty-five thousand knights from Alleble, Yewland, and Acacia had fought in the forest against Paragor's forces. Only half of those returned to their homeland. And among those still missing, there were names very dear to Kaliam: Sir Gabriel, Mallik, Sir Rogan, Antoinette, and Aelic. So Kaliam waited by the gate.

It was as the sun went down on the third day that Kaliam saw hundreds of knights ride across the plain on the backs of unicorns. He leaped upon one of the guard's dragons and flew out to meet them. Kaliam looked at them hopefully as they rode past. They saluted their Sentinel, and he smiled and saluted back, but Mallik, Sir Rogan, Lady Antoinette, and Aelic were not among them.

Kaliam returned to his bench and waited. Then two lone knights appeared on the horizon. As they neared, Kaliam recognized them. Leaping from the bench, he ran to meet them.

"Mallik! Sir Rogan!" he cried. "I feared the worst, but here you are! Praise to King Eliam, you survived!"

Mallik and Sir Rogan dismounted, and each in turn embraced Kaliam. But they were weary and somehow changed. They did not speak much—even days later—but they stayed in each other's company and exchanged knowing glances.

Kaliam stayed at the gate for many days more, but Sir Gabriel, Antoinette, and Aelic did not return.

45

BEYOND THE GATES
OF DESPAIR

The guards brought Antoinette through many dark, smoky passages and up a long, winding stair. At the very top of the stair, they opened a thick wooden door and entered a chamber that had one small cell within it. They roughly dragged her into the bare cell which smelled of dust, rot, and worse things; locked manacles around her ankles; and chained her to a ring embedded in the cold stone floor. A wall of iron bars divided the chamber, and the Paragor Knights locked her in. Finally, they slammed the wooden chamber door behind them. Antoinette heard a faint metallic click, and she knew they had locked the chamber door too.

There was one small window. When Antoinette dragged her chains to their full extent, she was able to look out. But she found the view inside her cell much more to her liking. For the window looked out upon the Grimwalk in the land of Paragory. Antoinette sighed and twisted at the silver ring the merchant had given her in

Baen. At that point in her journey she had still been able to convince herself that going after Kearn was a noble thing. Now, the grim reality was all too clear.

Antoinette had betrayed her commander, her friends, and her King. She had failed to keep her promise to Aidan. Robby's Glimpse was not willing to turn his allegiance from Paragor and accept King Eliam. Antoinette slid away from the window, dropped to her knees, and curled into a ball. And there she shivered upon the stone until at last she fell asleep.

"A morsel, my dear," said a voice. Antoinette woke with a start and scrambled to the back of the cell.

"Come now," the voice said. A metal tray scraped along the stone floor. On it was meat and bread. A dark boot nudged it into the light from the window. "You must eat. You must build your strength for the trial to come."

Antoinette suddenly knew the voice. "Kearn!"

"Yes, it is I," he replied. He stepped out of the shadows and peered out the window of her cell.

"What have you done with Aelic?" she screamed.

"What have I done?" he said, turning and walking toward the cell door. "Why, I have done nothing. His fate is a result of your actions."

"Nooo!" Antoinette moaned and sank to the floor. "Why didn't you just kill me too?" she whispered.

Kearn stepped out of the cell, locked its door of iron bars, but paused at the huge wooden chamber door. His eyes flickered red, and he replied, "I keep asking myself that same question."

TURBULENCE

She's still not back, Dad," Aidan said, inserting the plane's phone back in its slot on the seat in front of him. He looked out the window of the plane and watched streaks of lightning crawl among the purple cloud tops.

"Relax, Aidan," Mr. Thomas said, munching on some peanuts. "I'm sure she's fine."

"But she's already been gone longer than I was—earth time, anyway," Aidan complained. "I thought for sure she'd be back before we landed in Baltimore."

Mr. Thomas gave his son a reassuring squeeze on the shoulder. "I'm sure she's okay. We're about to land now, but you can call her from the hotel."

The intercom came on. "Ladies and gentlemen, we have some storm clouds up ahead. We might be experiencing a little turbulence. Please keep your seat belts fastened for the duration of the flight. We should be on the ground at BWI in about thirty minutes. Thank you for your attention."

Mr. Thomas stretched and put his arms behind his head. "Just think how surprised Robby'll be when you show up at his front door!"

Yeah, Aidan thought. *'Surprise, Robby! Are you ready to believe yet?'* Aidan shook his head and went back to looking out the window. The plane had already sunk into the clouds. Now it began to bounce a little. Aidan's stomach tightened. Lightning flickered in the hazy distance outside the window.

One of the flight attendants hurried up the aisle. Aidan watched her buckle herself into a little seat behind the cockpit. The plane shuddered for a second. Aidan's stomach felt like it did sometimes in an elevator. One of the little overhead compartments popped open. A pillow and a child's teddy bear fell out.

Aidan gripped the armrests so hard that his knuckles went white. He turned and looked out the window, and there in the reflection, he saw Gwenne's pale face. Lightning struck, blinding light filled the cabin, and the lights went out.

Never Alone

Aelic stared up from the bottom of a deep pit. His vision was unfocused, and what looked at first to be dark, feathery hands reaching down from the pale sky above turned out to be layers and layers of massive roots. They burst out from all sides of the deep hole he had fallen into.

"Arghhh!" The pain awakened Aelic fully. His legs throbbed. His arm burned as if a white-hot blade had broken off under his skin. And he felt a tightness in his chest, as if a heavy weight lay on him, compressing his lungs.

Aelic tried to sit up, but it was such excruciating agony that he almost lost consciousness. He lay back in the dirt and gasped. Eventually, the pain evened out to a dull pulse, and Aelic could think again.

The darkness is gone, he realized, looking at the circle of gray sky above. It all came back to him then. Fighting the wolvin Sleeper . . .

if it hadn't been for Gabby . . . *Gabby!* Aelic thought with a start. Aelic felt certain that Gabby had sacrificed herself so that he might live.

Aelic's left hand bumped into something. He reached for it. It was Fury! And with what little strength he had, he lifted the blade from the soil. He stared at the hilt, at the engraved image of the sun rising between the sacred peaks of Pennath Ador. It brought him hope. For there the sun had risen, a bright new dawn, marking the return of King Eliam. There, as in the forests of Yewland, had been suffering and tragedy. But King Eliam had proven to be greater still, even greater than death.

"I am never alone," Aelic whispered. And then he heard voices from above.

Adventures are
funny things.
They offer dark, uncertain
times,
forks in the road,
and choices between comfort
and peril.
And in such times,
heroes can be
made
or undone.

Acknowledgments

Twelve years ago, a special woman took an awesome and wonderful risk, choosing to spend the rest of her life with me. It has been an adventure of a lifetime, and I am so grateful to be sharing it all with Mary Lu, the beautiful wife of my youth. 1C13.

To my four young adventurers: Kayla, Tommy, Bryce, and Rachel . . . you are precious beyond all the gold and jewels in all the mines of the world. Your daddy loves you always.

To the Dovel family: Olin and Lorraine for giving me your incredible daughter, first of all, and for your remarkable support of The Door Within Trilogy. To Andy and Denise Dovel whose ministry and music opened my eyes and continues to enrich my life. Thanks, too, for sharing *The Door Within* far and wide. To Ed and Deanna Dovel for lending me your house so that I can write in peace and for showing up at just about every book signing! To Diana Dovel for buying like a gazillion books and making sure that all your patients hear about *The Door Within*!

To Bill and Lisa Russell: You both have sacrificed so much of your own time and resources to get *The Door Within* off the ground. Let's continue to pray BIG things for each other!

To Dave and Heather Peters, Doug and Chris Smith, Todd Wahlne, Danny Sutton, Chris and Alaina Haerbig, Dan and Courtney Cwiek, Steve and Janet Berbes, Chris and Dawn Harvey, Dan and Pam Pantera, Eric and Deb Southan, Don and Valerie Counts, Mat and Serrina Davis, and Warren Cramutola . . . with friends like you all, I will never run out of characters! (And I mean that in the nicest possible way!)

John and Diane Martindale: Thank you for taking *The Door Within* to so many who might not otherwise have known!

To Valerie W., Sean H., Krista G., Pat D., Laura B., Kim L., Mary O., Robin K., Linda G., Harry S., Susan P., Hannah C., Amy M., Marsha

A., Conrad O.: You were among the first to step through *The Door Within*. I won't forget.

To director Peter Jackson, whose vision and passion brought LOTR to the screen at last and reminded the world of why we love fantasy. Your work may have opened the door for mine. Thank you. P.S. Any chance you'll do The Hobbit?

To the clever, creative, insightful, enthusiastic children at Folly Quarter Middle School: Thank you for lending me your brilliance in the development of this novel. Pip, Pip Cheerio! Also thanks to every one of my colleagues, my friends at FQMS! You inspire me daily! Thanks for understanding my many "gray moments" as I sought to meet my deadlines!

Special thanks to Michelle Black and the noble folks at His Way Christian Bookstores. I am in awe of your efforts to open *The Door Within* for others. I am honored to raise a sword with you!

To the staff of Eldersburg Public Library: Thank you for letting me "live" in your little private study room. About a third of Wyrm Lord was penned there! P.S. I'll be back for *The Final Storm*!

To Kris Buker for sharing so much great literature with young people AND for setting me up with so many book talks and signings!

To Paul Peluso, Joe Burris, and Katie Champion: Thank you for your kind and eloquent words! To WBAL TV and WRBS Radio, thank you for broadcasting *The Door Within* over the airwaves!

Thanks to Leanna and Gordon Webb for being so trustworthy with our greatest treasures!

Special thanks to Gregg Wooding, my agent and friend, for stepping with me into uncharted territories! Who knows where this path will lead us?

To Dee Ann Grand, Beverly Phillips, June Ford, Patti Evans, Katie Broaddus, Andy Peterson, Brian Mitchell, and everyone at Tommy Nelson: Thank you for letting me be a part of this mission. I am still in awe when I consider how so many have poured their lives into The Door Within Trilogy!

To Brian, Jeff, Leslie, and Mom and Dad: For many memories such as Cross Country in a little white car, Fireworks in Atlanta, Dallas Dates, and frequent visits to Waffle Houses and Dairy Queens—thank you for this adventure of life we've been on together.

THE FINAL STORM

The torchlit passages in the heart of Paragor's stronghold twisted and turned like a den of serpents. "Please tell me you aren't lost," Antoinette said when Aidan stopped suddenly at a fork in the path.

"Quiet, I'm thinking!" Aidan barked.

Antoinette raised her eyebrows and looked at Aidan with wonder. She still couldn't believe he had found a way to return to The Realm. She was grateful, for together they might be able to escape and do something about Paragor's plan to destroy Alleble.

Zabed, the old sage they had liberated from a lower tower cell, placed a withered hand on Aidan's shoulder. "What place does thou hope to find?" he asked.

"It's a huge balcony," Aidan said. "On the northern side of the great tower. I tied the dragons there."

"Does thou mean that tower, the one crowned with thorns?"

"Yes!" Aidan exclaimed.

"Then take the passage on thy left," Zabed explained.

There came a strange rumbling from below. It grew louder, and Aidan recognized the sound as the tromp of many iron-shod feet. Paragor had not emptied his fortress completely after all. "Soldiers!" Aidan shouted. "Antoinette, they know you've escaped! We must hurry!"

They could hear shrieks and the shouts of many voices, distant but growing ever closer.

"The rats in this cursed hold will smell us out, I fear," Zabed growled. "I have told ye the prophecy of thy scroll. You have no longer need of me. Leave me behind."

Aidan looked at Zabed, who was starved from his long imprisonment, thin and frail with age.

"Maybe there's another way," Aidan said, and he handed Fury to Antoinette. Then he grasped Zabed's wrists and carefully slung him onto his back.

"Nay, lad!" Zabed protested. "Leave me be! I will slow ye down to the demise of all!"

"Zabed, I won't leave you," Aidan said, hefting the sage and taking a few steps. "C'mon, Antoinette!"

Aidan ran surprisingly fast, bearing Zabed's extra weight more easily than he had thought he could. The passage curled and then sloped downward. Aidan whispered a quick thank you to King Eliam and charged on. Antoinette, Fury in one hand, the Daughter of Light in the other, raced after him.

Heavy footfalls fell in the passage behind them. *Too close!* Aidan thought. *They'll catch us before we can—*Then he saw it. The passage opened up at the bottom and strange gray twilight fell upon the stone beneath a wide arch. Aidan knew that arch. The balcony and the dragons were just beyond it!

"It's just ahead!" he cried. "Hurry!" Just then an arrow swooshed over Aidan's shoulder, struck the ceiling of the passage ahead, and clattered to the ground. Angry screams blared from the passage.

Aidan dashed down the hill. The arch was closer. Almost there. Suddenly, Zabed groaned. His arms stiffened and then went limp in Aidan's grasp. Zabed's gray head fell on Aidan's shoulders.

"No!" Aidan exclaimed. "Zabed?!" But the old sage did not answer. Aidan surged beneath the arch into the ethereal gray of night in Paragory. But the moment Aidan stepped on the stone of the balcony, his feet slid out from under him. He skidded as if on ice and fell backward. His weight came down hard on Zabed. Antoinette was right behind him. She lost her footing as well, flailed to keep her balance, but crashed to the stone. Her sword and Fury clattered across the balcony.

Antoinette pushed herself up from the ground. Her hands felt wetness. She stood awkwardly and looked at her palms. Even in the shroud of gray night, she could see glistening blood. Blood! Antoinette looked around. They were in a great wide pool of blood.

With Nock and a legion of Yewland's best archers defending Alleble's parapets, Paragor's great siege towers could not get close to the walls.

But Kaliam knew better than to relax. He knew only too well that the enemy had a devastating weapon at his disposal. He looked out over the wall into the murky darkness breathed into existence by the evil Wyrm Lord.

"Kaliam," Farix shouted as he ran up, "what are your orders, my Sentinel?"

"Farix, good. I am glad you have come," Kaliam said, pointing out into the shadows. "What do you see?"

Farix stared into the gloom. "I see a thousand knights on foot," he replied. "They have also pendulum battering rams, and siege towers, but beyond that, I can see nothing."

"That cursed darkness! It hides the enemy's designs. We see only those within range of a short bow, but what lies beyond? And where are the Wyrm Lord and the Seven Sleepers?"

"Perhaps Paragor is waiting to release them at the time of greatest opportunity," Farix said.

"Now is the time of greatest opportunity!" Kaliam shouted out in frustration. "The Wyrm Lord in his weakest state razed Clarion to the ground, and together with the sleepers, they devastated our combined forces in Yewland! By now Paragor has no doubt nursed them back to full strength. Why does he delay?"

Farix was silent.

"We must be ready," Kaliam said. "Farix, go and find Kindle and make sure he has his force of spearmen near at hand. And see to it that Mallik and his folk fill the turrets should any of their siege engines win through to the walls!"

"Yes, Sentinel," Farix said, and he vanished down the stairs.

Kaliam stared out over the enemy into the darkness. He paced the parapets until he could bear it no longer. He raced along the wall, ducking into and out of massive turrets, until he came to one of the guard towers near the main gate.

As Kaliam approached, seven sentries ran to him and stood at attention. "What news?" Kaliam asked.

"The gates hold," answered the first guard in line, a clean-shaven Glimpse who wore a gleaming conical helmet. "In fact, it has barely been assaulted since the battering rams were turned back."

Kaliam went to the wall and peered between two stone merlons down at the enemy. There were knights as far as the eye could see in that gloom, but they were armed with swords and milled about almost casually.

"We sent the archers to the outer walls," the sentry continued. "They are needed more there to repel the siege towers."

"Yes, good," Kaliam replied. But he was not so sure. He looked again down at the enemy. As thick as ants on a carcass, they were, but they had no ladders or devices for scaling, no great rams for smashing the gates. Why would the enemy abandon the gates? It was the weakest point of entry. "You have done well," Kaliam said at last. "But do not be caught unaware by a lull in their assault. Send word to bring a host of archers back to the gate. I feel the enemy will strike here again."

The sentry nodded and sent one of his knights racing along the wall. Then he and the others returned to their posts.

"What is Paragor's plan?" Kaliam thought aloud. He turned and looked behind him, up Alleble's main thoroughfare, past the Seven Fountains to the castle. He longed to speak with the King. Surely he would know what to do. But King Eliam had gone to a place where his Sentinel could not follow. And there had been no report of his return. Kaliam would have to lead the defense of the kingdom himself.

Suddenly, the sound of metal grinding against metal ripped through the din of the siege. Kaliam whirled around. What are they doing?!" The enormous deadbolt arm of the main gate was being drawn back. He pointed to the sentries. "Go!" The sentries dashed from their post and flew down the spiral stairs to the causeway leading to the gatehouse.

Still the great murynstil bolt continued to slide back. Shouts came from the enemy knights on the other side. Kaliam went to the parapet and saw that they were aimless no longer. Hundreds had gathered at the gate, and to Kaliam's astonishment, they were form- ing ranks at the gate. Kaliam looked back along the walls, and there, running swiftly along the parapets, was Nock, and he led a great team of archers.

"What is happening?" Nock asked when he drew near.

"There is evil afoot!" Kaliam exclaimed. "Someone has begun to withdraw the great bolt to the gate!"

Nock and the others stared.

"I sent a team of guards to the gatehouse, but—" Kaliam looked back to the gate just in time to see the last of the bolt slide away from the guides on the portcullis. He felt a tremor of fear creep along his spine, for slowly the gate itself began to rise. "Nay! This is not possible! Nock, I must go myself to the gate! But see, the enemy is forming on the other side—lining up—as if they might simply walk in!" Kaliam locked eyes with Nock, and in that moment, he was not speaking captain to knight, but friend to friend. "Do not let the enemy enter our city!"

"They stand in line to perish," Nock said, motioning to his team.

Kaliam's broadsword unsheathed, he sprinted down the stairs and across the causeway to the gatehouse. He paused at the ramp and watched. The triple portcullis continued to rise. It was nearly high enough for the Paragor Knights who clamored there to squeeze through. *I will put a halt to this!* Kaliam thought as he hur- ried up the ramp.

But Kaliam stopped short. There before him was a trail of twisted bodies. He recognized the Glimpse warriors strewn about the road like broken toys, and their eyes were frozen open in fear.

"What madness is this?!" Kaliam exclaimed. Few weapons could inflict this kind of damage—Mallik's hammer, perhaps. And that led

Kaliam to a very disturbing thought. *Could one of Mallik's folk, the Glimpses of the Blue Mountain Provinces, be a traitor like Acsriot or the false ambassadors?*

Kaliam held his broadsword in front as he climbed to the top of the ramp. And there, turning the giant chain-driven wheel that raised and lowered the triple portcullis, was a single knight. *That is impossible!* Kaliam thought. *It takes three stout warriors to turn that wheel!*

The knight stopped and stood to face Kaliam. Dressed in the armor of Alleble, he smiled grotesquely at Kaliam before walking toward him. And as he drew near, he seemed to change. It was as if with each step, he grew larger. Then Kaliam saw his eyes. They flashed blue at first, but then they flashed red. The warrior began to convulse. . . .